# IN A LEAGUE OF THEIR OWN

# IN A LEAGUE OF THEIR OWN

## FOOTBALL'S MAVERICK MANAGERS

### Jeremy Novick

MAINSTREAM
PUBLISHING

EDINBURGH AND LONDON

First published in 1995 by
MAINSTREAM PUBLISHING COMPANY
(EDINBURGH) LTD
7 Albany Street
Edinburgh EH1 3UG

ISBN 1 85158 780 2

A catalogue record for this book is available from the British
Library

All photographs courtesy of Colorsport

Typeset in 11 on 13pt Adobe Garamond

Printed and bound in Great Britain by Butler & Tanner Ltd,
Frome, Somerset

*For Gilly, Maxwell and Elly – more than*
*a boy could ever wish for*

# CONTENTS

# ACKNOWLEDGEMENTS

Without whom it would not have been possible . . .

Way up there is Rob Steen, a Mount Rushmore of a mensch who's been put on the planet to prove that journalists can also be human beings. Thanks Rob, for having faith.

A big hand to Chris Lightbown, a top man who came good when it really mattered – as if there was a question. Thanks, too, to everyone who helped me in my endeavours with this weighty tome.

Thanks to my mother – maybe one day she'll get her hair cut – my sister, Tina, and her delight of a family, and my father, Louis, who's probably read this already.

To the existentialist Maxwell C. Wolf for clearing the woods of those pesky squirrels, and to Elly for providing the inspiration.

Finally, thanks to the patient, loving, kind and commissioning Mainstream folk. Judy, Janene, Richard and Bill – listen, grey hair can look distinguished.

Lastly, but firstly, a special thanks to Pete Watts, a researcher among researchers and a shooting star whose day won't be far off. If you ever need a hand . . .

And, of course, Gilly, but I'll tell her what I think when you're not listening.

So now I know how those Oscar-winners feel.

# PROLOGUE

TOMMY DOCHERTY: 'There are no characters on the managerial side now and very, very few on the playing side.'
MALCOLM ALLISON: 'They've gone back again. People are backing off again.'
DOCHERTY: 'There's a fear element now. In Manchester, no one says a word against United because Ferguson's got them eating out of his hand. He more or less tells them what to print and if they don't print it, if they say a word against him, they'll get nothing out of Old Trafford.'

*But they don't take the piss now like you used to.*

DOCHERTY: 'You've got to have a sense of humour to take the piss, and Alex isn't a funny man. He's created a team of whingers. I think Alex Ferguson is a great manager and he's done great things, but as a bloke he's a prat.'

*But he's a successful prat, isn't he.*

DOCHERTY: 'You know, people say to me, "What makes a great manager?". I say great players, they make a great manager. A good chairman is very important too. Luck plays a part, but the most important quality is a sense of humour. If you haven't got a sense of humour, you're dead.'

*If you came along now, do you think you'd be able to pull off the same stunts?*

DOCHERTY: 'We didn't pull off any stunts. We were asked questions and we answered them. . . . What you don't realise is that Malcolm enjoys a cigar, that's the most important thing. He actually enjoys a cigar.'
ALLISON: 'We wouldn't be any different now to how we were then. We've just got a little bit of a sense of humour in our character. We're able to laugh at situations and tell stories and say things.'
DOCHERTY: 'Even against ourselves.'

*Do you think it ever counted against you?*

DOCHERTY: 'It didn't bother me. I wasn't interested.'

ALLISON: 'I really enjoyed managing and I really enjoyed training and I've been very fortunate because I've spent my life doing what I love doing and I've been paid for doing it.

'You know, people are individuals. They don't have to follow what everyone else does – I think that makes them different and I think that makes them better as well.'

DOCHERTY: 'Look at some of the boxers, look at some of the snooker players. Higgins is a character. You might not like him, but he's a character. Ali, he was a character.'

ALLISON: 'Cor, not 'arf. Just because it's different from the majority of people, who's right and who's wrong?'

DOCHERTY: 'All it is is opinion. That's all it ever is. When people ask me something or ask Mal something, all we do is give our opinion. I'm not saying I'm right and Mal's not saying he's right. All we're saying is, "This is our opinion". That's one of the great things about our sport.'

*So is there any room for the 'characters' now? The charismatic type of manager?*

DOCHERTY: 'Well, obviously not, because we're out of work.'

*Introduction*

# INFAMY, INFAMY, THEY'VE ALL GOT IT IN FOR ME

*'The game is about glory. It is about doing things in style, with a flourish, about going out and beating the other lot, not waiting for them to die of boredom.'*

Danny Blanchflower, Spurs (natch)

WHO HASN'T BEEN IN A SITUATION WHERE THEY FEEL THAT their natural flair, their quite extraordinary talent, is being stifled by a boss who's got the dress sense of a dead bear and who is more concerned with their pension rights than with your rights of expression? Who hasn't found themselves frustrated by this mediocre safety-first jerk, the type who's got a red cross in their diary to remind them when their television licence is due. God knows how they got the job. Money? Connections? Who hasn't fought their corner, arguing all the way down the line, right up to that point where they've got to put their job where their mouth is? And who hasn't cursed their way through the rest of the day, fantasising about their boss in relation to the wheels of a particular silver Saab parked outside a house not too far from where we're sitting now? They're jealous of me and my talent, these no-good dullards with their standing orders and their residents' parking permits and their tax-deductable life assurance schemes. Life assurance. What a phrase. What type of adventure is an assured life?

Now imagine this. Imagine being so convinced of your talent that you're willing to step beyond that point. Imagine being so self-willed, so strong that, no, no, you won't dilute it for their safety. No, you won't bow down to their more-than-my-job's-worth fear. This is me and, if necessary, I'll go, but this is me. Take it or leave it. Imagine that. To be more concerned with doing things your way than with security or with the opinions of others. What a treat that would be. Where would that leave the Davies's and the Tuck's of this world? (Choose your own organisational automatons. These belong to me and my 900 GLS.)

So who are you kidding? Talent, we've all got talent. The dictionary describes it as 'a particular aptitude, gift or faculty; mental capacity of a superior order'. It also says, 'attractive members of the opposite sex', though

I think we can leave that to one side for the moment. (There's also a mention of talent once being a weight and denomination of money, but let's not focus on Brian Clough just yet.) We've all got talent. But if talent is the gift, then confidence is what makes it sing. You need a confidence that doesn't so much border on the arrogant as live there full time. What's the point of possessing a prodigious gift if you let others – others whose talent is mediocrity – dictate your actions?

Being gifted to the point where you just cannot accept anything less than your own viewpoint. Maybe it burns so hard that you implode; maybe it turns you into a not particularly nice person. And maybe it makes you a bit of a menace to those who stand in your way. Which takes us back to Davies, Tuck and a particularly hungry Saab.

Perhaps that's where the fascination of our heroes lies. It's not particularly that they were outrageously gifted – though their supporters would probably claim that they were; it's more that they had the guts to live out our fantasies. They were prepared to say 'This is me. This is how I do things. If you don't like it, I'll be on my way.' It's a talent that's as much a curse as a gift, but what it would be to be cursed with that gift. Guaranteed fun (if not a lump sum at sixty-five) and, for most people, it's as much a fantasy as scoring the winner at Wembley against the Arsenal.

There's one further talent that all of our heroes threw in the pot that turned their skill and arrogance into a lethal concoction. It's that magic ingredient 'X' that's needed to turn a success into a big league media-friendly success. They had the talent to get up people's noses.

Looking back, maybe it was the early 1970s that were to blame. Economics aside, it was the last era of innocence, when money was important but not *that* important. Maybe it was that we all knew it had to end, that someone had to pick up the bill, but there was an undeniable feeling of joy in the air. In the pop world, everything went glam and glittery. In the football world, things were similar. A new breed of players emerged, players like Alan Hudson, Stan Bowles, Rodney Marsh and Tony Currie. Players who were skilful enough not to give a toss. Fourteen million pounds a week at AC Juventus wasn't an option; entertaining was.

They were characters. But what is a 'character'? A non-conformist. A loud, too-talented-by-half maverick. In our terms, perhaps we can say someone who had so much talent they couldn't handle it. That's why Gerry Francis or Kevin Keegan could never be 'characters'. No disrespect; they were both top players and they're both fine managers, but do they fire the imagination? Are they fuelled by wit? Our heroes cannot be defined by any criterion other than this: they were all stroppy, self-willed self-publicists who were only interested in doing things their way. Mostly, this ideal meant entertaining. Throwing caution to the wind. Sometimes it meant the opposite. Invariably it meant getting a new job.

Maybe that's why they got up people's noses. It's not as simple as saying something like 'people were jealous of their talent' or 'people were jealous of their success' although both those propositions were true. Curious as it seems, they pissed people off because they lived life to the sound of laughter. Laughter is, you'd think, such a happy sound that people would pay to hear it. And they do. In the cinema, in the theatre, in comedy clubs . . . but in the workplace? No. Not in the workplace. Work is a serious thing. To laugh about it? No. People define themselves by their work – it's that old work ethic thing. Work is such a sacred cow in this society that belittling it is damn near anarchistic.

Maybe we shouldn't blame the 1970s. Maybe we should blame the 1980s and Thatcher and Lawson and all those other 'free' marketeers whose real intentions towards the notion of freedom stretched as far as their own kind and no further. Free market? What they did was to impose a fear on the people who actually worked in that market and tried to create a world where the sun only shone if you had enough coins to put in the meter.

It's no coincidence that the last few years have seen a resurgence in interest in the 1970s, the economically shot but spiritually still optimistic 1970s. And it's no coincidence that much of that interest has focused on football, a forum where that optimism blossomed.

The men in this story – Bill Shankly, Malcolm Allison, Tommy Docherty, Ron Atkinson, Brian Clough, Jack Charlton – are united not by any conventional notion of success, nor by association, appearance or achievement. Though we'll touch on all those things, the one thing they had in common was the desire, the *need* to do things their way, regardless. They had a combination of qualities – the ego, the ability and the chutzpah – necessary to take on the establishment. They were prepared to put their mouths where their mouths were, and laugh about it.

*Chapter 1*

# THAT'S ENTERTAINMENT

*'One of the problems with the media is that they like to pigeon-hole personalities.*
*Some managers are described as "dour" and others are "deep-thinking". Then*
*there are the "great tacticians" and the "marvellous motivators". My time as a*
*player and my early days in management hardly brought me to national*
*prominence, but later in my days with West Bromwich Albion I was projected*
*more and more as a personality in the same groove as John Bond, my good*
*friend, and Malcolm Allison. There were many descriptions of the personality I*
*was supposed to be, raging from "flash" to "nouveau riche". Sure, I've always*
*liked the good things in life and I believe in living life to the full . . . and I've*
*always been prepared to graft hard for my luxuries. But suddenly I was depicted*
*as a champagne-swigging, cigar-chomping Jack the Lad who could hardly move*
*his body because it was weighed down by gold trinkets.'*

Big Ron Atkinson

IN A BOOK NOT DISSIMILAR TO THIS ONE, IT IS WRITTEN THAT
'the meek shall inherit the earth'. Well, that may be true, but here in the
West no one is too interested in all that hanging around, waiting for the will
to be read. Inheritances, inschmeritances. Get yourself a couple of sharp
lawyers, a Marvin Mitchelson or a Whiplash Willie-era Walter Matthau
(check *The Fortune Cookie*), and contest the thing. The meek? Whaddya
mean, the goddam meek? Get outta here! I lived here all my goddam life!

By the time the 1960s turned into the 1970s (some time around 1972),
pop culture – the media that since Elvis had provided our societies with a
public face – had come to recognise the truth about this meek nonsense. It
was all very well if you just wanted peace, love and understanding, but what
if you wanted something a bit more? If you wanted something a little more
– how you say? – tangible than a small piece of card with a pretty picture
on it that sent you up there to the sky with Lucy and her diamonds? Yeah,
well, forget all that sitting cross-legged with an acoustic guitar, a bongo and
a bong.

Take Marc Bolan. How Marc Bolan was loved. Everyone loved Marc

Bolan – well, everyone apart from my mum. (We grew up in Stamford Hill, North London, the same mid-urban neighbourhood that fed the young Bolan and his boy, David Jones. They used to hang out in the local bowling alley and my mum, a kindly soul who knows one end of a chicken from the other, gave strict instructions that the bowling alley was to be avoided. Odd types hung around there, she reckoned. Me, in my green-and-black crushed-velvet loon pants, didn't buy it. But Bolan's dead, Bowie's on an iffy art trip and the bowling alley is now a deceased Sainsbury's. Mother knows best.)

Anyway, Bolan. Everyone loved Marc Bolan. Throw a free festival and he was there. He'd turn up at the opening of a packet of rizlas. Loved. Him and his sidekick. He made a record called something like *My People Were Fair And Had Sky In Their Hair But Now They're Content To Wear Stars On Their Brows*. Nice tunes, sweet lyrics. Sensitive. It was a great success, bought by about maybe thirty people. (No doubt they passed it around, but that's not the point.)

But Bolan had been brought up in Stamford Hill and had been Chosen to know the value of things. Enough was enough. Cult love fed the chakras but left the tummy empty. Something else was needed. Bolan had seen how his erstwhile friend, the boy now known to the world as Bowie, had taken the world by storm. That story is well known. First there was *The Man Who Sold the World* where our David appeared on the cover in a dress. Then, when that didn't do quite enough, there was *Ziggy Stardust*. Eating Mick Ronson's 'guitar' on *Top of the Pops*. That did the trick. The tummy was still empty, but by now the nostrils were so full it didn't matter.

Bolan watched and learned. Out went the dippy hippy and in came the Electric Warrior. Loud hair, loud clothes, loud looks. More to the point, loud sales and serious cash. Meek schmeek.

It was the same everywhere, the same in every field. The twentieth century had matured into what it had long promised to be, an era of style over content. Politicians had, naturally enough, been among the first animals to recognise their essential truth: look nice enough and smile brightly enough and no one will notice that you've just lied through your teeth and completely contradicted what you said yesterday. Theirs was the art of charming mendacity. And that isn't a criticism – it's a job description.

After the débâcle that was Alec Douglas-Home (nice geezer, just a shame he was born 150 years too late), it was as easy for Harold Wilson to clean up as it was for the Sex Pistols over a decade later. With his mac and pipe and mannered vocal inflections, Wilson was someone the people could relate to. Never mind that he was a brilliant academic prodigy who'd hardly seen the street since he left home to go to Oxbridge, he was an ordinary lad from an ordinary family. His accoutrements were banner headlines reminding people – voters – of his ordinariness. Alec Douglas-Home didn't lose to Harold Wilson because Labour had a new set of dashing radical policies. He lost because Wilson understood the power of the image. Douglas-Home, the televisual precursor of Scott Tracey, was no match for Wilson's mac and pipe. It didn't take the Tories long to catch on. Enter Ted Heath, an acceptable Tory with an acceptable name (if little else). Ted. A good solid name. Just like Harold.

Sport was hit by the communications revolution more than most other areas of life. The parochial became national and the national became global as television brought the myth of the legendary to life. Would Cassius Clay have had the same impact if he had made his stance in an earlier age against not Vietnam but Korea? Tennis was in hiatus, caught in a no-man's-land between amateur and professional. The result was never in doubt, just as it was never in doubt many years later when Kerry Packer took on the cricket world.

Symbolically, the change took place at Lords – where else? – on 30 June 1962, the last ever Gentlemen *v* Players match was played. Cricket. Wasn't it ever cricket. The idea of the match was an anachronism that would have seemed ridiculous fifty years earlier, and its passing heralded a move towards a more honest state. Even writing now, one of the last bastions of the Gentlemen ideal, rugby union, is crumbling and its supporters privately acknowledge that a merger with the dreaded league is inevitable. All that remains is the Boat Race, but in a way it's right that that should stay. Think of it as a crocodile. One of nature's curios, a croc is a dinosaur that, by rights, should have become extinct millions of years ago. But it's still here and we can look at it and think back to how life once was. It's the same with the Boat Race. Show it to your children and explain to them about gentlemen, players, money and American students who study at fine British universities for two weeks a year. It will give them all the knowledge they need to survive in England.

For football, the people's game, the differences were even more black and white. Spurred on by their new status and the new media's need to fill column inches, the players began to respond like stars. All that football needed now was a platform, a catalyst. As chance would have it . . .

While winning the World Cup in 1966 was obviously crucial to England, hosting it was of equal, if not greater, importance. Up and down the land people could see top-quality football being played by the cream. Together with the new splash media, it was an irresistible combination. A new generation of stars was created, both inside the game and outside, as the innocence of age was visibly eroded. The game began to be dominated by characters – individuals who, like Wilson, understood the power of the image and thrived on it.

Everyone with a bit of front knew what it was they wanted. They knew what they had to do. The rest was detail. What accent? What type of trousers? What hairdresser? Surf on board the *Zeitgeist* express and the world can open up in front of you like a delicate oyster. It only opens a little way and only for a little while, but if you can catch it right . . . The grief is that if you get it wrong it could be fatal. Approach that oyster with a bubble-perm haircut when it should have been a bleached number-two crop, it's likely to piss itself laughing. You've got to be different from the crowd, but the same as the people who matter.

There were, and are, two types of people: those who risk everything and those who risk looking the twat. Be honest now. Would you have been that geezer who stepped outside his front door with the first bubble-perm? (In this particular case, it would have been better to have been the first than the second. At least the first had the excuse of trying something new. The second person knew that he'd look a complete twat and yet still did it. It's like being the second on your block to buy an Allegro or an Arsenal season ticket.)

The point of any fashion-cum-uniform is that it says more about you than words ever can. You can justify your stance, write a manifesto or rationally state your point of view and people will understand where you're coming from – if they can be bothered to take the time to do it. You can be more forceful and stand up tall and shout all you like and people will understand more easily, but they'll still have to listen. If you want people to know immediately where you stand, you have to hit them hard and straight; you have to become a walking noticeboard; you have to wear the right dress.

Fashion in the early 1970s went two very different, distinct ways, yet despite these external differences, both looks were saying the same thing.

On the one hand there were the glitter merchants, all look-at-me glitz, powder-puff peacocks, colourful and flash. It was a complete reversal of all that 'proper' society held as good and true. Then, as now, this was a man's world where men were men and rabbits ate lettuce. Only in Israel, bless her, were women taken seriously; back here in the West, only a woman would want to be a woman (they're the only ones smart enough to, but that's a different story). Making it so that you couldn't tell the difference between the sexes like the hippies did was bad enough, but a fashion that positively made men look like women with all that make-up and fancy hair and those effeminate gestures . . .

The other fashion direction was equally anti-Establishment. Skinheads were all clean, austere lines, smart and pressed, dressed to kill. Clothes were of paramount importance. The right label (Ben Sherman, Levi's Sta-Press, Loakes loafers . . . ) and the right amount of starch on the collar, the creases, the press. A crombie with a dark velvet collar was a coat that, if worn over a different suit, would have found its way easily enough into any father's wardrobe. Skins – and this is Skin before it was hijacked by the lame-brained jack-booted fascists – looked immaculate and this was their anti-establishment stance. It was a time of economic depression, of unemployment, of poverty. What were working-class kids doing looking smarter than us? It was a pride thing.

These fashions flourished precisely because they were a reaction against the times. Coming directly after the 'white heat' of the 1960s, a time of believable dreams and unbelievable possibilities, the 1970s were a dread-filled disappointment. The early 1970s was the bill – service not included. Unemployment, three-day weeks, strikes in place of strife, Leyland, Michael Edwardes, Red Robbo, oil grief, Thatcher the Milk Snatcher (June 1971 – you were warned), Ireland, poverty. Even the Apollo programme blew up in our faces. If we'd have known then what we know now about pollution, whales and the ozone layer, life would have been complete.

As politics got greyer and life became more depressing, people needed a break, needed – literally – larger-than-life figures to take them away. That's where the Bolans and the Bowies came into it. What joy was there in watching a dirty gratefully dead hippy who was happy to play long, meandering instrumentals because it meant that he didn't have to get up from his stoned-out stupor?

For Marc Bolan, glitter was a definite decision, a uniform, a look that defined him. Some eyeliner, a bit of something to make him stand out, something that made him sparkle. Like glitter. It worked a treat. Bolan hit upon something that inspired an army of clones who revelled in his success. He shone a light in the hearts of kids who were being brought up in a grey world. It was escapism and realism combined. Don't watch that, watch this. You don't have to believe what the grown-ups are telling you. *Metal Guru* was no accidental title.

There's nothing radical in this. It's one of the only virtues of the British character, this ability to conjure up joy to flaunt in the face of the grey. In the 1980s, when Thatcher was busy selling England by the pound and caring more about some southern hemisphere sheep than for 'her' people, the youthful reaction was the Blitz, Boy George and Marilyn. And if that wasn't enough, there was always Frankie Saying No.

*'No other decade changed the fabric of British society like the 1960s. It was a time when the rules were broken. It started with something like Mick Jagger being allowed into the Savoy without a tie on and finished when terrorists realised they could let off a bomb in a city centre without getting caught.'*

Philip Norman

If you think that all this is irrelevant to our cult of the football manager, well, look a bit more closely. The spur for all this activity was, as ever, not politics, not economics, but the media. The 1960s saw the communications industry explode in a way that allowed the individual to flourish, and style to win out. Take the Profumo affair. In 1963, the scandal probably seemed hugely important, but now who do we remember? Profumo? No, he's just another faceless name in a long line of sleaze-bag politicians. We remember Christine Keeler because she looked good and she talked good. She also had the good sense to sell her story to the press for £23,000. (With more style than a Profumo could muster in two lifetimes, she bought her parents a shop with the proceeds.)

In February 1962, *Private Eye* published its first issue. But while that was fun, it was essentially a class thing – the privileged classes taking the piss out of the privileged classes. A much more profound publication also started in that month. *The Sunday Times* printed the first colour supplement. With features on pop art and Mary Quant and her 'absolutely twentieth-century clothes', the supplement marked the beginning of the 1960s. Advertising-led and thus necessarily image-obsessed, it marked the dawn of the age of style over content and we entered the PR dreamtime.

Newspapers changed too. On 15 September 1964, a grey broadsheet, *The Daily Herald,* was transformed into the grey broadsheet *The Sun.* One week in October 1968 gave a taste of what was to come. On the 16th, Robert Maxwell bid £26 million for *The News of the World.* Rupert Murdoch's News Ltd joined in the chase on the 23rd. On 1 January 1969, *News of the World* editor Stafford Summerfield wrote an editorial proclaiming that the paper would remain 'as British as roast beef', a thinly veiled attack on Maxwell's Czech origins and another reminder (as if one were needed) of the pervasive racism of the British ruling classes, and it was announced that Murdoch had won. Summerfield found out about the new world order rather earlier than the rest of us. Just a year later, Murdoch sacked him.

Later in 1969, another media insitution fell to the voracious Australian, and another Summerfield was found in the shape of the print unions. Murdoch had long been angling for *The Sun,* a daily title which, shall we say, had potential. The print unions, possibly on the advice of a soothsayer, put up the barricades and did everything in their not inconsiderable power to stop the takeover. On 15 October, after a lengthy period which was more a courtship than a dispute, Murdoch bought *The Sun* for £250,000, having finally received the unions' permission. Up, up and away soared the super soaraway *Sun*. The fabric had changed and, out there in the material world, life was never really the same again.

Everything became entertainment and entertainment became everything. Showbiz, it was all showbiz. Image became all. If you gave good copy, you'd be written about. If you were colourful and larger than life, you'd be noticed. *Time* magazine wrote, 'In this century every decade has its city and for the 1960s that city is London. The rising star of the scene is a seventeen-year-old model, Twiggy, a six-and-a-half-stone Cockney with huge eyes and waif-like looks who can now earn ten guineas an hour.'

In 1967, the advent of colour television on BBC2 put everything on fast-forward. Okay, so the first seven hours' coverage was Wimbledon, but it was a start. The ITV network underwent a radical change as the staid Rediffusion network was replaced by the hip Thames/LWT duo. Academic notions such as McLuhan's 'global village' became merged with reality as The Box gave everyone a front-row seat.

Back in our real world, the meek didn't stand much of a chance under this media onslaught. Ask Manchester United about meek. Manchester United was about winning, being flash, cutting a dash and splashing the cash. As the last of the great meeks, Frank O'Farrell, was on his way out of the door, it slammed in his face, thrown back by the force of Tommy Docherty's entry.

There were plenty of nice guys knocking around, men who'd spent their lives in the game, respected figures. And they got by, people listened to them and they had steady jobs, regular incomes. For some, this was okay. It was like a Civil Service but without the security (who was it who said in the 1970s that being a football manager offered marginally less job security than being policy adviser to Idi Amin?). You could work in the field that you loved, doing the things that you loved, working with people whom you respected and who respected you. Lovely work, but anonymous.

For others, there was another world out there beckoning. It was a new world, a world where anything was possible. Football was one of the few professions still awash with cash. And it was new cash, novelty money. After all, it wasn't that long ago that there was a minimum wage. Now there was sponsorship, television, advertising. As a working-class entertainment just like any other, football sought to create the illusion of getting away from it all. If there was more money in the game, there was more money to be had from it too.

There were newspaper columns there to be written; televised football had discovered the panel – someone had to be on them; supermarkets had to be opened. This was the dawning of the age of football's Aquarius and all you needed was desire. Desire and an ego the size of the Grand Canyon. Bigger, if possible. Big cash, big fame, big name. And big was the password. Big was the name of the game. Malcolm Allison turned into Mal Content via Big Mal. That it was a double-edged sword is a different thing and a different story.

The decade had begun with the abolition of the minimum wage in January 1961, and that meant that players, like pop stars, could now be paid according to their worth, according to sales, and it gave notice of the imminent shift from sport to showbiz. And so a new breed of players came of age, long haired, sublimely skilled entertainers, these egocentric stars danced in the footsteps made by George Best, arguably the best of the lot but weather-beaten and worn out like pioneers so often are. (Right about here, we could slip in a couple of books about George Best. Suffice to say this: George Best was the first and he paid the price for being the first, but historically life would have been so much better for all concerned if he'd been as good a driver as James Dean. Athena would never have stopped the print run.)

Rodney Marsh, Charlie George, Frank Worthington, Alan Hudson, Stan Bowles, Tony Currie, John Pratt . . . loved by the fans and reviled by the Establishment, these players were the pop stars of their world. It wasn't only their talent that set them apart (though God knows, that was enough), it was their *joie de vivre*, the way they played the game. When someone like Marsh or Bowles got into their stride, taking the piss out of the hard, grey men around them, they were saying to the fans, 'It doesn't have to be like that. You can be like me. You can be like me if you adopt my value system and don't buy into theirs.' No wonder they were seen as a threat. No wonder they won about two and a half caps between them.

Maybe for the Establishment, this was right. A footballer is a cog, a cog in a wheel. If one cog starts acting in isolation, then the whole shebang can go down. It's no coincidence that Manchester City blew their chances of the League Championship in 1972 when Rodney Marsh joined them.

It was all very well to grow your hair and pay lip-service to the pop ethos of glitz, but that's where the similarity ends. A profession like football cannot go against the gender grain. The players lived most of their lives in the environment of the game, an exclusively male club where anything less than Charlton Heston was viewed with suspicion. Was? Is. Listen, it's still like that now. If one in ten are gay, and each football team has eleven players . . . How many gay footballers can you name? Well, there's Justin Fashanu and . . . ? And coming out did Justin's career a world of good, didn't it? While we're on it, how many gay cricketers or rugby players (league or union) can you name?

For managers, the choice was both more and less stark. They wouldn't go down the peacock route – being that much older than the players, it was that much harder for them. But they could do something that the players could never do. Unlike them, managers were individuals. They didn't have to fit into a mould, they didn't have to work in a unit. They were also higher up on the food chain than players. Because they had more authority, they could take the piss in a way that players couldn't. Managers had to inspire people, but they were the lion-tamers, not the lions. They could project any image they wanted. Theirs was not a team game.

So they went down a different route, something that combined traditional male values with traditional (working-)class desires: money. The signifiers were bought with cash (on a first names basis).

Natural showmen, they took to their task like elephants to castles. But they were more than showmen. They were more than team players. Riding high on the burgeoning cult of the individual, they were determined to do things their way. Though they'd deny it, it sometimes seemed as if the winning came a poor second to the size of the quotation marks in the next day's papers. The figures that counted were the column inches, not the 'points for' total, and the notion of being publically quoted had very little to do with the stock market.

It can be argued that things really changed during the 1970 World Cup. Even though England had its best-ever team there, it was nothing to do with the football. It was during that World Cup that the panel was born. Ostensibly a group of talking-head experts brought in to offer analysis, what the panel actually did was create a platform for show-offs. And show off they did. It's no coincidence that the first batch included Malcolm Allison, Brian Clough and Jack Charlton. Mouths vied with mouths as these 'characters' fought to get the biggest laugh or, more often, to say the most outrageous thing. Everyone knew that the more outrageous the comment, the bigger tomorrow's headline would be.

And if you were going to sound outrageous, then you had to look outrageous too. For pop's glitter and sparkle, read shades and leather. Over everything was the quintessential sheepskin coat. There was the all-weather suntan. (Let's not forget that suntans were originally desirable because they showed that you were wealthy enough to be able to afford a holiday in the sun.) The gold identity bracelet. Blow-dried hair. The shoes – Gucci – were leather slip-ons, the type that have the little gold chain across the top. The tie was one of those dual purpose efforts: it acted as an effective scarecrow and, if the weather turned, you could happily camp in it. As the right hand was holding a glass of Moët, the left held a furiously puffed-at Havana, while the mouth spat out an endless succession of quotable quips, one-liners that sounded as if they couldn't make up their mind whether they wanted to be Bill Shankly or Jimmy Tarbuck.

When Big Ron Atkinson was offered the job of managing West Bromwich Albion, the chairman tried to tempt him by saying that the company car, a Jaguar 3.4, was to be thrown in with the deal. Atkinson's legendary response was, 'You'll have to do better than that. My 4.2 is sitting outside.' Later, he changed this version of events: 'I can't think where that story came from. My Jag at the time was a 3.4,' which, while laughing at the first story, actually reinforces it. What fun there is to be had ripping into this Cointreau sensibility – we could start by calling it something like Ferrero Rocher chic. But it's crap. To everyone but the hereditary rich (who don't have to care) and the anal middle classes (who really care more than anyone but are too dishonest to declare it) money is necessary. It is self-empowerment and, for good or ill, it's our society's mark of success.

Money is important, and if you've acquired a stash, why not go shouting it from the rooftops? Like the young black male rap stars of a later generation, they were proud to show off their acquisitive wealth. Be loud, be proud and set out your stall.

A cliché? Of course it's a cliché, a caricature. No one really looked like that, did they? Well, curiously, yes. There was an A-line route to success – articulate, arrogant, ambitious – ploughed by Malcolm Allison, the George Best of managers. Allison was as much pop star as football manager. Loud and brash, good-looking and severely talented, Big Mal was news for what he was more than for what he did. As far as the media were concerned, he was a star. The football bit was incidental. It might have entertained him and fed his gargantuan ego to be the toast of the tabloids, but what really warmed his heart was seeing a free-kick that he'd dreamt up in training work in a match. Allison might have been all hat and cigar, but he'd still forgotten more about the game than ninety per cent of jobsworth managers would ever know. (Listen, Keith Richards might have spent the early 1970s in a smacked-out haze, but he still knew enough and cared enough to knock out *Exile on Main Street*.) In the end, though, Allison paid the price just as the Establishment always hoped he would. While pop stars were fêted for being wasted, football types who tried the same trick ended up just being wasted.

In *Heartbeat*, the film about the Beat lives of Jack Kerouac and Neal Cassady, Jack turns round to their wife and asks plaintively what they did wrong. 'We did nothing wrong,' Carolyn says. 'We just did it first.' (Kerouac was wrong even asking what they did wrong, but then again his heart was never in it.) Carolyn was right about Big Mal, too. He never did anything wrong. He just did it first.

Allison was the Sex Pistols of the era, the William Burroughs, the original sheepskin-coated, shade-wearing character manager who had more front than Selfridges and who spent too much time watching *Starsky and Hutch*. Allison was the trend-setter, the style guru who blazed the trail that others walked in. A hat, a coat, a bird on his arm, a cigar in one hand, a glass of champagne in the other and a headline in his mouth. Allison was the consummate manager, a grotesque Spitting Image puppet come to life.

It was all wonderful, and it was all wonderfully naff. Like champagne. (Is there anything that's so irredeemably tacky? Since time began, it's been held up as the measure of all sophistication. All smoking-jackets, Noel Coward and cool elegance. Maybe there was a time when champagne was cool and elegant. And maybe there was a time when the Costa Del Whoyoulookinatpal was picturesque and peaceful. Whatever, it was a long time ago and it says much for our powers of imagination that champagne, the Aqua Libra of the used-car salesman, is still held up in this way. At the same time, it's sad that something loses its appeal just because, for whatever reason, the great mass of the population can suddenly afford it. It's as if it had no value of its own and was merely judged as a social yardstick. Heaven forbid we do something like that. Just think, though, how apposite it is that champers ended up sharing a name with a bunch of Eurovision Song Contest winners.)

Allison's downfall had the same root cause as Best's and Cassady's. They'd all have been that geezer who stepped outside his front door with the first bubble-perm. Not that they would have had a bubble, but plenty of their followers did.

For more than a decade, that's the way it was. Then the money-men moved in in earnest. Football was big business and it couldn't be run in the cavalier way that it had been. Like pop music, it was swept down the glitz-fuelled highway so quickly that rules tended to be *à la carte*. The glare of stardom blinded many to the iniquities of the business. Money was dealt with in an 'informal' way – cash and first names. Come the 1980s, it had to change – business is business and progress is progress. If the rise of the character manager was a reflection of its time, then so too was its demise. Like a small independent record label, football had been taken over by the corporate mindset. Solidity and success became the buzz words, words that the quixotic character actors didn't have too much truck with. Even the panel has gone, replaced by the nice Alan Hansen and the nice Gary

Lineker with their sensible suits and interest-free smiles. As Docherty says of Lineker, 'If Gary would have been a chocolate he'd probably have eaten himself, but he's a super player and as a pro he's been a credit on and off the pitch.'

One of the first of Big Mal's acolytes was, coincidentally, a contemporary of his at West Ham's 'academy of football' back in the 1950s. John Bond was someone who, for a brief period, took the job of being a flash bastard gob-on-a-stick manager very, very seriously. So much so that when Peter Swales sacked Big Mal from his second stint as Manchester City boss in 1980, Bond was the man he called in.

Wonderfully arrogant and with an eye for the main chance, Bond had established himself as someone who was good for a quote. You know those MPs who you never hear about in the context of Cabinet reshuffles or policy or anything remotely important but who are always being quoted in the tabloids as being outraged, such as Terry Dicks? That was John Bond. The paper goes to bed at 11.30 on a Sunday night and that story needs spicing up: phone Norwich 1212.

Bond had been at Norwich since 1973, Bournemouth before that, and was a regular big fish in a small pond. Down on the south coast, he traded on the old West Ham academy nonsense (it came complete with a lifetime's guarantee: win nothing ever, or your money back), made and sold Ted McDougall, and applied a huge amount of Mr Sheen to his larynx; he practised speaking with a Havana and succeeded in sounding as if he had a dick in his gob. The advantage with teams like Bournemouth and Norwich is that they're not expected to be 'Big'. You get half a success there and people notice; you get half a success in Manchester and people also notice, but it's a different type of noticing.

Bond made a visible difference at Norwich. In 1973, when they made the League Cup final under Ron Saunders, the players wore light-grey suits with a club tie. When they were back there with Bond two years later, the League Cup again, and against Saunders' Aston Villa (football's a spooky old game sometimes, isn't it?), their outfit had subtly changed. Dark-green velvet suits, lime-green shirts, dark-green ties with yellow stripes and polka dots. I'll just repeat that in case you missed it. Dark-green velvet suits, lime-green shirts, dark-green ties with yellow stripes and polka dots. When you're wearing an outfit like that, who cares that you've just lost another Wembley final?

While Bond's mouth attracted the attention – it took someone with the astute footballing brain of Bob Wilson to point out in his 1979 column that 'Bond is not the sort of man to seek self-publicity' – Norwich's football attracted the points and, in 1979, for a brief period, they were top of the tree. Players like Justin Fashanu and Kevin Reeves are remembered more for their failures than their successes, but in this team they were young and bright and shiny – a bit like Bond himself, really. Reeves, in particular, was attracting a great deal of attention. Martin Peters was the captain, shrewdly picked up from Spurs for a song. The Canaries were cooking, but by the spring they'd done and finished the season in mid-League obscurity.

*'History repeats the old conceits, the glib replies, the same defeats.'*

Elvis Costello, 'Beyond Belief'

In the early-1970s, Manchester United hired The Doc to counter Big Mal at Maine Road and, almost a decade later, exactly the same thing happened. John Bond was in charge at Maine Road giving it loads of gab and flashing the cash like every day was Christmas. There was only one response that United could make: lose Dave Sexton and get Big Ron Atkinson. 'We both loved clothes, both loved to look our best,' says Bond now. 'And we've never changed. We were both flamboyant. He wore jewellery. I had a couple of rings. We were both good for Manchester.' They said it at the time, too. Their clubs might have been death's-head rivals but Big Ron and Bond were thick as thieves, media-wise. Both knew that their 'rivalry' meant only one thing: column inches. For a while, the papers couldn't get enough of them. Big Ron this, Bond that. Ron grew his rings and Bond coiffed his barnet and both rubbed fake tan into their cracks.

'Of course the back pages are full of us,' Ron crowed just after his appointment. Poor City, always the bridesmaid to United's bride. Typical that they got Bond and United got Big Ron. 'A lot of big things have been going on. I've been making major signings – and Bondy's been just missing them.' Boys, boys. What Ron was referring to was that he'd just signed Frank Stapleton – 'the best centre-forward in Europe' – for £900,000 while Bondy had just missed out on reuniting Justin Fashanu with his old Norwich partner, Kevin Reeves.

Bond enjoyed the trappings and got into the swing of things quickly, signing, ironically, Trevor Francis for a million pounds. Ironically because when Clough had signed Francis for the same amount in 1979, the Bond gob went into hyperdrive about spiralling transfer fees, the morality of the market, blah, blah. So then he signs Francis, and Clough gets a chance to knock out a quick exclusive. Roll-up, roll-up. Column inches for everyone.

A sort of greater-spotted Mal, Bond coped with the pleasure of Swales for three years, during which time he managed to take City to Wembley for an FA Cup final. The night before the final, he went to a Chinese restaurant and pulled a fortune-cookie: 'Never play Spurs at Wembley when there's a one in the year.'

City did well and took Spurs to a replay. But you cannot argue against the football gods. To rub salt into the wound, City hit the mighty Spurs with a goal that, in any other year, would have been remembered long into the night. It would have been called the MacKenzie final. Steve MacKenzie. That he was at City at all was the result of one of Allison's brain haemorrhages. A teenager with not a minute of first-team experience, MacKenzie had been plucked from Crystal Palace reserves by Allison in 1979 for the princely sum of £250,000. Compared to Kevin Reeves, Steve Daley and Michael Robinson, young Steve was one of Mal's more astute purchases. 'I thought he was going to mature,' Big Mal said ingenuously many years later.

At Wembley it looked as if that quarter of a million would be paid back in the most spectacular fashion. The ball flew across the edge of the Spurs penalty area harmlessly enough. Then, as if by magic, in one fluid body movement, MacKenzie swivelled and volleyed the ball into the back of the net. It was the sort of thing you dream about doing in a game of three-and-in in your local park. While the headlines flashed before his eyes and Bond rehearsed the quotes, Ricky Villa decided that he'd had enough of being 'the makeweight in Spurs' audacious Argentinian raid'. Ossie might have been going all trembly, but the bumbling Villa sorted him out. That was Wembley then. And that was John Bond.

In the end, his own arrogance betrayed him. Now arrogance is a good thing in a quote-merchant, but let's keep things in perspective. City began to lose. Some of the players expressed unrest. Bond said that if things didn't improve, he'd quit. They didn't. He did.

'If you are in a man's world you have to make a man's decisions . . . I might be out of work for evermore, but that's a risk you have to take. I certainly won't be applying for any jobs.' Walking out on a £175,000 contract. It was an act of outrageous arrogance, taken in a land way beyond the place where rational thought lives. Perhaps he thought Liverpool would pass over Joe Fagan once they heard that Bondy was a free man. They didn't. Neither did anyone else, and Bond was out. Quite why he had to pay such a high price while others continued to bumble along is a mystery. Maybe he just wasn't good enough. Maybe a dodgy haircut is no match for a decent coat. He took Bournemouth from the Fourth to the Third, but no higher. He took Norwich to the top and City to Wembley, but what did he actually win? It's that old West Ham academy deal.

Bond, of course, had a different explanation. 'It all started when I slagged off Bobby Robson [the England manager]. I said that sometimes I wondered whether he knew what he was doing. Well, I was fined £750 by the FA and one of their members asked me how I would like to wake up and read such things about myself. I said, "Do me a favour. Margaret Thatcher gets up every morning to hear people saying things like that and you don't hear her crying. She just gets up and fights back."'

Possibly she didn't complain because she knew she deserved everything people said about her. It's only a thought. Anyway, carry on.

'But from that moment it was as if people were saying, "We aren't going to give him a job." And I was told that there had been talk at a meeting of top managers about not co-operating with me.' Great. A conspiracy theory. We're twenty-odd pages into this book and it's about time we had a good conspiracy theory. The bosses ganged up against me. Love it.

In 1991, when he had been rescued from soccer's slag-heap by Shrewsbury Town, Bond said, 'Oh yes, I see it now. I should have kept my trap shut, not gone for the fame and vainglorious big time and headlines and star players and all that and always stuck where I was happiest, at a small-town club, somewhere unfashionable.' You can't put a wise head on young shoulders, but admit it, John, it was fun.

Tommy Docherty came up with another quip to put down the daddy of the carbon 'characters'. 'It's all very well copying Malcolm's style. It's just a shame that he took the later Manchester City version as his model when he should have taken the earlier one.'

*'Are you a better manager for your experiences?'*
*'No. I always thought I was good.'*

Big Ron, Sheffield Wednesday manager, 1990

Big Ron Atkinson. To take the music analogy again, this time punk, if Big Mal was The Sex Pistols, then Big Ron was The Damned. Or, given his exemplary record as the complete misogynist, The Stranglers. He looked perfect. Every inch the manager, right down (or up) to his hair, a perfectly balanced, bouffant Bobby Charlton complete with its own ozone hole.

From the off, Ron went out of his way to be 'Big'. When he took over West Bromwich Albion on 13 January 1978 and came into the public eye for the first time, he was like a kid in a sweet shop. Quotes came gushing out of his mouth quicker than you could say 'What do you think, Ron?'. To nick a joke about someone else, the message on Big Ron's ansaphone was 'Yes'.

Managers are no longer the headline-makers they once were. Maybe it's a fashion thing; maybe the public gets bored with the same cast of characters – after all, there are precious few Ken Barlows in British soaps. Characters and storylines are replaced and updated. Keep on moving. The current vogue in the back-page soap is for figures. It's transfer spiral time – the mini-skirt in the lexicon of football stories. Suddenly, according to the papers, if you're 'worth' less than £5 million, you're going to struggle getting into the Orient reserve team. It's all money and figures and X is getting £Y thousand a week and Y is getting £X thousand a week. And if this one is worth that, how much is that one worth? But it's not a new story – in March 1972, Philip Whitehead MP (a man Clough would later take under his wing) called for the government to 'take control of this flesh market'. Flesh market? In that season, £5.5 million was spent in 150 deals. That's an average of £36,000 on each player – two weeks' wages for some of today's starlets. But it's just one of the stories on football's wheel of fortune and it must keep spinning.

So where to next? Well, next we go right to the top. For a mega-multi-million-pound industry, the feudal nature of British football never ceases to amaze. And it's not just the familiar stuff about players calling managers 'The Gaffer' or 'The Boss'. It's the way the thing is set up. The land is divided up into big catchment areas, each of which is under the control of the local moneyed bigwig. He employs a manager who, in turn, controls the workers. And while the manager has the right to hire or fire his underlings, so the bigwig – the chairman – has the right to hire or fire him. In the late-1980s and the 1990s, it was clear who ran the show, and while in the past the chairmen were, with a few notable exceptions, prepared to be faceless backers, now things were different. The stakes were higher and there wasn't any room for egocentric fancy dans with fedoras and car-boot coats. As football has become more and more money-orientated, it's only natural that the people with the ultimate control over that money have got more and more powerful. And with that money and power comes ego. Is it any surprise that today the charismatic figures are not so much the managers as the chairmen?

They too are subject to the changing times that we live in. The estate agent culture that was Thatcher's great invention has resulted in the very nature of the people who run the game changing. In the 1992 election, John Major promised us a classless society, but in truth what he and his predecessor gave us is a society without any class. We who crave classlessness may bemoan the passing of a generation of Old Etonians – and what sort of society is it that defines people by which primary school they went to? – but replacing 'old money' with 'new money' is like changing your car from a Mercedes to a BMW (preferably a model with the letter 'i' tacked on the end – and we mean tack). Invariably these people, shrewd nuts, players rather than gentlemen, aren't in the game for purely financial reasons. They want to wear the sheepskin. They want the glory. No doubt in a few years' time, there'll be another book sitting on your shelves, *One Lump or Two? The Chairmen of the Bored*. If we're real lucky, it'll come out just before *Hall or Nothing: Agents of Change*.

The whole manager schtick is a curious one. What are their qualifications? What do they do? What exactly are they? Sports coaches? Public-relations officers? Financial wizards? Man managers? They're all of these things – or rather, they become all of these things – and they do all of these things. Now. At one time the manager was just that: a manager. It was only with the influx of big(ger) money and the all-knowing, all-seeing eye of the media that things changed. The 'character' manager came about because the job specification changed faster than anyone realised. Faster than it took anyone to write the manual. No one knew the rules, so it was left to the managers themselves to write their own rules. And, as ever, those with the loudest pens wrote the loudest rules. In terms of qualifications . . .

Once upon a time, the qualification was a purely football-based one. Now, though, it's a little more complex. Part footballer, part CEO of a multi-million-pound corporation, it's little wonder that a generation grew up committing (knowingly and unknowingly) the most horrendous financial *faux pas*. Bungs. It's a different story in a different book, but how many footballers do you think are financially qualified for their job? The mind scans back to the television sitcom *Porridge* and the Richard Beckinsdale character, Godber, who was considered an intellectual because he had a geography O-level. Tony Galvin (Spurs' nymph-like winger) stayed away from the management game – and he had a degree in Russian!

Times change. There are no revolutions, only successive evolutions. So pop music traded The Rolling Stones for East 17, the Labour Party swapped Harold Wilson for Tony Blair. And football? Roy Evans for Bill Shankly? Frank Clark for Brian Clough? Glenn Hoddle for Tommy Docherty? But then again . . . Atkinson for Phil Neal?

Big Ron. Of all the figures here, only Big Ron Atkinson remains. The oldest manager in the Premier League, Ron has survived and has turned into what all survivors eventually turn into: an elder statesman. A respected figure. Jack Charlton remains the same and that's because he was never like anyone other than Jack Charlton. No cigar, hat or *Starsky and Hutch* threads. Even when he was at Leeds, Jack looked like a relic from a bygone era. Jack has what he's always had: a fishing-rod and an attitude, good solid things that are built to last. Shankly's gone, Docherty and Allison are still entertaining the boys, though in a slightly different form. And Clough? Well, Clough . . . you can work out Clough. He always was on a different planet.

As Jack Charlton said, 'It would be the best job in the world if it wasn't for Saturdays. I love working with players, love being involved with a football club. It's just a shame that every Saturday you have to put it all on the line. But that's what the game is all about. You enjoy five days and suffer the sixth. And like most football managers, I wouldn't change it for the world.'

## Chapter 2

# THE FIFTH BEATLE?

*It is widely recognised that the courageous spirit of a single man can inspire to victory any army of thousands. If one concerned with ordinary gain can create such an effect, how much more will be produced by one who cares for greater things!*

Chuang-tse, Chinese Taoist philosopher

WAS IT REALLY SO DIFFERENT BEFORE? THOUGH IT COULD BE argued that before things were the same, only smaller, it would not be true. Life – entertainment life – really was a different animal before the early-1960s. It was parochial and heroes were strictly local. Football clubs were huge community focal points, players were of the people and managers were little more than community leaders, more akin to a parish vicar or youth-club leader than a flamboyant pop star. For every loudmouth local warrior like Burnley's Bob Lord (who often stated that he wasn't going to let the fact that his Lord-ship came after his first name rather than before it stop him achieving his aims), there were a hundred anonymous men doing an anonymous job. Men who were known and respected within their city walls, but unknown outside. But that was in an era when managers were just that. They managed. They didn't have to bother with mega finances, the commercial side of things, the media intrusions. They just got on with the job.

Probably the first football manager to make it big outside of his immediate constituency was Arsenal's Herbert Chapman. Autocratic leader of Arsenal's all-conquering team which won a hat-trick of titles between 1930 and 1934, it was Chapman more than anyone else who built the monolithic edifice that we still see today. But Chapman was an exception. In Wolverhampton, the name Stan Cullis still holds true. But where else? Spurs fans know the name Arthur Rowe, he of the push-and-run. Anyone know anything else about him? Every programme-collecting schoolboy worth his salt knows that Huddersfield Town won a hat-trick of Championships between 1923 and 1926. And their manager's name? Who'd want to be the sad schoolboy who'd know that? (Herbert Chapman, said the sad schoolboy at the back).

The night that Ipswich won the League Championship in 1962, their manager, a Mr Alf Ramsey, a one-time greyhound-touting wide(ish) boy turned admiral of the fleet, was so overjoyed that he did a solo lap of honour around a deserted Portman Road stadium in the dead of night. If it had happened a decade later, the light from the flashbulbs would have made Las Vegas look like a provincial town in the middle of the desert.

Shankly. Everything can be traced back to Bill Shankly, the man who first developed the one-liner as a weapon when managers were only just coming into the public perception. Though the nearest he ever came to a sheep was at Sunday lunch, Shankly changed the rules of the game forever.

It's not difficult to find someone to speak ill of Shankly, it's impossible. And if it's difficult to talk about Shankly without gushing and getting slushy, then maybe it's best not to try. If gush slush is what's required, then it's best to gush and slush. Tommy Smith, the hardest – and best – of all hard men and not a man to throw compliments around lightly, says, 'He was treated as a god on Merseyside. He didn't have a bad bone in his body. Every time he stepped into the room everyone stopped talking. He had an aura about him that just made you take notice of him whether he was talking or not.'

In conversation, Smith still refers to Shankly as The Boss as if it were the most natural thing in the world, as if The Boss was a name, like John. It's worth remembering here that Smith played most of his football under the most successful manager football has ever seen, The Boss's successor, Bob Paisley.

So be cynical. Smith might have been harder than hard, but he's not going to mouth off against the father of the Anfield family, is he? Loyalty still has some meaning, even in this age of the computer. The curious thing, though, is that even players not versed in the ways of Father Shankly are of the same opinion.

Alan Hudson, former Chelsea and Stoke City firefly, tells of the time his heart jumped a beat. 'I was playing for Stoke against Liverpool and at the end of the game, Bill Shankly came into the opposing dressing-room – our dressing-room – and came up to me and told me that that was probably the finest ninety minutes he'd seen from a footballer. I couldn't believe it. My manager, Tony Waddington, told me Shankly never did that. He never went into the opponents' room. You've no idea what sort of buzz that gives you. No disrespect, but if someone walked up to me on the street and said that, it'd be nice, but, you know. You've got to put it in the context of who it was – and it was Bill Shankly.'

And this is Alan Hudson, one of the most talented players of his generation, someone who knew one end of a football from another, someone who must have had compliments coming out of his ears. Hearing Hudson talk like this is sweetly reassuring. It's like hearing one of your best mates admit that he hadn't really been a tough-hanging hooligan when he was younger; he had, in fact, been a train-spotter. Tearaways, huh? Pussy cats.

It's interesting, this one, and whether you're reading about him or talking to people about him (or, truth be told, writing about him), you can't help but get sucked into this notion of Bill Shankly as a deity. You have to repeat to yourself, as if a mantra, 'He was only a football manager'. But then you think, why adopt such a snobbish attitude? He gave pleasure to thousands – millions? – of people and how can you belittle that? 'He was only a football manager.' Are you seriously going to have more respect for a government minister? John Gummer? John Major?

There's an old Polish saying which is important to remember here: 'Behind every great man there's a great myth'. Without wishing to take anything away from Shankly (couldn't and wouldn't), that's as true here as it is anywhere. There are a number of things that help his cause. Firstly, he, the person, is long dead – he died of a heart attack on 29 September 1981, aged sixty-six. So he's safe. He can't damage the myth. If Bill Shankly were a rock musician, he'd still be selling by the bucketload. Kurt Cobain, Buddy Holly, Jimi Hendrix, Bill Shankly.

Second, and we can call this (take that tongue out of your cheek) the 'Harold Wilson Factor', the world – both the football world and the world outside – is getting murkier, scuzzier, sleazier by the minute. Shankly stands tall and proud and clean, a memory of all that was once good in the game (the world). He had morals. Where are the morals today? He's a reminder of what it was once like, an age when footballers wore only the colours of their club and weren't mobile advertising hoardings. Bungs, iffy transfers and ridiculous greed-fuelled wages, that's what we've got now. In Shankly's day . . . If Shankly were here . . . It's all, of course, complete bollocks – point two is not called the 'Harold Wilson Factor' for nothing. Everything that we've got today, they had then. It's just that today there's more noise. If you doubt this, think back to three particular Sheffield Wednesday players, a £100 bet, a lifetime ban and the phrase 'the tip of the iceberg'.

Third, Shankly was at Liverpool. Yes, yes. Look, Shankly might go on about the grit and honesty of the Scousers, but think about it. During the same period that Shanks took hold, Liverpool suddenly became the centre of the universe. Beatlemania had just broken loose and the world was beating a path to the city. Everyone wanted to be Liverpudlian. Everyone tried to look Liverpudlian. In short, all eyes were on Liverpool. Shankly couldn't have had a better platform. He might well have performed the same miracle at, say, Leyton Orient, but it's unlikely. There couldn't have been a more perfect place for football's first media-friendly figure than Liverpool. If Gerry and the Pacemakers could make it big, think how easy it was for someone like Shankly.

For someone who eschewed the notion of the individual so strongly – is there a single player you associate with Shankly's great Liverpool teams or is it the great teams you recall? – Shankly was a fully signed-up member of the cult of the self. The more the legend of Shankly grew, the more he seemed to enjoy it. Things reached ridiculous proportions by the time he quit, as was seen after the 1974 FA Cup final when Liverpool beat Newcastle 3–0.

It was a time when the new media frenzy had reached a fever pitch and the television hype-machine was going overboard at every opportunity. The final started at around ten in the morning and there was all that Meet The Wives and Cup Final It's A Knock-Out nonsense. Malcolm MacDonald – inevitably SuperMac – had been shooting his mouth off about what he was only going to do, how many goals he was going to score, how he was going to beat Liverpool on his own. That he was basically a pair of walking sideboards didn't matter, he was good copy and the press bought it. Come the match and come the team. Liverpool didn't beat Newcastle, they destroyed them, and the match became a kind of joyous (or sad, depending on your colour) exhibition. At the end of the match, Shankly walked up to the Liverpool end. Mothers thrust their arms out, holding blind babies, desperate for Shankly to touch them. Cripples threw away their crutches. Fans clambered over the crash barriers, ran up to Shanks, fell to their knees and kissed his feet. He made no attempt to stop them.

Like all great mythical men, Shankly's errors have been brushed over. His 'retirement' is a perfect case in point. Even now, no one will say what's obviously the truth: he screwed up. He was only fifty-seven when he quit and, in retrospect, it was a ridiculous thing to do, a decision borne out of a classic mix of ego and stupidity. He made the time-honoured mistake of thinking that he was bigger than the club, of forgetting that he was an employee. Taking on the management and calling their hand . . . history is full of these people.

He quit at the end of the 1974 season, a season that reached its climax with that FA Cup final against Newcastle. They were irrepressible, magnificent. The footballing world seemed to be at their feet. Then Bill Shankly quit. He resigned as manager of Liverpool. Why? Together with the question of why dinosaurs became extinct, this is one of the most perplexing questions in recent times. There are more theories about this than there are trophies in Anfield (well . . . ), but one thing seems certain. As Tommy Smith says, 'He didn't realise that the directors didn't like him.' It sounds strange, but then again . . .

What Shankly was after, more than anything, was a place on the board. He wanted to be up there. But – Smith again, 'He wasn't a very good schemer or an operator. He had, in the past, treated the directors with disdain, thinking that he was more important than them and when they got their chance to get rid of him, they did. It killed him.' Shankly, it transpires, had regularly used the threat of resignation as a tool to get his own way and never figured that the directors would react. And while it may be true that he 'didn't have a malicious bone in his body', it was naïve to think the same of others. It's also more than possible that the directors were frightened that, if they let him on the board, he might try to take them over. And who's to say that they would have been wrong?

Shankly himself recognised his mistake. In 1977, the year that Liverpool won the European Cup for the first time, the League Championship for the tenth time and were stopped from winning a unique treble when Jimmy Greenhoff scored a freak goal to rob them of the FA Cup, he was asked to speak at the ceremony crowning Bob Paisley as Manager of the Year. Shankly said his piece but there was a hint of bitterness in his words. He finished by saying, 'And if you think I'm feeling a wee bit jealous, then you're bloody right.'

By drawing attention to all this, I'm not trying to diminish the legend or suggest that he was any less 'great' than he was. It's just that if we don't, then the only reminder we have of his humanity, of his fallibility, are the completely horrible shirts that he's wearing in every photograph. But away from the myth, what was Bill Shankly?

Shankly's attitude to the way that things are was externalised in the shape of his haircut. Marine chic. A fierce razor job in which every hair knew its place – and woe betide it if it got caught in the wind. A socialist autocrat who knew when not to get involved, Shankly was always doing what a manager should be doing if he's doing it well. Asking Tommy Smith what made Shankly different to other managers is like asking Shankly what makes Liverpool different to Everton. Where shall we start?

'He instinctively knew when to do things and when not to. He delegated very well, but then he had very good people to delegate to. He didn't drink or smoke – there was none of that cigar stuff that the other managers got into – and he was a great role model. He didn't give a shit about anybody apart from Liverpool Football Club and always had the club at heart.

'If you were doing well, you'd be on first name terms, but if it was "Tommy Smith", you knew you were in for a rollicking. He didn't hold grudges or carry on an argument, but he definitely had his favourites.' A chink of light. He had favourites. In this context, that's almost a fatal character flaw. 'No, it wasn't really like that, but in a group of people that big, there are always going to be people who are difficult and who have to try and make themselves special.' Who? Who? 'No, no, you don't want to go into all that. By the way, did you know that two of Emlyn Hughes's kids are called Emma and Emlyn?' So that's the dinner-party guests sorted out then.

'The Boss was just interested in the way that things were supposed to be done. I think it's all down to ego, whether you are prepared to put the club first and not yourself. Most managers are on ego trips; Bill wasn't. He genuinely wasn't.'

You're beginning to wonder if the adoption agency's got any of these Shanklys left, aren't you. And just in case you had any doubts (as if), Smith comes in with 'He was the most generous man I knew.'

Shankly was not really a football manager in the sense that the word had been used before. That football was his life there's no doubt, but in many ways he had more in common with, say, Billy Graham than Alf Ramsey. Shankly was an evangelist. A fundamentalist. A religious fanatic whose religion came to be Liverpool Football Club. Only Brian Clough can claim to be cut from the same cloth but, even then, the cloth was cut in such a different style as to make the comparison almost meaningless. Almost, but not quite. Both were men with a mission, both had a fire that inspired a loyalty from those around, both were touched with genius and both were exempt from the rules that govern ordinary men.

Putting Shankly in this book seems almost sacrilegious, for he was as far from the modern image of a 'character manager' as it is possible to be. Big Bill Shankly? A cigar and a glass of champagne? C'mon, it's not going to happen. But still, he's the daddy, the one they all look up to. There's film of Chelsea, Tommy Docherty's 'Little Diamonds', playing Liverpool and Shankly is talking to Docherty after the match. The look in Docherty's face, in his eyes, is one of pure devotion. Like a Tibetan monk meeting the Dalai Lama. Even now, talk to Docherty or Allison or any of our other heroes and the gags stop and a reverence takes over. Respect from your peers is something everyone craves, and Shanks had it in buckets. He was a football man above all else and above all others. His famed one-liner – 'Football isn't a matter of life and death. It's far more important than that' – is a joke. Isn't it?

In another sense, though, he belongs. He was loud, witty and, in every sense, larger than life. He fired gags like an Uzi and spun tales like the grandfather you wished you had, laughing, as journalist Eric Todd said in a wonderful phrase, 'like a corncrake in search of a mate'. Shankly was the link between the old school and the new. He was what connects someone like Bill Nicholson to a Big Mal or a Big Ron. But whereas Bill Nick was content to let his Spurs do the talking, Shanks wasn't. Maybe it was that he was shrewd enough to see which way the wind was blowing.

While it might be asking too much of even a Shankly to stand out in the early-1960s, look at Ian St John and Jimmy Greaves and see the Saint and Greavsie of today, it really wasn't that hard to see the way the media were moving. In fairness – and this gush slush caper can go too far if you're not careful – it was probably something much more basic. Like ego. His fame spread far beyond the confines of the field, dragged into the national consciousness by a charisma on fire. Ask my mother. She'd have heard of Bill Shankly.

The Shankly legend has it that, in essence, Shankly was football-obsessed and Liverpool-obsessed. Both ideas he milked. He took his wife to a football match during their honeymoon. More. He was spotted celebrating his wedding night at a Central League game in Huddersfield. Maybe it was true and maybe it wasn't, but everyone was prepared to believe it and he was prepared to let everyone believe it.

Shankly loved Liverpool and Liverpool loved Shankly. While espousing Liverpool's cause, he focused on belittling neighbours and rivals Everton. 'There's only two football teams in Liverpool, Liverpool and Liverpool Reserves.' Ironically, he lived almost directly opposite Everton's training ground, Bellefield. He enjoyed telling visitors that, if they got off the bus quickly, they'd probably not get contaminated. Maybe, the way he saw it, the more attention he got, the more attention Liverpool Football Club got – a Good Thing. It would have been interesting to see how he'd have reacted if one of his players had demonstrated such a ready and vocal wit.

Even before he was at Anfield, there persists the feeling that he knew that was where his heart was. As a Glaswegian, the son of an Ayrshire miner, he understood Liverpool. A strong, solid working-class community which used humour to bolster a pride that had survived the ravages of economic depression, where football was both high church and escapist cinema. He once said, 'If I wanted a workforce I would pick it from Merseyside and we would wipe the floor with everybody. All they need is to be treated like human beings. The people here have a hard life but a great spirit. When they're on your side and all working together, then they take some beating.' It was the people, says Smith, who first alerted Shankly to the real Liverpool story. 'He realised that Liverpool was a sleeping giant and did it so passionately that they couldn't resist. He understood the people better than anyone.' Later in his life, he recalled a time in 1958 when, as manager of a ten-man Huddersfield team, he beat Liverpool 5–0. His team had thrashed Liverpool yet, he said, he felt a certain sadness. Perhaps somewhere deep inside our psyches, we all know where our destiny lies.

When he arrived there in December 1959, Liverpool was a middling Second Division club, muddling along with not much ambition to be anything else. And Anfield, far from the hothouse temple that it was to become, was tatty and in need of more than a lick of paint. But it wasn't all bad news. The bricks might have needed a bit of grouting, but Shankly found a rich vein of human talent waiting to be exploited. Bob Paisley, later to prove himself as the most successful football brain in British history, was the first-team trainer, Reuben Bennett was chief coach and Joe Fagan was in charge of the reserves. Ronnie Moran was also there, playing at full-back. Roy Evans. Roger Hunt. Shankly took this lot and did something strange to them. Even now, no one's really too sure what he did. Everyone talks about the loyalty he inspired, the 'simple things' he initiated and the honesty he espoused. But the way he changed Liverpool makes you think that he, too, arrived floating out of the sky on an umbrella. And, like Mary, Shankly believed that a spoonful of sugar helped the medicine go down, only in his case the sugar was football and the medicine was his methodology.

Football. It was always football. Break the word football up and you get foot and ball. And that, for Shankly, was what it was all about. He couldn't cope with ideas and theories and notions and concepts. Football was really a very simple game. Ronnie Moran talks of the time that Shankly was obliged to attend a seminar given by some great coaching guru. The coach was lecturing on something called 'shadow play' which involved players chasing each other around the pitch without the ball. Any practice that didn't involve the ball was, to Shanks, anathema. So, anyway, he was standing there listening to the great coach and waited patiently until he'd finished. Shankly then looked up at the sky and announced, 'There's no sun today so we can't do this shadow-play. Here's a ball. Let's play some five-a-side instead.'

*'No one was asked to do more than anyone else. We were a team. We shared the ball, we shared the game, we shared the worries.'*

Bill Shankly

Like all decent-minded people, Shankly was a socialist. What made him great above others was that he lived it. He applied the basic socialist principles to his life and his work and, while it may be pushing the point to say that it was no coincidence that Liverpool played in red, it certainly did help in defining them as the good guys.

Maybe it's not pushing the point. After all, it was Shanks's idea, that red strip. To briefly tangentalise, let's say it now and get it out of the way. It was Shanks's idea. The red strip, the THIS IS ANFIELD sign, the chemical make-up of the bricks in the west stand . . . it was all Shanks's idea. Everything was Shanks's idea.

About that THIS IS ANFIELD sign. It was the perfect opposition psyche-out. As if going there to play Liverpool wasn't enough, Alan Hudson remembers going there and walking out onto the pitch through the tunnel and past that sign. Standing next to it was Shanks. 'He stopped to talk to our players going out, and because it was Shankly, you'd stop and listen. And he was wishing everyone good luck, telling them not to worry about a thing, telling them how it'd be a good game. Then he'd start telling them what great players they were going to play against, how it would be a great experience and he'd start reeling off the names of the players in the Liverpool team, and saying, but don't worry, they're only human . . . By the time you got onto the pitch, you'd be 3–0 down.'

Anyway, the strip. It was November 1964 and Liverpool had just set off on their first European Cup jaunt. Their first match was against Reykjavik, a fine pipe-opener but their 11–1 victory wasn't what was needed in terms of tournament preparation. In the second round, they were to play Anderlecht, a proper team. Shankly was, as ever, looking for an edge, and the idea came of a new strip. Big Ron Yeats ('a fantastic man' – Shankly) was his model. 'One day after training, he asked me to try on this new kit and run out of the tunnel at Anfield while he stood on the pitch to study the effect. I came out and he stared hard at me and said, "Jesus Christ, son, you look eight feet tall in that. You'll scare the living daylights out of them."'

Nearly all the Shanks stories revolve around this kind of football pop-psychology, some of which is just funny and some of which is frighteningly effective, so effective that the thinking behind it would probably cost around $200 an hour in New York. In his book *The Boot Room: An Anfield Legend*, Ivan Ponting relates a classic Shanks story. Three days after Liverpool had beaten Leeds in the gruelling 1965 FA Cup final (who said that the good guys wear white?), Liverpool were due to play Inter Milan in the semi-final of the European Cup. Now, Liverpool were no slouches but Inter? Inter then were as Inter usually are; the holders and a class apart. With players like Facchetti and Mazzola, they were a top team.

Anyway, Bill knew that the Kop were on for it, Liverpool just having won the FA Cup. So, after having taken the trouble to direct them to the Kop end, he made Inter go out first. The noise – the row – was so loud that the Italian players looked at each other, gulped a bit, turned about face and headed for the marginally quieter Anfield Road end. Then Big Ron Yeats led out his red army and the ground erupted. To use a contemporary analogy, it was like a heavyweight champion fighting in his home town – and milking it. By now Inter – and you've got to remember, this is no backwater team, this is Inter Milan who play in the San Siro, the most impressive stadium in the football world – were wondering what was on the telly. Can't we just get this over with and go home?

Not yet. Just before the match kicked off, just as the players were warming up, Shankly pulled off his master stroke. Out came Gerry Byrne, who had broken his collar bone against Leeds, and Gordon Milne, who had missed the FA Cup through injury, with the trophy. As the two crock heroes traipsed around the perimeter of the pitch – slowly – the ground, which already sounded as if it were going to erupt through sheer noise-force, blew a gasket. Someone turned the amplifiers up to '11' (© *Spinal Tap*). Just when you need to go that little bit louder, when you need that little bit extra, Anfield goes to '11'. (Don't even bother to ask why they don't just make '10' louder.)

Milan had packed their bags before the game kicked off and Liverpool won 3–1. Sadly, Shanks couldn't pull off the same trick in the return and Milan went on to win the Cup.

Liverpool BS were, as we've said, a bit of a shambolic shambles. They'd last won the Championship in 1947, but since then? Nothing. In 1954, they were relegated to the Second Division and there they'd remained – until Shankly took over in 1959. In 1962, they were champions of the Second Division. At the end of the 1963–64 season, Shankly was holding up the League Championship trophy, and that's the way it's been ever since. Championships, FA Cups, League Cups, European trophies . . . Just as Shankly was the bridge between the 1950s, the 1960s and the 1970s, so that first Liverpool side was, along with Tommy Docherty's Chelsea, the bridge between the old and the new; and while Docherty was beaten by youth, so Shankly was beaten by age.

Perhaps that's the difference between a pessimist and an optimist. A pessimist would bemoan the passing of a great team. An optimist would say that it was only the blueprint for something better. Great though the 1960s' Liverpool side were, they paled in comparison with the 1972–73 model. The players Shankly had available – Ray Clemence, Tommy Smith, Alec

Lindsay, Chris Lawler, Phil Thompson, Larry Lloyd, Peter Cormack, Ian Callaghan, Emlyn Hughes, Steve Heighway, John Toshack, Kevin Keegan, Brian Hall – were of a remarkably high standard. Look at the names, just look, and see if you can find a weakness. Take as long as you like. Even Shankly was moved to say – with his usual understatement – that 'the football we're playing is frightening. Frightening. Even I feel privileged to watch it.'

The peak performance came in the first leg of the UEFA Cup final in 1973 against Borussia Moenchengladbach, Liverpool winning 3–0. 'If anybody wants to know what Liverpool Football Club is about then let them study this match. We played football that was world class against world-class opposition. The second leg will not be easy but there is not a team on the planet that I would expect to overcome a three-goal deficit when we are playing as well as this.' He was right, too. Liverpool picked up the trophy.

The secret of Shankly's remarkable success was the 'Liverpool Secret', a magic ingredient kept in a cupboard in the mysterious Boot Room and known only to a few select men who were careful never to take the same flight.

The Liverpool Secret. It's up there with Nessie (the Loch Ness Nessie, not Bill Shankly's wife Nessie), the Yeti and the lost civilisation of Atlantis. The odds on finding it are marginally greater than on finding Big Foot. And it's one of those things that, the more its existence is denied by those in the know, the more everyone else is convinced that they're lying. The truth is, of course, that there is a Liverpool Secret. (Just like there's a Nessie and all the others. Curiously, part of the Secret is that we should learn to trust our instincts more.)

The first ingredient of Shankly's Secret – he called it the 'Recipe' – is outlined in that Milan story. As Smith says, 'The first thing he did was realise that it was a great advantage to have the crowd on your side, and so he made the crowd part of the club and the club part of the side. He energised everything and made everyone pull together. It was some combination.'

Shankly's Secret was actually more an ideology. And like all successful ideologies, it worked because it was simple, straightforward and logical. You didn't need a slide-rule to work it out, you didn't need a minimum of two megabytes of RAM (and don't be pedantic), you didn't need to have it explained more than once. 'You can't score until you've got the ball, so when you've got it you must keep it.' There. You can remember that, can't you? Don't boot the ball uphill. Don't run straight up the field by yourself. Play short, sharp passes to feet. Pass the ball and move to the next position.

Never stand still. Keep moving, keep looking, keep aware. The instructions he barked out were easy to follow. As he said to one of his players, 'Look, laddie, if you're in the penalty area and aren't quite sure what to do with the ball, just stick it in the net. We'll discuss your options afterwards.'

By playing the ball around this way, no one was required to do more than anyone else. No one was subject to any great strain. Injuries were infrequent. Continuity was maintained. Confidence grew. It's so obvious. Like all great doctrines, you look at it and scratch your head in wonder. Why doesn't everybody do it like this?

It was football socialism. Every player knew that he was being supported by his team-mates. Like ants, they poured forward (or backwards) safe in the knowledge that their backs were covered. Individuals didn't sparkle, the team did. And because the team sparkled, all the individuals were lit up. Socialism as it should be with everybody getting richer as the society's strength grows. Compare that to the capitalist model. Spurs, for example. They'll glitter and sparkle and glisten, but only for a brief period and only if the X of the day (Hoddle, Klinsmann, White, Beal, Moores) is performing. As for continuity, there is none because, when push comes to shove, everyone involved has different priorities. That's why Spurs are the quintessential Cup side and Liverpool win Championships. The glitz can only flatter for so long before deceiving. It's also why the social fabric of the country is breaking down, optimism is at an all-time low and morality has been abandoned. You wouldn't catch Bill Shankly leaving Liverpool and going to work for a tobacco company.

Another tenet of Shankly's secret is an idea that's more often hijacked by the Tories. (The Maoist model of communism also espouses this, but then again we've long suspected that Mao was the original Thatcherite.) This one's about how everyone has greatness inside them and if you apply yourself correctly then you can achieve it. Never sit back and smile at past successes. That's done with. Look to the future and improve on the present to be part of it. Get better to be better. It sounds like some slogan a Thatcherite spin doctor might come up with – the difference is that in Shankly's hands it was done for the common good. 'The beauty of Shanks was that he made you believe it,' said Ron Yeats. 'He made every player think that he had it inside him to achieve greatness. Having instilled that belief, he would then send them out onto the pitch to prove it.'

The next Liverpool legend concerns Shankly's attitude to the injured. To the outsider his attitude seems, at first, to be a little on the odd side. Bluntly put, if you were injured, he wouldn't speak to you. Wasn't interested. Occasionally, he'd pop his head around the door of the treatment-room. 'You still here?' As Roger Hunt said, 'At Liverpool you didn't get injured –

you couldn't afford to. If you did, Bill didn't want to know you.' So players didn't get injured. It wasn't worth the aggro.

As with all of Shankly's quirks, it makes sense if you stand back from it and just think about it. Logic aside, though, it says stacks about Shanks's attitude to good old working-class concepts like honesty, laziness and cheating. And about his attitude to prima donnas. For Shankly, the most important thing was for a player to be 'honest' on the pitch. You could be the best player in the world, skilful to the nth degree, but if you weren't 101 per cent honest, forget it. Honesty here is a very pre-war, Hovis concept, and refers not so much to verbal truths as to physical loyalty. You don't hide. You don't shirk your responsibilities. You never give less than your all – your mate's life might depend on it. One player was told that he had 'a heart like a caraway seed'. He didn't last.

For this reason, Shankly focused on players, not stars. If his players became stars, then it was all well and good. If, however, they became stars and, in the process, forgot they were players . . . 'He had,' says Tommy Smith, 'an uncanny ability to get the best out of an ordinary player'. (Even in a self-deprecatory world, I don't think we should take that as self-referential.) Shankly bought raw talent from the lower divisions and Liverpoolised them. It was a talent he shared with Brian Clough. Neither would do particularly well with big-money, big-name stars, but both could inspire someone like Ian Bowyer or Brian Hall to heights that God, perhaps, hadn't originally intended.

Sometimes he bought big, but only when he was sure and only when he had to. Alun Evans (£100,000) from Wolves and John Toshack (£100,000) from Cardiff stand out. Sometimes he made a mistake, although, typically, he didn't admit to it. 'People often ask me if I ever made a mistake. Well, tae my mind "mistake" is an overused word in football. For example, you might say it was a mistake for a club to buy such and such a player, but that might not necessarily be true. The player might not suit his environment. Just bad luck. A footballer's not like a hat or a coat that you can leave at a shop if it doesn't fit or suit you.' While you try and work that one out – a hat or a coat? – ponder his purchase of Tony Hateley for £100,000. That's the same Tony Hateley that Shankly later dubbed 'the Douglas Bader of football'.

In today's world, where Chris Armstrong is worth £4.5 million and Warren Barton is worth £4 million, quoting figures for Shankly's buys doesn't really mean much, but try to get the flavour of the thing. Gordon Milne (£16,000) and Peter Thompson (£40,000) came from Preston; Willie Stevenson (£20,000) from Rangers; Ian St John (£37,000) from Motherwell; Ron Yeats (£30,000) from Dundee United. Another player bought during this period was a young lad called Roy Evans. He only played eleven times for the first team, but was to make a more valuable contribution later.

He'd buy players, get them in and put them straight into the team. The reserve team. There, they'd learn about the Liverpool way of doing things, the Liverpool way of playing. When they'd done learning, then and only then, they'd get their first-team chance. Again, it makes perfect sense. Your car's broken down on the motorway and you pull into the hard shoulder. When you're ready to go again, you drive along on the hard shoulder until you're up to speed and then you join the flow. If you dive straight into the flow, the chances are you'll risk an accident. And it doesn't matter if you've got a 3.4 Jaguar or a Morris Ital.

If he made a mistake, it was in underestimating how quickly his first great side would age. He said later that he figured a player's peak should be between the ages of twenty-eight and thirty-three, but some of his men faded earlier than expected. Roger Hunt, for example, was sold to Bolton for £32,000 in December 1969. So he bought again. And again it was wisely. Emlyn Hughes (£65,000) from Blackpool; Larry Lloyd (£50,000) from Bristol Rovers; Ray Clemence (£18,000) from Scunthorpe; Alex Lindsay (£67,000) from Bury.

Shankly bought Kevin Keegan for £35,000 from Scunthorpe five days before losing to Arsenal in the 1971 FA Cup final – the Charlie George final. It was a match that stunned him. 'Nobody comes from behind to beat us. Nobody. I wouldnae've believed it if I hadnae seen it with my own eyes.'

Keegan relates how Shankly sold the club to him – as if he needed to. 'He drove me to Anfield in his Ford Capri and said, "You're joining the greatest club in the world, son. We've got the greatest ground and the greatest players. Emlyn Hughes – great player. Chris Lawler – great player. Tommy Smith – great player and harder than a brick wall. Roger Hunt and Ian St John were great players for us, but they're gone now. Now we're building a new team and you can be part of it provided you're ready to give it your heart and your soul."' He offered Keegan £45 and Keegan, cheeky sod, bargained him up to £50. Shankly told him, 'That's it. You'll never have to ask for a rise again.' And he didn't. Every year, apparently, Keegan's wage was cleanly and precisely doubled. It's a cute story, but there's something that stands out and cries for attention. Something that is just so out of kilter that you immediately see it and think, '. . . uh?' 'He drove me to Anfield in his Ford Capri and . . .' Bill Shankly drove a Ford Capri?

There was one player that Shankly tried to buy who stands out like a peroxide quiff from this lot: Frank Worthington. Really. Shankly, the man who once said, 'If I'd wanted a juggler I'd have gone to the circus for one,' tried to buy Frank Worthington. The deal fell through because a routine medical revealed his blood pressure to be way too high, the consequence of 'living a little bit too much in the fast lane'. Not everyone at Liverpool was upset. Tommy Smith, for one, wasn't too bothered. 'We only played players who fitted in. Frank Worthington? No chance. Any player who has more than two clubs in their career is suspicious. You'll soon find out that they're not putting everything in.' While it might be difficult imagining Tommy Smith and Frank Worthington sharing a flat (a distinctly odd couple – you choose which one's Tony Randall and which one's Jack Klugman), just close your eyes and fantasise about what might have been if the skills of someone like Worthington had been welded to the Liverpool machine. If any criticism can be made of the various Liverpool incarnations, it's that there has been a distinct lack of maverick flair. The unexpected. There have been supremely gifted players but, Dalglish aside, no real individual sparks.

It wasn't that Shankly avoided, distrusted or baulked at the idea of individual stars. More, it was that in the Liverpool scheme of things, the team became the individual. It may sound trite, but in Shankly's ideal, the pinnacle of achievement was that the team was seen as one. Paisley carried this idea, as did Fagan.

The way that legends grew up around the 'Liverpool Secret' reminds of one of those old Hammer horror films like *Dracula: Prince of the Night*. A mysterious Gothic house high on the hill where strange things go on and things happen that no one really talks about. The locals are suspicious. They want to know but are frightened. It sounds exactly like the Boot Room.

A room twelve foot by twelve foot – more a cupboard, really – the Boot Room more than anything else sums up Shankly's Liverpool. Even the name of it sounds so quaint, more like a shed you'd find on an allotment than the inner sanctum of the War Cabinet. Hearing tales about the Boot Room conjures up an image of Ronnie Moran, Roy Evans and Joe Fagan sitting around a steaming cauldron chanting ancient spells about newts' eyes. Maybe it actually was like that. Maybe it wasn't really just a space where they kept the booze and their notebooks and their gossip pads. Maybe all that was just a ruse. Sometimes it's too easy to get hooked up on the truth.

Players weren't banned, they just didn't go in. It wasn't their place. Opposing managers would often be invited down for a drink, but only a few accepted. Brian Clough rarely went. It was long believed that this was just another quirk of Old Big 'Ead's arrogance, but it transpires it was much more respectful than that. Whenever he was invited and whenever he declined, Clough sent down a polite note of apology. The Boot Room. Curiously, Shankly himself rarely went into the Boot Room. It wasn't his space and, respectfully, managers ever since have treated the Room accordingly. Except Graeme Souness, who pulled the thing down.

Routines seemed routine but, invariably, there was a good reason for it. Take, for example, the habit of players meeting at Anfield and then getting taken *en masse* over to their Melwood training-ground, a twenty-minute coach-ride away. They'd train the day away, and then get back in the coach to Anfield where they would shower, change and go. Habit is actually the wrong word at Anfield. There, habits tend to be orders writ deep in stone. At first glance, it might seem another example of this 'we're in the army now' attitude which treats individuals like small, irresponsible children. Even in the days before salaries were Cantona'd and cars that cost as much as a good full-back, you'd be pushed to find a club not letting its players make their own way to the training-ground. But look again.

In Ponting's *The Boot Room: An Anfield Legend*, David Johnson – just one in a long line of Liverpool forwards afflicted with an unfortunate moustache tendency – explains: 'It made sense for three reasons. First, it made everybody get used to Anfield as their working environment. That meant that it was not unfamiliar on a Saturday when you got there for the match. It was your workplace. You knew all the non-footballing staff and there was a bit of banter. When I was at Everton, we went to Goodison only on match days, an experience twice as nerve-wracking as it might be.

'Second, if you drive straight to the training-ground, you shower and change immediately after training and then you're off. It is a pretty swift process which is not really suited to professional athletes. Your body temperature takes about forty minutes to drop after heavy exercise, so you'd still be sweating after your shower, your pores would remain open and you'd be more susceptible to chills and strains. In the Anfield way, you'd have a chat, a cup of tea and then a twenty-minute coach-ride before showering.

'The third reason was simple. It was good for team spirit. On those coach journeys, you'd get to know each other. It was a good time for play.'

Shankly swore by this routine. 'If you have a bath or a shower ten minutes after hard work then you'll carry on sweating all day. There's nothing worse than sitting around sweating, it's bad for your system. It doesn't seem much but it's very important to us.'

It doesn't seem much. It didn't need to. When Shankly spoke, people listened. Curiously – not – when the main stand was being rebuilt in 1970 and the team had to go straight to Melwood to train, they suffered one of their worst spells of injuries ever. The worst spell ever, that is, until Graeme Souness took over and, while he was throwing the bathwater out, threw the going-to-Anfield-first baby out too.

The routine of winning trophies was another strange but logical Liverpool quirk. Ronnie Moran: 'We all enjoyed winning things and when we had won we would always enjoy ourselves that night. But the next day we got straight back to normal. The lads got used to that routine over the years; it was the drill, right back to Bill Shankly's day. That way, it stopped the lads getting too carried away with themselves. The only time there was a ceremony was when we came out of the Second Division.'

Listening to all this, you can't help but wonder. To the dilettante writer (and, no doubt, the dilettante reader) it all sounds a bit of a nightmare. A psycho cross between a particularly fierce army outfit, the boy scouts and the worst public school, co-ordinated by a secret male institution such as the freemasons and run by a despot. But if that's the way it seems to me, it might explain why I'm not a competitive sportsman obsessed with the notion of winning.

Simply put, when Shankly spoke, people listened. The reason for this is, like his ethos, very simple: he won things. You can be as strong and forthright as you like but, especially in a competitive environment like football, if you don't win things, it's unlikely you'll be listened to.

But Bill Shankly isn't the legend that he is because of the trophies that his Liverpool won. They didn't even win that many. Remember, under Shanks Liverpool won nothing between the 1966 Championship and the Championship/UEFA Cup double in 1972–73. No, that reads wrong. Anywhere else that wouldn't seem such a bad deal. What would a Spurs give to be on a seven-year Championship itch? The trophy record only looks a bit thin because Shankly was succeeded by the most successful English football manager of all time, his faithful adjutant, Bob Paisley. (Strictly speaking, it isn't relevant here, but let's say it anyway. Earthquakes don't happen every day. Paisley won thirteen major trophies – three European Cups, six League Championships, one UEFA Cup and three League Cups – in nine years. Twice they came second in the League. In 1980, they came fifth, but 'compensated' by winning the European Cup.) Shortly after he took over, Paisley said, 'I am not Bill Shankly and never will be. He is a one-off. I feel privileged to have worked with him for so many years and I have learnt an awful lot from him. We continue to play his way – the Liverpool way. Team work will always be all-important with us and the success we have had this season is down to our players doing the simple things well. That's the way we intend to continue – the Liverpool way.'

Shankly's achievement was that he laid the foundations for an empire. Alone among modern managers – with the curious but possible exception of David Bassett's Wimbledon – Shankly laid down a Liverpool way of doing things that long outlasted him and which became the envy of all football. (Take away those last eight words and the Bassett comparison doesn't sound so daft. Together with chairman Sam Hamman, 'Harry' – we can be familiar here – set into motion an institution that long outlasted him. Wimbledon are forever cast in his shadow. Long balls, sharp elbows and players that are the envy of the big boys.)

Shankly founded a dynasty which still survives today, twenty years after he stepped down. From Bob Paisley to Joe Fagan to Kenny Dalglish to Roy Evans today, Liverpool lives life according to the rules laid down by Bill Shankly. Only Graeme Souness strayed from the path of righteousness, and we all know what happened to that ill-starred reign. 'It doesn't seem much but it's very important to us.'

*'If you take one straw, it's easy to snap it. But put a hundred together and they are unbreakable.'*

David Johnson on Shankly's Secret Recipe

Shankly was eccentric, but he knew what the story was. 'The professional game is all about two sets of people – the players and the public. They are the most important of all and I honestly try to do my best for both.' It's an ethos that all concerned can learn from. Big Ron Atkinson said that, not Shanks. But you were fooled for a moment, weren't you?

*Chapter 3*

# HERE'S ONE WE MADE EARLIER

*'A lot of people in football don't have much time for the press; they say they're amateurs. But I say to these people, 'Noah was an amateur, but the* Titanic *was built by professionals.'*

Malcolm Allison

What do you think your greatest strength was?
'Well, I was probably the best coach in the world.'
Probably?
'No. I was.'
Why?
'Because I was better than everybody else.'

1964. IF LONDON WAS PREPARING FOR THE FULL-BLOODED onslaught of the Swinging Sixties, Plymouth was still recovering from Bill Haley. Rowdy naval antics aside, the town cryer was rarely bothered. The occasional cat in a tree, the two-day-old milk left outside Mrs Jones's, the strange goings-on at number 72 . . . Something, nothing. It was typical of a hundred and one English towns of the time. Halfway through the 1960s, yet still firmly living in the post-war 1950s. It was a nice place full of nice people who had never done nothing to no one.

All this changed the day that the elders of Plymouth Argyle had the bright idea of asking Malcolm Allison to be the manager of their football club.

It's easy to imagine a kind of cartoon set-up. Big Mal (drawn as a kind of mutant offspring of Leslie Phillips and George Cole) arrives in perhaps a soft-top beat-up American car, fedora and cigar blowing in the wind. The car makes an enormous noise – of course – and the streets are lined with groups of Mary Whitehouse lookalikes tut-tutting at this noise-spitting metal monstrosity. Men stand taking the piss while their young glamour-starved wives look on, not saying anything but knowing.

So much for fiction. But, for once, the truth wasn't so far away. When

Allison joined Plymouth Argyle in 1964, everything changed before he even stepped into his office.

As he pulled his car into the club carpark for the first time, he was confronted by two police detectives. As the words '£94', 'unpaid parking tickets' and 'arrest' fell out of the official mouths, the net curtains of the offices at Plymouth's Home Park ground twitched like those on a suburban street late on a Saturday night. If there was a pianist in the house, he'd have stopped playing.

'I think it dawned on Plymouth Football Club that their new manager was a bit of a lad. I think they were a little perturbed that they might have introduced some sort of tearaway to the town,' said Big Mal later.

A little more of that sort of understatement and Plymouth's directors might have slept a bit more soundly. Sleeping soundly wasn't, much to their chagrin, one of Allison's major concerns. Neither was the survival of Plymouth Argyle. Survival. No, it's not really an Allison word. If Big Mal's welcoming committee didn't impress the Plymouth faithful, if that didn't make them sit up and take notice, then the next thing Allison did must have.

When he joined Plymouth Argyle, Allison found a situation familiar to nearly all new managers. The best way to explain it is to say that the previous season the club had avoided relegation to the Third Division by one-hundredth of a goal. The team's in a bad way and the first thing the Messiah does is get nicked by the long arm. The next thing he does is spend £1,500 on some non-League player who's nearly thirty-one. To Big Mal, signing Tony Book was obvious, but put yourself in the position of a Plymouth director. What'd you do? Tell yourself that the Lord moves in mysterious ways, and hope?

Big Mal. If he didn't exist, you'd have to invent him. Two stories, both from Allison's 1975 autobiography *The Colours of My Life*, explain it better than words ever could.

'I was once carrying enough cash to outbid Richard Burton and Liz Taylor for the waiter's attention at Toronto's most luxurious night-spot, The Swiss Bear. I had been irritated by the service, which was inevitably sluggish when you consider the number of people hovering around the Burtons' table. I snapped to a waiter, "Give me half a dozen bottles of champagne, send some to the band and here's a handful of dollars for the head waiter." Service improved. Someone in my party wanted the singer to sing "Hello Dolly", but she said it wasn't on her list. So I bought some more champagne and she ended up singing "Hello Dolly" six times. I know that it all sounds rather flash . . .'

'I suppose Christine Keeler was a bit of a challenge to my ego. Here was the most infamous woman in the land, a girl whose ability to fascinate and enslave men had torn to pieces the morale of a Tory government. And I had heard in The Star pub in Belgravia – a place she visited regularly – that she had seen me on television and, shall we say, quite fancied me . . . I found her a strong and interesting woman. We went out, in fact, a couple of times. I recall that we made love . . . I take no pride in any of this. The whole affair was over almost before it began. My reaction to the whole affair was, I suppose, the one of the male mind working at its lowest level.'

But that's only half the picture. The other half is the story of the coach who first introduced the sweeper system to England, the breath of fresh air which dragged Manchester City out of the shadows cast by their more illustrious neighbours in the north of the city, the man who inspired his team to win four major trophies in three years – and we're not talking Ronco Presents the Freight Rover Autoglass Trophy here, we're talking the three domestics, plus the European Cup-Winners Cup.

In the semi-final of the Cup-Winners Cup, City were 1–0 down going into the second leg against FC Schalke 04. Their coach had been voted Coach of the Year in Germany and was assistant to national team manager, Helmet Schoen. It was a Spassky-Fischer situation. You can imagine it, what with Malcolm's mouth. But five goals later, there were no arguments. 'After the game he said he couldn't believe what we'd done to his sweeper system,' said Allison of his German counterpart. 'We outplayed them in every department and he said it was the finest performance he'd ever seen by a British club.' Forgive the self-promoting hyperbole, but a 5–0 win is a 5–0 win.

There's yet another side to the Allison story which involves hats, cigars, coats, porn stars, baths and a cabaret show with Tommy Docherty, a man he once called 'one of the biggest losers in the game'. It's that side which is perhaps best known, but patience. First things first.

The story of Big Mal really begins at exactly that moment he probably thought it was ending. It was 1958 and Allison was now playing for West Ham. He was a good player, not a great one. It's a fact he readily admits to now. 'I was born to be a coach. I knew it from when I was nine or ten years of age. I wanted to play but when I played I was always telling people what to do. Terry Venables was another one who was born to be a coach. He wasn't born to be a player. His mother told me that when he was fourteen and I agreed with her. We both had the same failing, we both lacked pace.'

True enough, but that logic was a long way off to the thirty-one-year-old medium-sized Mal. Anyway, he was playing in an evening match, away to Sheffield United. A United player ran up to him with the ball, dummied as if to go one way, stopped, and went the other way. He needn't have bothered. Allison couldn't have stopped him if he'd just strolled along. There was nothing in his legs. It was an era when men were men and substitutes weren't allowed – can you imagine Big John Wayne going to fight the Cheyenne and calling for a sub because his leg's feeling a bit iffy? So Malcolm played on. But the next morning his room-mate, Noel Cantwell, went to see the boss. Allison had been up the whole night coughing like an Olympic champion.

A couple of days later he was in the London Hospital listening to the specialist saying, as though to someoneone else, 'Mr Allison, I think you will have to forget about playing football. You have TB quite severely. We will have to remove one lung.' To make it worse – it couldn't have made it better, we're talking about human beings here – West Ham won the Second Division Championship that year. Guess who didn't get a Championship medal. It's an old story. People don't like being surrounded by the sick. It reminds them of their own mortality.

It was a gutting blow for a man who'd been football crazy, football mad since before he could remember. Allison had been the little kid who'd always wanted to be a footballer and who'd never grown out of it or developed a more sensible ambition.

He'd been that way since he was a boy. 'The first job I had was in Fleet Street. I was going to become a photographer. After I'd been working there three months, the boss called me in one day and he said, "Malcolm, you like football, don't you?" And I said, "Yes, boss." And he said, "You're going to the Cup final tomorrow. You're going to see Arsenal against Preston North End." I thought, marvellous, marvellous. So the next day I go to Wembley with the photographer and we take our position next to the goal and Arsenal come out. For a fourteen-year-old boy, it was unbelievable. Leslie Compton, Ted Drake. Preston were led by Bill Shankly, Tom Finney. Anyway, after seven minutes, Arsenal get a penalty. Leslie Compton comes up, puts the ball on the spot, takes five paces back and smashes the ball against the post. The photographer took the shot and looked at me, took the plate out and said, "Take that back to the office." So in no uncertain terms I told him I wasn't going to take it back. I got the sack on Monday and that was the end of my career as a photographer.'

Football won. It always did. And he did it. He'd become a top footballer. But then it was taken away. It hit him hard. Where was the logic? Where was the justice? Good God, Malcolm even went to a church. When there was no response there, Big Mal did something that was, for him, much more in context. He went horseracing.

There's something else you should know about Malcolm Allison. It's true that he'd been the little kid who'd always wanted to be a footballer and who'd never grown out of it or developed a more sensible ambition. It's also true, though, that after exclaiming to his mother that he'd be a professional footballer and after she'd said 'Oh, Malcolm', the little Big Mal turned around and said 'I'll give you thru'pence ha'ppeny at 5 to 2 that I do it.'

Malcolm was a natural-born spieler. Looking at his life story, it seems superfluous even to say it. Gambling, playing the odds – it's been a part of everything he's ever done. Can you imagine Malcolm Allison saying that gambling was irresponsible and proposing that it's possibly a better idea to put your money in the Abbey National because you get a nice steady rate of interest? No. It's not going to happen, is it?

As a sad footnote to this train of thought, in 1991 he lost his life savings in the Bank of Credit and Commerce International crash. When he took over as manager of the Kuwait side in 1985, he invested in the BCCI after 'somebody advised me it was a good bank. Of course it was a blow when I lost the money, but there's nothing you can do, so there's no point worrying about it.' That's one thing about Allison. He might so often appear to be the bumbling goon, the clown, but he's always had the fire of eternal optimism burning bright to keep him warm while others around him have fretted and stressed their whiles away.

Anyway. The doctors have written him off, West Ham have rejected him in favour of a clever young prospect called Bobby Moore and he's skint. What can a poor boy do?

While he's at Epsom race-track, he bumps into Arthur Shaw, the old Arsenal player (a defender, naturally). Now Shaw is a spieler *par excellence*. A nod of the head, a tip of the tifter, a couple of 'good things' here and there – it was a marriage made in heaven. 'We didn't keep a ledger but I estimate that we must have won something in the region of £80,000 that first year. Of course, I bought a few suits – the notes seemed to burn through the expensive linings. Do I need to add that I bought a flash car?'

His sojourn lasted two years, during which time he won more money than is kept at the Bank of England and lost more money than is locked deep at Fort Knox. Necessarily, the tales are told. 'We had lost £160,200 in six minutes . . . Gregory Peck was at the races . . . Dining with a Rothschild at Deauville struck me as good progress for a recently retired West Ham centre-half.' What all these bullshit tales tell more than anything is that, even when he had been kicked by life, even when the one thing that he really loved had been taken away from him, Big Mal remained good value. 'Do I need to add that I bought a flash car?' No. No. Of course there's no need to add that at all. And for those who care, it was 'an American-styled Simca Cadet'.

Between his twilight bark at West Ham and his appointment as manager of Bath City in 1962, Allison's CV reads like a script for Peter Cook and Dudley Moore's 'Derek and Clive' sketch, 'The worst job I've ever had.' A car salesman? Would you buy a used car from this man? Probably not. No one else did. The high point was when he took a part share in a nightclub off Tin Pan Alley, the musicians' row. 'The clientèle was promising. The place was filled with showbusiness people, footballers and villains.' Harry Secombe, Dorothy Squires, Jimmy Greaves.

And then there were the birds. Beth, whom he had married at twenty-six, had left the scene, and, well, what was a young boy to do? There was a blonde called Suzy – no doubt her friends called her Crêpe – and, of course, Ms Keeler. Later there was a beauty queen Jennifer Lowe ('it was a small, pleasant affair') and Miss United Kingdom, Jennifer Gurley ('she would tidy up my flat a bit, cook a meal and we would talk or watch television. It never went further than that'). It was just after this time that he met his long-term partner, Serena Williams ('as she passed me on the way to the cloakroom, I took hold of her arm and said, "I would like to take you to dinner, young lady." She said, very coolly, "The name is Williams, third from the bottom of page 262 of the telephone book"'). Oh, and there was one other thing about Serena Williams. She was a bunny girl. A minor detail.

But even Big Mal could recognise that all the club offered was a one-way taxi-ride to Losers' Alley. Football was his game. The offer to manage Bath came after a spell at Romford (playing!) and a period coaching at Cambridge University. All this was very well and rewarding, but did little other than whet his appetite for the real thing.

When Allison joined Plymouth Argyle, he found a situation familiar to nearly all new managers. But having a bad team is not a problem. All managers know that taking over a Championship-winning team is like winning the Lottery. It only happens to other people, and even then not very often. If managers get sacked because teams are doing badly, it stands to reason that managers get employed because teams are doing badly. What might seem like a classic 'frying-pan and fire' situation is, to the manager, acceptable for two basic reasons. Firstly, taking over a struggling team may be a bore but it is a job, and to most people having a job is preferable to not having a job. The other reason is probably more applicable to footballing types. So the team is struggling: it's only a short-term thing. It wouldn't struggle under me. How could it? I'm a better manager than he is. Belief: for a football manager's ego, it would be very difficult to accept that he could not do a better job than his predecessor.

Bolstered by the arrival of his adjutant, Tony Book, and armed with a handful of bright young sparks, Plymouth started the 1964–65 season with a charge. Things were going well. They were challenging at the top of the division and, more satisfying to Allison, they were beating people with their style of play. After knocking Stoke City out on their way to a League Cup semi-final place, Allison heard Stoke manager Tony Waddington complain that Plymouth had played very negatively. From Waddington's point of view, it seemed that Tony Book was just hanging around at the back, a kind of 'extra defender'. To Allison, it was perfect. It was the first time the sweeper system had been used in England, and it was perfect. Little wonder Waddington was perplexed.

By the end of the season, though, the cons had begun to outweigh the pros. On the footballing side, things fell apart a bit after goalscorer Frank Lord picked up an injury. Rather than put in a reserve and preserve the structure and balance of the team, Allison changed things around to try to accommodate new players. It was a mistake – 'my first big mistake in football' – a lesson he said he'd learn. Eighth position and a League Cup semi-final place may have been an improvement on avoiding relegation by a hundredth of a goal, but it wasn't good enough for the Plymouth board. Maybe they were more ambitious than that. Or maybe it was the fact that Allison had started to get into trouble with the FA. Or maybe 'there was the fact that I didn't exactly lead a monkish life'.

And that was that. In truth, the Plymouth directors probably got a collective nosebleed just thinking about how high Allison could take them. Best avoid that. Best sack him. For his part, he didn't care. He already had his eye on the Maine chance. 'This city is not big enough for the both of us, so Matt Busby will have to go.'

If Plymouth was a good place for Malcolm Allison to try out some of his embryonic football theories, Manchester was the perfect environment for Big Mal.

Allison joined Manchester City in July 1965. After leaving the south coast, he'd phoned up Joe Mercer, who had just returned to the game after a stress-related illness had sidelined him. Possibly Allison had figured that there might be a window of opportunity, that Mercer might need a younger, fitter assistant. But, then again, it's just as likely that he phoned simply to see how he was. Mercer was one of the game's great figures, a real establishment boy, and Malcolm had always had an innate respect for the greats. Whatever could have been said about Allison's personality or attitude, there was never any doubt that his heart was married to football.

'We just got on great together; we had a good style. He used to come and see me work and used to love the work I did and he'd ask me about players. You see, he'd been ill when he came to Manchester City. He had hypertension and terrible stress and it took him about a year to memorise things, but that year we won the Division Two Championship – it was such a lift for him, it was great, you know. [Five years later,] we were walking out of a restaurant and he said to me, "That was the best five years of my life." I said, "What about when you played for Everton and Arsenal and England?" And he said, "Yeah, that's true, but these last five years have been the best five years of my life. We've had a wonderful time." Which we did. He used to keep me in place more or less – like sometimes I used to get annoyed and he'd say "Okay, Malcolm, okay". He was very good like that.'

Allison's feelings about the Joe Mercers of the world go back to 1958 and that night at Bramall Lane. Robbed of a glorious playing career, Allison knew that he'd never have a place in the pantheon. If his name was going to be remembered, then it would have to be for something else. It's a condition you could call Cloughitis.

Whatever, if it was shrewd of Allison to phone, it was shrewder of Mercer to pick it up. It was a marriage made in heaven. As Francis Lee said, 'Malcolm was probably the best coach I ever worked with in terms of how he motivated the players and got them to play, and Joe was the father figure. Joe gave City the same dignity as Busby gave United. It was a nice balancing act.'

A nice balancing act. In July 1965 when Allison joined Mercer, City were a mid-table Division Two team dying from lack of sunlight after having lived in United's shadow for too long. Three years later, they were champions of Division One. Two years after that, they won the European Cup-Winners Cup. It was their fourth major trophy in three years.

When Allison arrived at City, Joe Mercer had just bought Mike Summerbee. As rebuilding blocks go, it was a good start. The next piece of the City jigsaw was Bury's twenty-year-old midfielder, Colin Bell. By now Allison had been charged with the task of shopping for talent. He'd go out, look around and report back to Mercer. Almost invariably, Mercer trusted his judgement.

'I told Joe about [Bell] and he said okay, but Bury wanted forty-odd thousand and we didn't have £40, so I thought, "I know what to do." I knew Colin was being watched by lots of other clubs, so I used to go along to their games and sit with the other people watching and I just criticised him for the whole game: He's got no left foot. Can't head the ball. The others would listen to what I was saying and the word started getting around. I did this until we had enough money and then I went back to Bury and bought him. The first match he played for us, I was sitting in the stand next to Joe – I'd been warned off the touchline at the time – and Joe said to me, "Why did we pay £42,000 for that rubbish? He's got no left foot."'

Curious how that 'I'd been warned off the touchline at the time' just passes by without a second thought.

'So Joe's sitting there saying "Oh my God, what have I done, what have I done". I said, "Don't worry, he's a good player, just wait and see". Anyway, he makes this great run into the box, the keeper comes and kicks the ball as hard as he can it hits Bell's back and rebounds into the net. I turned round to Joe and said, "There. What did I tell you?"'

The next year they were back in Division One – winning the Division Two Championship was never in doubt – with a style that seemed to come as a birthright. In October 1967, the chequebook flapped again and another inspired piece of the jigsaw arrived at Maine Road. Francis Lee, a strutting, swaggering goalscorer blessed with the dimensions needed for a low centre of gravity (make that short and squat), was top dog at Bolton, and not particularly lacking in confidence. City weren't the only club interested, and when Allison said to him 'If I had you I'd make you a great player', Lee was less than impressed. 'What an arrogant bastard,' said Lee, and with the insight that was to make him a millionaire by the time he was thirty, he signed.

He joined a team built for success: solid at the back, strong in midfield and sparkily efficient up front. When you think of Allison and what he's like – or, rather what you think he's like, the Allison that he likes to project – the make-up of his teams sometimes comes as a surprise. Straightforward, strong and not a funny hat in sight.

'If you don't live at risk, you don't live. You've got to work out the odds and go to win all the time.' Working out the odds was something that Allison was once good at. Like all spielers, Allison started good. Working on knowledge. Playing the percentages. And Allison's City were a good bet.

Whereas you might expect him to name someone who you felt – someone you hoped – was nearer the Allison ideal, he would always say that the best player he ever had was Colin Bell. Bell was indeed a great footballer, a thoroughbred, a classic athlete, someone who, apparently, could have been a class hundred metres runner, a footballer who'd fetch mega-millions today. Well respected, too. 'Colin Bell is probably the best Manchester City player since Peter Docherty,' said Joe Mercer. And Kenneth Wolstenholme, during the 1969 FA Cup final, said, 'He finds oceans of space,' before adding, in the spirit of the true commentator, 'He finds space that doesn't even exist!'

Now, and no disrespect to Colin Bell, you understand, you can't help but feel a little disappointed. But if he shaped up to hit the ball from X to Y, you'd know that the ball was going to go from X to Y. There's a little bit inside that hoped that Big Mal's favourite player would be the maverick who'd assume the X to Y shape, swivel and split the defence with a quick X to W. Someone like, say, Rodney Marsh. Perhaps on reflection though, it's not so strange that Allison shies away from Marsh. If Allison hadn't bought him in March 1972, City might have won another League Championship and Allison might have lasted more than a year at Maine Road. But those mights belong to another story.

When Summerbee, Bell and Lee played their first game together in October 1967, at home to Wolves, the City forward line was completed by a young seventeen-year-old runaround called Stan Bowles. Bowles. You'd have thought that he'd have been the perfect Allison player. He had the ego of the supremely gifted, and the arrogance to match. More, he had a passionate love affair with the horses.

Maybe it was that Bowles just didn't display the love for the game that Malcolm so obviously had. Maybe it was just that he was too young, too headstrong. Maybe they just met each other too soon. 'The older players were a handful, but there's this seventeen-year-old kid who was breaking every rule in the book. I didn't care about the gambling so much because I was a professional gambler myself for two years, but I worried about the drinking, and the drinking and the gambling are linked. You have a good night gambling, so you celebrate.'

As he relates in *The Mavericks*, Rob Steen's splendid study of the 1970s, Allison gave up the ghost after one Bowlesism too many. After a missed flight to Amsterdam, Allison admitted to Mercer 'Look, I can't control this guy. You've got to get rid of him. He's going to cause a problem for me with the other players.' Anyway, what did City need with Bowles when they had Tony Coleman?

Tony Coleman was . . . Some footballers are described as 'hard men'. Tommy Smith, Peter Storey, Norman Hunter – you know the type. Coleman wasn't hard in that sense. He was more the 'You lookin' at me, pal?' type. 'That's my pint you spilled.' Tony Coleman was . . . After being thrown out by Preston as 'unmanageable', he went to play non-League football with Bangor before being rescued by Doncaster. And was he grateful? He was so grateful that in his first match, he laid the ref out cold with a punch to the face. Charming.

There's a lovely story about how Big Mal contrived to get Coleman – his own player – sent off one day. City were playing Coventry, the team managed by his old pal and compadre, Noel Cantwell. Malcolm and Cantwell went back a long way. They were contemporaries and room-mates at West Ham when Allison contracted his TB, and it was Cantwell who first alerted West Ham boss Ted Fenton to his condition. And it was Cantwell who advised Fenton against picking Allison in favour of Bobby Moore after Allison had sweated his balls off trying to rehabilitate himself. This effectively ended Mal's career, but in the land of Real Men, grudges aren't held. Anyway, Coventry full-back, Dietmar Bruck, had committed a bad foul against Coleman. Coleman squared up to him and Allison knew that big-time retribution could not be far off. It wasn't the sort of thing you did to Coleman. So Allison jumped out of the dug-out and shouted, 'That's disgusting, ref. You send them both off and there will be no complaints from me.' Hilariously, the referee dutifully obliged.

Still, Coleman had a baby face and angelic skills and Malcolm needed a left-sided player. 'I can handle him,' he said, and he could – up to a point. For two years, Coleman – and City – burned like a Coronation Day bonfire. Being champions of Division Two in 1966 wasn't much use if United were champions of Division One in 1967. There was only one thing that could alleviate this neighbourly pain.

That year, City were on a roll, cooking. It was a great team - fast, fluid and exciting. It was a team that reflected both Allison and the times, but more importantly for their supporters, it put a sock in the mouths of the United faithful. What price Best, Law and Charlton when you've got a forward line that reads Summerbee-Bell-Lee-Young-Coleman?

After – oh, joy – Manchester United lost at home to Sunderland, City needed to win at Newcastle to be sure of the Championship. It was a classic match worthy of the occasion, City winning 4–3 with goals from Lee, Summerbee and two from Neil Young. While Lee grabbed the headlines with spectacular strikes, the ever-dependable, ever-reliable Young was always there when he was needed. If Young's mouth had been as loud as his left foot, he might have made more of a name for himself, but Allison's Maine Road wasn't the place for nice, quiet types.

It was, said Francis Lee, 'a great relief for everyone in the side because it was the first and only trophy any of us had ever won. It really whetted our appetites for more.' Allison was rather more Allisonesque. At the press conference the next day, he said, 'There's no limit to what this team can achieve. We'll win the European Cup. European football is full of cowards. We will terrorise Europe. We will terrorise Europe.' And the West Indies would grovel.

It seemed possible. Manchester United had, in typical one-upmanship style, followed Celtic's lead by winning the European Cup. The whole thing was opening up, and the way City were playing . . . At the Charity Shield, the curtain-raiser to the 1968–69 season, FA Cup-winners West Bromwich Albion were made to look like a bunch of Turkish part-timers. It was everything football should be. Total.

The third goal was pure City, pure Allison. Smart, audacious and clever. There was a free kick on the edge of the area. Colin Bell and Francis Lee stood over the ball, and it seemed that the only question was who was going to shoot. Suddenly, Lee burst forward, Bell pushed the ball to Mike Summerbee who was standing next to Albion's wall. One touch. Summerbee knocked it behind the wall into the path of Lee who had run around them. Two touches. The WBA defence were still trying to guess who was going to shoot as the ball struck the back of the net. Three touches. Match commentator Kenneth Wolstenholme couldn't contain himself: 'Oh, what a goal. That was football perfection.' It was as manic as Wolstenholme got. Perhaps the time had come for Brian Moore to be invented.

Meanwhile, back in Europe, City met a real-life bunch of Turkish part-timers. And once again, there were shades of Hungary as collective Englishmen scratched their heads and wondered who taught Johnny Foreigner our game. Still, what did it matter? The next year City won the FA Cup and the following year they added the League Cup and the European Cup-Winners Cup. Beating first Schalke 04 in the semis and then the top Poles, Gornik FC, in the final vindicated Big Mal and silenced his detractors. But as Paul McCartney has found out, living a long and full life has its downsides.

While it could be easy to say, 'Well, so what did Mercer do then?', you don't really have to look too far for the answer. You don't have to look much further than Allison's post-Mercer career. Mercer did Allison. Mercer said, 'Okay, Malcolm, okay.'

Another Big Mal story. So Joe Mercer was driving through Moss Side in Manchester doing about 80 mph as you do round there and all of a sudden he's surrounded by police cars. So he stops, winds down the window and says, 'Okay, what's Malcolm done now?'

Married couples pledge eternal love and promise to take each other on 'to the exclusion of all others', yet one in three marriages ends in divorce. Mercer and Allison were engaged in the survival business and promised to take themselves on to the exclusion of all others. That it came to a sorry end should surprise no one. That it came to a sorry end at the height of their success is just another example that 'greed is good', 'me' and all that 1980s bollocks is, in fact, just bollocks.

The details are unimportant, really. He said neither, and I said neither. He said tomato, and I said tomato. Neither, neither. Tomato, tomato. Let's call the whole thing off.

For what it's worth, in his biography Allison claims that Mercer took him on as his heir apparent but, then when the glory got going, the only thing that was apparent was that Mercer wouldn't leave. One more year. One more. Now this ate away at Allison's unbridled ambition. 'I don't blame him for his attitude. Success is like a drug and we had both become mainliners.' As it became more and more apparent that this heir business was never going to come off, Allison colluded in an ill-fated takeover venture which involved local businessmen, people willing to put up large sums. A rainwear manufacturer with half a million pounds in his pocket.

Now. There's a horror story called something like *The Monkey's Paw*. A couple find a magical monkey's paw and ask for untold riches. Their son is killed and they get the insurance wedge. The moral of the story is . . . sometimes a coach shouldn't forget what he's good at. Allison got his way, he became the manager; but at what price?

In March 1972, City were six points clear and looking good for another Championship. But then something – possibly two things – happened. Allison and Mercer swapped offices. Suddenly the coach was a team manager and the team manager was a 'manager'. This turned Maine Road upside down and – like any finely balanced unit – it was thrown out of synch. Six points clear suddenly didn't mean so much and, despite beating Derby County 2–0 in the last game of the season, they lost out to Clough's mob by one point.

In retrospect, Allison thinks differently. 'Yeah. Actually, I think that football is two people. I think that there's no one person who's got enough to offer both ways in running a football team. I think two people have got to do it. I think all the most successful teams have had two people - Clough and Taylor, Shankly and Paisley – one levels out the other.'

There was one other thing that threw the season out of synch. Now this may be a coincidence, but, on 6 March 1972, Manchester United signed Ian Storey-Moore from Nottingham Forest for £200,000. Storey-Moore, incidentally, had just been involved in one of Brian Clough's more outrageous ventures – and you can read that how you will. (Briefly, Clough had wanted to sign him, hadn't managed it but paraded him at the Baseball Ground anyway. Maybe he thought it would chutzpah Forest into action. Maybe not.) Anyway, Storey-Moore was big news. Hot. That was on 6 March. On 8 March, Allison signed Rodney Marsh from Queen's Park Rangers for £200,000. Now this may be a coincidence, but really, what's the point in having an ego if it's continually going to get trumped?

To try and imagine the effect Marsh's arrival had, try this test. Imagine you're Mike Summerbee. Or Colin Bell. Or Francis Lee. Imagine you're Queen Bee. Then this dandy dilettante comes along and instead of playing the nice passing game you're used to, he's doing other things. Beating three players, putting his foot on the ball. Well, if he can do that, you're kind of obliged to do it too. What? And people might think you couldn't? It might not be the definitive test, but it's as near as dammit. Summerbee said, 'We're all big fans of Rodney and all good friends now, but when Malcolm decided to sign Rodney, we lost our formation. It cost us the Championship.'

In fairness, it was true. Marsh did upset the system. He did upset the other players. His car number-plate, a Lotus Europa, famously contained the letters E, G and O. It's true. He did upset the system. Curiously, Mike Doyle and the other anti-Marsh delegates didn't moan quite so loudly when Wyn Davies arrived. Marsh's early experiences at City are disarmingly similar to those of free spirits the world over. If it's different, it's a threat.

While it's true that he thought that Marsh would be better alongside Francis Lee than Ian Bowyer, it's also true that when our Rodney turned up at Maine Road, in a full-length leather coat with matching sideburns, Malcolm's heart probably sang.

In many ways, Malcolm Allison changed profession that day in March 1972. When Joe Mercer stepped unceremoniously aside, Allison ceased to be purely a football man. He became a one-man branch of the entertainment industry.

In 1970, the television companies decided to spruce up their coverage of the Mexico World Cup and, for the first time, they included the dreaded panel. Not so much a forum of discussion and debate as a precursor to *The Comedy Store*, the panel was a sign of the times. It was football mixed with pop, Simon Dee and the sensibilities of Alf Garnett. Be loud, be proud. It was ITV's idea, really, and one inspirational idea begets another. They signed Malcolm Allison.

It was around this time that Malcolm Allison turned into Big Mal and started to bear an uncanny resemblance to Huggy Bear's long-lost brother.

*Chapter 4*

# SOME KIND OF SATIRICAL INTENTION

*'When I ran a club off Tin Pan Alley I saw too clearly that sharp dividing line between enjoying yourself and merely seeking to submerge your failures, your fears and perhaps a growing boredom with life. I once helped a rich customer out of my club. He was quite drunk. He had no control over himself. He had become a clown. I have never forgotten the thought that came into my head: "So this is being a playboy?"'*

(from Allison's autobiography *The Colours of My Life*)

IAN MELLOR. NO DISRESPECT, IAN, BUT IT'S NOT A NAME THAT shines bright in the annals of British football. Best, Charlton, Law, Mellor. No. It's not there. But Ian Mellor was the straw that broke Malcolm Allison's back at Maine Road. After all the Bells and Lees and Marshes, it was Ian Mellor.

On 6 March 1973, the Manchester City board sold Mellor to Norwich for £65,000. Big Mal thought this was a ridiculous price. Not that he'd have complained about it when it happened. He didn't complain because the board didn't tell him. It was a slap, a humiliation, but the show must go on. 'My directors have gone against my wishes and my advice. But I will not resign. There are some things you have to learn to live with.'

Words that aren't worth the air they're spoken into are something else you have to live with. On 30 March 1973, the new manager of Crystal Palace was announced. 'My relationships with some Manchester City players have soured recently. I couldn't motivate them. So I've come home after too long a stay in the provinces. London is where my heart is. I now want to give Palace a team and a style that can meet the ambitions of the directors and supporters.'

While it fired Big Mal's image and fuelled a hundred headline writers – how many puns can you make along the lines of 'Big Mal Gets Call From the Palace'? – it was never going to be easy. The 'I love a challenge' bit is all well and good, but this was one Palace that had to be knocked down before it could be built up again. Allison joined a team that was about as happy as the one he had left behind. If City, with nine matches without a win, were in a bad way, then Palace were one of the few teams that could match them. Since their promotion to the top rank in 1970, they had done nothing. Two seasons in twentieth position and one at eighteenth – not the sort of stuff to get the Liverpools and Arsenals breaking out in a cold sweat. When the new Emperor rode into town, the Palace was, as usual, in need of a bit more than a lick of paint. Twentieth position and falling fast. Still, a five-year contract at £13,000 a year is a five-year contract at £13,000 a year.

The relegation threat proved not to be an empty one. While no one could really blame Allison for their demise – 'I never believed Palace could be this bad,' he said – no one really seemed to mind too much either. Malcolm was beginning to find himself cast in the role of Dr Frankenstein as his monster alter ego, Big Mal, slowly but surely took over.

The papers were having a field day. There were blondes around every corner, loud suits, louder quotes and, if there was ever a break in the proceedings, why, there was always Serena, the bunny girl. The one Palace star, Don Rogers, was a dead ringer for Jason King. That helped too. Everyone knew Big Mal. Everyone knew he smoked Montecristo A-size cigars, drove a fawn Jaguar 4.2, drank Louis Roederer Cristal champagne at £5.63 a bottle down at the White Elephant Club in Mayfair.

Quotes flew out of his mouth like water out of a tap that someone had forgotten to turn off. Ever since he appeared on the ITV World Cup panel in 1970 it seemed that he'd had a microphone as a permanent appendage.

Big Mal walks into a café and orders a coffee. The waiter asks if he wants sugar. No, no sugar, thank you, says Malcolm. The next day, odds on, there are screaming headlines: 'Big Mal turns his back on sugar', while inside the paper there are leaders speculating about Big Mal and the sugar. Does he have a weight problem? Is there diabetes in the family?

It was on that 1970 World Cup panel that Allison had out-Big Malled himself by describing some foreign players as 'peasants'. He laughs at the memory now. 'Actually it was the German team I was talking about. I said that he was rubbish, Beckenbauer.' You remember the old adage, 'Don't count the words, just the column inches'?

'In 1970 we had the best England team, the best chance ever of winning the World Cup. Even though we won it in 1966, the 1970 team was much better. Someone had doped Gordon Banks, someone had poisoned his food and doped him and I took my spite out on the German team. Actually, Beckenbauer was crap as a sweeper, honest, because if you attacked him he had no pace. He could read the game great, but he had no pace and that's why I was really upset in 1970, because I knew how to beat the German team.'

As usual, the crap thing about Big Mal was that he was ninety per cent right. The 1970 team was better than the 1966 team. England should have beaten the Germans. It was true. It was also true, though, that Big Mal was mighty pissed off that his boy Colin Bell had been one of Ramsey's substitutions that had attracted so much flak.

So 1970 was one thing. Mal was at City and City were winning and all the world loves a winner. You win, you can get away with all sorts of nonsense. What happens, though, when you start losing? You know what happens. The things you got away with before, you don't get away with them now. It's as true for football managers as it is for politicians.

During her heyday in the 1980s, Margaret Thatcher's vindictive words – her social cleansing – could have fertilised every farmer's field in Britain. But the people loved her. God rewarded them with negative equity, but we all know about His sense of humour. As soon as the people started to get the bills, and did they get them, and her popularity began to fade, she was on her bike quicker than you could say 'free transfer to Orient'. Equating a place with the mighty O's with a job as a PR for a cigarette company is horribly harsh, but there you go.

So while all the shenanigans kept the quotes boys at bay, there was a cloud that just wouldn't go away. Big Mal was no longer at City, he was at Palace and Palace were doing a very fine impersonation of a parachutist who'd had his silk cut. 'This not winning is killing me. Everything is right about the place. The only thing wrong is that we cannot put it together on the pitch,' he said. 'I've never gone this long without a victory in my life. It's the first time the pressure has got to me, but I'm not going to let it get me down.'

Frank McGhee wrote in *The Daily Mirror*, 'Malcolm Allison reminds me of a character in a film scene that has become a classic. It's the one where the vultures circle, hover and perch. Then the hero – the dinner – suddenly sits up, starts making a few noises and the vultures go away. But not very far.'

A League Cup defeat to Fourth Division Stockport County had the vultures tucking their napkins into their collars, ready. A club director said, 'We support and admire Mr Allison one hundred per cent.' Some hyaenas joined the vultures. There was enough for everyone. Big Mal reacted in a way that was set to become the way for all football managers. Out flapped the chequebook and in came Peter Taylor for £80,000.

That year – again – the relegation threat proved not to be an empty one. None of this seemed to diminish the legend of Big Mal. A vacancy occurred. Mal was linked. A headline was shy. Mal filled it. When Sir Alf Ramsey was unceremoniously retired, who was the paper's favourite? 'No, no. Not me. They'll want a nice fella. The way it's run, it's more like a part-time thing, a couple of days a week. Perhaps it would suit a retired person.'

Division Three and the team were in free-fall. Pundits and fans alike were quite sure where the blame lay. Palace had bought Dr Jekyll but had found themselves lumbered with his idiot sidekick whose ego was matched only by his shirt collars. Trying to locate what had gone wrong is ridiculously easy. The shenanigans had outweighed the football. And yet . . . what had happened to the man who had introduced the sweeper system, who had outwitted Schalke in the Cup-Winners Cup, who had masterminded the winning of four major trophies in three years? Maybe it was as simple as this: there was no genial Uncle Joe there to say 'Okay, Malcolm, okay'.

In the January of his final season at Palace, there were two newspaper features that had pictures of Big Mal strolling along – Apollo collar, kipper tie, sheepskin coat. The first related to a drink-driving ban: 'Mr Allison was stopped in his Daimler on 28 December.' The second was notification that a bankruptcy charge had been filed against him by a credit card company. 'His agent and former girlfriend, Serena Williams, said it was a ridiculously small amount . . . Big Mal was reunited with his wife, Beth, after a much-publicised affair with former Bunny Girl Williams.' The vultures were sending out invitations to their friends and were being fitted for new dinner-suits.

There's a point that every media star reaches. They court the press, they play up, they use its publicity and they fly. Suddenly the wind changes and things start to go wrong. Their work suffers. It all kept the column inches flowing and the name of Big Mal in the public eye, but with no substance to back it up, the game started to become a nightmare.

The media interest becomes an addiction and the star slowly turns junkie. The power relationship changes, the hunted becomes the hunter and the star becomes the paparazzi, chasing the elusive exclusive. The flamboyant quotes become almost confessionals. It's a stage every star from Boy George to Brian Clough reaches. Big Mal got there too. In 1975 he said, 'For about forty-seven years I've been carrying this great ego around with me . . . well, it's gone, overnight. I'm not saying that I've lost pride in myself or in my ability to do certain things, but in the last month or so certain things have happened to me to make me really think.'

The 'certain things that made me think' made him think for about thirty seconds. About how long it takes to say, 'A bottle of champagne, please.'

A useful insight into this period is given by Terry Venables who had moved to Selhurst Park from Queens Park Rangers on 14 September 1974 in exchange for moustachioed winger Don Rogers. In his autobiography, Venables says, 'He told me that when he went to Palace a lot of the players were very confused by what he was doing. After seeing me coach them, he realised that he had made a big mistake. I started off with the very basic things, and it reminded him that he should have started at Palace as he had started at Manchester City, by building from the same principles. Instead, he had started there as he ended at City, and without the basics, his ideas were all too much for the players.'

A few thoughts occur, the most obvious of which is that, with diplomacy like that, Venables could one day be manager of the England team. Another thing is that it is especially magnanimous given that it was Allison who gave Venables his final orders as a player.

Though the official announcement was made on 27 February 1975, the actual deed was done much earlier. Venables was still a week shy of his thirty-second birthday and had played a mere fourteen games for Palace. It was on 31 January that Allison called him into his office, and Venables says now that he thought Malcolm had called him in to wish him a happy new year. It didn't quite work out like that.

Malcolm relates the story: 'It was me who had to tell Terry that he was finished. I said to him one day, "Look Terry, I think you're at the end of your career." I said to him that "I think you better finish playing and you'd better come on the coaching side. You'll be more valuable to me on the coaching side than on the playing side." Telling someone that they're finished is the hardest thing in the world. It's the most difficult thing I've ever had to do. Two people I had to do it with were Terry and Colin Bell and it's a really difficult thing to do. The next worst thing is to tell a young lad that he's not going to make it; that he's not going to make it professional. Anyway, I said to him "You're finished. Playing in the Third Division, with the players we've got here at the moment, you're going to be much more use to me on the coaching side."

'He said to me, "I wouldn't take this from anyone else. I'm not sure I'm going to take it from you. I might, but I definitely wouldn't take it from anyone else." I said, "Listen, never mind you might, you're finished. Come on the coaching side and you'll be more useful to us than you will as a player." It was funny with Terry. A few minutes after he left my office, there was a knock on the door and it was Terry again. He said, "I just wanted to wish you a Happy New Year." It was New Year's Eve and I'd been too wrapped up in my own world to even realise it. I know that he went out with Bobby Moore and Frank McLintock that night and they told him to carry on playing, but I said, "No, no way. You've got to concentrate on coaching now." But the thing with Terry is that he was always cut out to be a coach. He was always coming out with ideas. Terry was getting so slow he used to put on weight in training.'

It's possible that with Venables at his side, Big Mal thought he could forge another partnership like the one he'd had with genial Uncle Joe. Certainly, when he bought Venables he had more than half an eye on his coaching abilities. Perhaps they could have been another team but, from the outside looking in, it would seem a duplicatory rather than a complementary relationship deal. At City, Mercer was the respected authority, the establishment father figure and Big Mal was the young tyro full of brilliant, radical coaching ideas. 'Okay, Malcolm, okay'. But with Venables? Was Malcolm supposed to be the Mercer? The respected authority, the establishment father figure?

For a while it worked. The staff of fifty-five professionals – *fifty-five* – was pruned and the two old pros were charged with firing up the players. Some were fired up, some were simply fired. By the time Allison and Venables had them where they wanted them, there was the beginnings of a top young team: Kenny Sansom, Terry Fenwick, Billy Gilbert, Peter Nicholas, Vince Hillaire, Jerry Murphy, Peter Taylor . . . It was a good team. In 1976, they reached the FA Cup semi-final, the first Third Division side ever to do so.

It was a Cup run which, for the tabloids, had a special significance. Palace had beaten Walton and Hersham and Millwall and were looking forward to a money-spinning big-name third-round tie. A Liverpool perhaps. Manchester City if it pleased the gods. The draw came out and they got . . . Scarborough. Some would have been pissed off. Not our dynamic duo.

'The hat? I'll tell you about that. I'll tell you about the hat. Serena bought it as a Christmas present for me, and I always liked that sort of hat, always loved to wear them. Anyway, there was a man called Jack Tinn, manager of Portsmouth, and in 1939 Portsmouth were about 300 to 1 in the Cup and Wolves were about 3 to 1 on favourites. Portsmouth got to the Cup final and going to the Cup final he wore these spats on his boots. Going to the final he said these are lucky spats, we'll win the Cup final with these spats. It was just a thing, you know.

'Anyway, he went on and won the Cup final with those spats, so when I had this hat, we were going to play Scarborough in the Cup, I thought okay and I decided to wear this hat at the game. So we were changing at Crewe and were standing at the station and all the players are there and I said "Watch this, we'll have a laugh". I took the hat out and put it on. The lads took the piss, and I said "Never mind that. We'll win the Cup with this hat". I just meant it as a laugh, and then I thought about that Jack Tinn thing and I thought, "Right. I'll do it." There were about twenty or thirty photographers behind each goal and I sat down in the stand with this hat on and all these photographers ran from behind the goals to take a photograph of me sitting with this hat. I couldn't believe it. After the game – we won 2–0 – I was walking past their dressing-room and I heard one of their players say, "What do you think of that cunt? The only chance we'll ever get of getting some publicity and he wears that fucking hat."'

In the next round, they drew Leeds away. Allison knew that the players would be nervous, full of dread – they were a Third Division outfit, and Leeds hadn't been beaten at home for something like two years – and had a word with his assistant. Venables: 'Malcolm said to me, "We've drawn a First Division side away. When you all hear who it is get very excited, say what a lucky ground it is for you and really give it some hype." When we were all together and the news came out, Malcolm said, "You beauty! What a great draw for us!"' Venables duly chipped in, saying what a lucky ground it was for him, how he'd always done well there. 'The players sat there open-mouthed, staring at us as if we'd gone completely mad.'

Mad or not, Palace went to Leeds fired with belief and came away with a 1–0 win. Their mood was summed up by Stuart Jump, a young, unremarkable player. With something like twenty minutes to go, he smiled at the bench and feigned smoking a cigar. Easy.

Of all the clichés in football, one of the best is this: the team gets knocked out of the Cup competition and the manager, trying to grab some consolation, says, 'Good, now we're free to concentrate on the League.' There's another cliché, though this one isn't limited to football: 'Clichés become clichés because they're true.'

After Leeds, they and their fedora-clad manager beat Chelsea and Sunderland before losing in the semi-final to the eventual winners, Southampton. While they were concentrating on the Cup, they let their minds off the real target: promotion. Three teams were promoted. Palace finished fourth.

At the end of the season, Allison was given the vote. Maybe it was that they'd missed out on promotion. Maybe it was that they'd missed out on the Cup. Maybe it was because of that hat. And maybe it was Fiona.

'At Palace I had a good young team coming through, maybe the second-best I ever had after City, but then Fiona Richmond got in the bath and the FA said I brought the game into disrepute.'

Why d'you do it, Malcolm?

'I felt she'd been working hard, you know, and she said "Do you mind if I get in the bath?", so I said "Yeah, why not?".'

The mid-1970s was a time when a strange phenomenon called soft porn was at its height. While the rest of the world opened up, the parental British authorities, led by the tightly-bound Godslot campaigner Mary Whitehouse, banned real pornography from these shores. Sometimes it's so nice to have the choice taken away from you, though it's perhaps fortunate that Mrs Whitehouse wasn't too encouraged by her successes. Who knows where that might have led? Perhaps she could have ended up dictating what clothes we all wore.

No sex please, we're British. Anyway, the upshot of our guardians' good work was soft porn. It would have been less than a step away from those 1950s' *Playboys* with the pubic hair airbrushed out had it not been for that other great British invention, saucy humour. Double entendres, word-plays featuring key words like 'come' and 'up' and bags full of so-bad-they're-good jokes. Mix and match Donald McGill's seaside postcards, the *Carry On* films, Frankie Howerd and Max Miller and then add liberal doses of naked girls. No boys bits, you understand – why, the sight of them would probably make you go blind.

It sounds crap, but for a few short years, soft porn was glorious in a way only the Brits can be. A genre came and went in, maybe, five years. Like all genres, it created its own environment, its own language and its own stars. And in the world of soft porn, few stars shined brighter than Fiona Richmond. Legend has it she was a 'normal' housewife in a previous life before being born again as Fiona, one of those chesty girls with an all-over tan who never travel by plane. Allegedly, Fiona's car had the number-plate FU 2.

It was during that season that Big Mal brought off the most outrageous, most ridiculous, most bloody stupid stunt that he – or any other football figure – could have ever dreamt of. The players were at the training-ground, training. Out of nowhere, a Rolls-Royce pulled up. Out got a tracksuited Big Mal, followed by Fiona Richmond, who was in a fur coat. Both of them were wearing huge smiles. The photographer following them was too serious to be smiling. He was working.

The training session finished and the players went back to their changing-room to wash and change. Normal things, you know. Then it was not so normal. Into the changing-room strolled Big Mal, Bigger Fiona and the snapper. Quick as a flash, they were in the communal team bath. And, really, one flash was all that was needed.

Some of the players didn't mind. Others didn't mind, until the tabloids came out. Others were smarter. 'Terry [Venables] was coaching with me, but it was the fastest I've ever seen him move, and I thought, hang on, I might have made a mistake here. He's quicker than I thought he was.'

Now, Allison recognises the mistake. 'To tell you the truth, it was a great disappointment to me because when she got in the bath I realised that she had plastic tits. It wasn't worth getting the sack for.'

Fiona got back in the Rolls and Malcolm got on his bike. Palace were a million pounds in debt, Peter Taylor was on his way out and confidence in the manager was so high you couldn't see it. The Palace board got really pissed off when they had the chance to sell Taylor to Leeds for £300,000. Money was tight and they needed it, so what did Mal do? He rebuffed Leeds and took himself off to the Cannes Film Festival where he was 'seen with' Serena. There's somewhere along the line where the lovable rogue becomes the pain-in-the-arse con-man. Big Mal found that place and built a house there.

Allison left a legacy. He bequeathed his young Palace team – the Team of the 1980s, as his young buccaneers went on to be known – to Venables. Faithful protégés, the team proved that they had learnt all the lessons and all the wisdom that Big Mal had instilled in them because, dutifully, just as they were on the edge of something real, they imploded.

And that was Malcolm Allison. Oh, he was still being employed by football clubs as late as 1992, but everything after Palace was strictly Frank Sinatra. There were no new films, no new songs, only endless comebacks.

There's a story Venables relates. It's a few years later – 1978. 'A couple of years later, with Malcolm about to take charge of Plymouth Argyle, we were at Bisham Abbey on a coaching course together. Rodney Marsh, Don Howe, Ron Atkinson, Allan Harris, John Bond, Malcolm and I were all sitting in my very small room, drinking and talking football one evening, when Don Howe started telling Malcolm that he was throwing away his talent, and he had to make sure he didn't go out on the tiles any more. He must not oversleep and take days off; he had to be consistent, because he had so much to offer.

'All of a sudden, Malcolm launched himself into a great speech, saying, "You're right. I've got to start pulling myself together. I'm one of the best coaches there is, and I'm going to prove it. I'm going to get myself fit during the summer. I'm not going to have a holiday. I'm going to go to fitness camps and I'm going to do special weight-training. When I go to Plymouth, I'm going to get them back for pre-season training not four or five weeks early, but seven weeks early. Never again will I lie in. I'm going to be up every morning at 7.30 and I'm going to make sure I never break the régime right through the whole season. I will be the first one on patrol. Not one day will go by, through wind, snow, sleet, hail – no matter what the weather – I'll be there. This is a new Malcolm Allison. I'll mould and motivate that Plymouth team into a promotion-winning side."

'It was a great speech, and by the end of it, he had us all thinking that we'd like to be at Plymouth ourselves, to see this incredible transformation. But when I tried to wake him up for training the next morning, he just put his head under the covers and said, "Oh, piss off. I'm too tired to get up early," and finally appeared for the 9.30 session at 11.30.'

And that's the way it was. He went back to Plymouth, back to Manchester City, back to Palace and, along the way, picked up enough sacks to open a shop.

Outside Britain, he fared a little better. He enjoyed a brief renaissance in Portugal in 1981 when, as coach of Sporting Lisbon, he won the League and Cup double. It was, he says now, 'the best team performance I was ever in charge of. They won the double, but then again, that was the first time I ever went to a team that was in the first three or four the year before. Usually, you know you always get a job when a team is at the bottom or has just got relegated.'

But even that ended in tears. And, curiously, it wasn't Big Mal's fault. 'I still got sacked that year, the president was jealous of me. It was the club's seventy-fifth anniversary and he really wanted to win the Championship. It wasn't a bad team the year before I went there and then he bought a couple of players and I came there and we won the League and Cup double. We won the League with about four matches to go and the Cup final about 4–0 and no one took any notice of him. He'd paid all the debts, about two million or something, and no one took any notice of him.'

After he left Palace, he went to America to set up a 'football consultancy'; he went to Galatasaray in Turkey; he went back to America; he went back to Plymouth; but mostly he went to pot. It was where the newspapers lived.

In May 1977, he set the date to be married to Serena. Beth filed divorce papers. 'You can keep the champagne and the other girls. I'm just beginning to live now,' Serena said. 'We have both played the field but now we just want each other. Now Mal wears a gold pendant round his neck which says "No longer me, but we".'

In August 1978, when he was manager of Plymouth, 'he appeared in court accused of being drunk and causing £28 damage to Paddington police station. . . . He lunged at a photographer before being whisked away by two blondes in a taxi. . . . His much-publicised romance with former Bunny Girl Serena Williams ended in December [1977]. Since then the girl in his life has been twenty-seven-year-old receptionist Sally Anne Highly. . . . Allison recently predicted that 1978 was going to be his lucky year.' Sally was, it should be noted, 'a former receptionist at the Playboy Club'. It sold newspapers, I suppose.

Everyone, sooner or later, goes home, and in early 1979, Big Mal left his equivalent of the Betty Ford Clinic – the Cornish peace and Plymouth Argyle – and headed back up the M6 to Maine Road. In truth, they needed him as much as he needed them. City were a big club and a big club needs big attention and the only attention they were getting stemmed from losing their last eleven games. Big Mal was cheaper than the Pope. With his adjutant Tony Book now in charge, Mal was again to be Genial Joe Mercer. If he thought of Mal as Joe, Tony Book didn't need good luck, he needed his head examined.

'I suppose my role at City will be like that of a scientist. A scientist puts all the pieces together. That's what I'll be paid to do and the pieces at City are very valuable indeed.' Dr Allison's experimental idea was this: If you buy enough money players for enough money, will the team succeed? He then made his experiment more specific. If you spend enough money on players who aren't that good, will they becomes as good as their price-tag would indicate?

Exactly one year later and the scientist was beginning to see the fruits of his experiment as City were beaten 1–0 by Halifax in the FA Cup. 'I am upset about it, but it is all part of the soccer scene. I was just too good for them.' Allison's wife, Sally, said, 'Malcolm is very upset and has taken it badly. He loved City.'

A leader in *The Guardian* in the summer of 1979 predicted the story. 'The notion that money buys success in football will be tested as never before this winter after a close season in which something like £17 million has been spent. It will be tested most of all at Maine Road where Malcolm Allison has been buying and selling on a scale which almost suggest some kind of satirical intention.'

A kind of satirical intention. *The Guardian's* priceless sometimes. It was more than satire. It was madness. The favourites are, in reverse order, Steve MacKenzie, a teenage Crystal Palace reserve bought for £250,000; Steve Daley, from Wolves for £1,480,000; and Kevin Reeves, bought from Norwich for £1,250,000.

MacKenzie hadn't played a match yet. Daley was a runner, harmless enough but probably more useful to Loughborough College than Manchester City. And Reeves? Well, you can't blame Reeves. Anyway, Allison holds his hands up on that one: 'The worst player I ever bought.' Not that this was all Big Mal's fault. Perish the thought.

'I'll tell you the story. I went to see the manager of Wolves, John Barnwell, and I said, "John, how much do you want for that boy Steve Daley?" And he said "I want £700,000", and I said "Do me a favour. I'll give you £400,000". Anyway, we settled for £550,000. Three weeks later, John was in a car accident and he was in hospital for three months. He was very, very ill and I rang up Richie Barker who was looking after the team and I said to him that before John went to hospital I'd agreed a deal with him for Steve Daley for £300,000. So he said, no no no, he wants £650,000. So we left it and nothing happened for three or four months. The next thing I knew, we were playing at Southampton and it was the first time ever that Peter Swales came on the bus. We went to Southampton and came back on Saturday night and came into work on the Monday and Tony Book said to me "We've signed Steve Daley" and I said "Oh, good. How much?" And he said, "£1 million". I said, "£1 million. What are you talking about?" and this is where the bung comes in.'

What started out as a regular tale of 'it wasn't my fault' is suddenly sounding more interesting.

'Ten minutes later it was £1.1 million plus the VAT which was about £1.5 million. I said to Tony, "I'm not interested. It's nothing to do with me." Peter Swales and the chairman of Wolverhampton Wanderers did the deal. When Francis Lee took over at City, I told him to look at the books, look at the Daley transfer. He did and said that there was a discrepancy of £300,000. Now, where's that money gone?'

I don't know. Where's that money gone?

'You work it out, but I'm now suing Mr Swales for saying that I signed Steve Daley. When I went there he said to me, "Malcolm, you look after the team, I'm the financial genius." I didn't know what he meant at the time.'

You never really got on with Mr Swales, did you?

'No, I quite liked Peter Swales because he wore a wig, a blazer with an England badge on it, and high-heeled shoes. As a man he really impressed me.'

The manager-go-round was also suggesting some kind of satirical intention. It became a kind of sad cabaret that flattered no one. In October 1980 he was sacked by City and by December he was manager of Palace. Have we been here before? In his first match in charge, Palace drew 2–2 with . . . Manchester City. You know the idea: that if you give a monkey a typewriter, it will eventually come up with the complete works of Shakespeare? This was like a soap opera that it was practising with.

Allison lasted fifty-five days at Palace, just long enough for both of them to get back in the headlines. From here on in, Malcolm went to Middlesbrough (sack), the Kuwaiti national team (sacked), the Portuguese team Vitoria Setubal (sack), another Portuguese side, Farense (sacked), Fisher Athletic (left for 'personal reasons') and Bristol Rovers (ill-health). He'd done his bit. Fisher tried to resurrect the old spirit by introducing him to both their crowd in a helicopter. He was brought to the Fisher ground by helicopter. Even he's left speechless by that one. 'I didn't want to ask them why they did it.' In case you're wondering, his deal was worth £30,000.

Like Frank Sinatra, regrets he's had a few, but then again too few to mention. Well, maybe a few are worth a mention.

The biggest mistake? 'Just weeks after City's Cup final win, I was being fêted in Italy by one of the most powerful men in Europe, the Fiat magnate, Agnelli. He said to me: "Come to coach my team Juventus, Malcolm, and I will pay you £20,000 a year tax-free and give you your own private aeroplane." I thought the language would be a problem. I went there and said to Agnelli, "Look, I want to change the way they play. I don't want to play with a sweeper. I want to play with four at the back and I want to play with a defending midfield player," and he kept saying to me, "Do it with the reserves, Malcolm, do it with the reserves. Don't do it with the first team. You'll find it difficult to change, but you've got to do it." And I said, "Look. If I can't do it the way I want to do it, I won't," and also I was a bit concerned about the language and I said, "No". I should've taken the job and done it slowly.'

Taken the job and done it slowly. It's not really your style is it?

'No, I suppose not.'

He looks far away for a moment, thinking maybe of the black-and-white stripes, maybe of what might have been. More likely he's probably wondering why this twit with a list of questions and a microphone is so interested in the past. Whatever, he soon comes back and fixes me a grin like an old raddled version of Johnny Boy in *Mean Streets*. All cocky arrogance and fuck-off 'I told you so' confidence.

'Anyway, the coach they got instead of me lasted six weeks.'

Their loss, you see.

## Chapter 5

# UNITED WE STAND

*'The game is riddled with it – it's almost as bad as the House of Commons. When I look at my situation compared to some, I feel quite innocent.'*

Tommy Docherty

IT WAS JUST ANOTHER DAY IN JUST ANOTHER WEEK WHEN SHE first saw him. She'd gone to the training-ground to meet Larry, her husband and the team masseur, more out of duty than anything else really. Every morning they had the same conversation. He would ask her to come to the ground, she would refuse.

'But you'll find it interesting.'

'What's interesting about a group of muscle-bound neanderthals running around? Would you want to come to the classroom when I'm teaching?'

'Maybe you should bring your class along. It's got everything they'll need – athleticism, teamwork, skill, hard graft . . .'

'Oh, Larry. It's only a game. The way you go on about it, you'd think it was more important than life and death.'

'Someone else said that once. Anyway, your kids would love it. They'll learn the value of friendship and loyalty, honesty and principle. No one at the club would ever shaft anyone else.'

'Maybe. One day.'

It was a conversation they'd had a million times. Why she was there now, God knows. But she was and for some reason she found herself transfixed by the manager. Standing there in his sweaty tracksuit barking at his players, he looked every bit the bastard she'd heard he was. 'Laddie, you're to football what King Herod was to baby-sitting.' 'Call yourself a full-back? I've seen milk turn faster than you, laddie.' He was harsh and brutal, yet there was something about him, a kind of animal charisma, that made everybody listen.

It was the kind of charisma that wasn't an accident. It came from a lifetime of winning. He'd clawed his way up from the street to be in charge

79

of the most powerful club in the land, and he was loving it. It was where he belonged. He once said that he'd walked from his native Scotland to be where he was today and, looking at him, you knew what he'd walked on.

As the training session came to an end, Larry rushed up to her and started saying how glad he was that she'd come. Her head, though, was somewhere else.

'Marie, you don't look like you've been listening to a word I said,' said Larry.

Snapping out of her reverie, she said, 'Sorry, sweetie. I wasn't listening to a word you said.'

Later that night, she phoned Grace, her best friend. 'It's ridiculous. I can't get him out of my head. I love Larry and I'm pregnant with his child, but I can't get him out of my head. I can't believe this is happening to me.'

Grace said relax. Grace said calm down. Grace said nothing's happening. What did Grace know?

At breakfast the next morning, Larry casually asked Marie what she was doing that day.

'Oh, I thought I'd come down to the ground again. You were right. It was quite interesting.'

'Ha! See?' said Larry triumphantly. He turned to go out the door. 'Come a bit earlier. I'll introduce you to Timmy, our manager. He's quite a character. You'll love him.'

Relax. It's fiction.

If you're a romantic – and if you're not, well, I'm sorry – you can forgive Docherty almost anything for the Mary Brown business. It's a sense of forgiveness that's heightened by the beautiful irony that it all happened at Old Trafford.

It's 1966 and Georgie Best, the sparkly-eyed Belfast boy, is just breaking through as the first footballing pop star. His dazzling, audacious skills are matched only by his good looks. Whenever Burnley play away there are crowds of teenage girls, screaming at this boy wonder, this raven on the wing, this fifth Beatle. And his home ground of Turf Moor has been bursting at the seams ever since Best first appeared. Osgood was good, but Best was best.

No, it doesn't quite work, does it? Burnley could never have been George's club. Andy Lochhead's but not George's. No. George had to be a Manchester United player.

Manchester United was the footballing home of glamour, of romance, of love. As the 1960s turned into the 1970s and the media circus got a hold of football, different clubs' images became set in the public imagination. Leeds were Lee Van Cleef, all dark hats and snidey shots in the back;

Liverpool were Clint Eastwood, quietly getting on with the business of coming out on top; Arsenal were something else, but something too dull to remember; Spurs were flash new cash; and Manchester United were aristocrats, not actually winning anything, but superior through breeding.

More than any other, United was the club that had traded in love. Munich, Busby, the Babes, the Best–Law–Charlton era . . . the word United was soccer shorthand for romance. Love. There was a bottomless pit of the stuff that had been gathering at Old Trafford since 1958 and it was buried deep in the stands. As those fallow years turned into the cash crops of the 1990s, United changed. It would be too easy to say that the public sympathy left them as the trophies returned; sitting here you get the feeling that the trophies were an irrelevance. It was the attitude. Somewhere along the line, probably just about the time that the First Division became the Second Division, United turned from being classic aristocrats to being grubby money. Exit Bobby Charlton, enter Paul Ince. Neither would be the last to be picked in the school playground; they're both good players. It's just a question of attitude. Bobby Charlton's going to run over to the crowd and 'offer' to take on the lot of them? Perhaps it's unfair to blame United for turning into a cynical, nasty, shirt-manufacturing commercial enterprise. Perhaps we should just file it in that large, ever-expanding cabinet called Thatcher's Britain. It doesn't matter. For lovers of irony, the whole thing's a treat. Docherty lost United to love, just as United were themselves preparing to lose love to the god Mammon.

Whatever Docherty had done since hanging up his boots, it all seemed a warm-up for the Old Trafford job. Even when he was managing the Scottish national team, it was second best. United was 'the best job in football', he said, and, despite guiding Scotland through the qualifying rounds for the 1974 World Cup, he chose to hit the rock and give it all up.

'I always wanted to be manager of Manchester United and, within me, I believed it would happen one day. Everything that has happened to me in the past has been for my benefit.'

Britain's most famous club were deep in it. Since the walking legend that was Sir Matt Busby had stepped down (or rather, stepped up: Sir Matt didn't step down anything at Old Trafford) as manager, they'd had first Wilf McGuinness and then Frank O'Farrell. Both of them were nice enough blokes, honest and true, but sometimes nice just isn't the ticket. It's easy to get the impression that their niceness was exactly what the board at Old Trafford was looking for. Because they knew that nice wasn't what was required. Maybe the board knew that nice Wilf and nice Frank could be relied on. Not to challenge the Busby legend. Not to rock the boat. Not to disturb the status quo. Sir Matt had stood up as manager, but there was still only one boss at Old Trafford. And he wasn't called Wilf or Frank.

Something special was expected from Britain's most famous club, especially as the light-blue patsys next door had started winning trophies like they were going out of fashion. Worse, City had started to dominate the headlines. It was all 'Big Mal this' and 'Big Mal that' and then it was 'Rodney this' and 'Rodney that'. United had Frank, a genial enough soul who'd failed his basic communication O-level. 'He came as a stranger and went as a stranger,' said one player. Something had to be done.

If the board had already started to think about these things, then a trip down to London on 16 December put the final nail in Frank's coffin. Five nails. United were beaten 5–0 at Crystal Palace. If it had been Milan at the San Siro, that would have been one thing; but Palace at Selhurst Park? Something had to be done. Now, as chance would have it . . .

The dictionary defines synchronicity as a 'concurrence of two or more events in time'. To some people it's spooky. To some, it's proof that there really is a God. Docherty being at Palace, that to some was synchronomous. To Frank O'Farrell, it probably seemed more than spooky. The spooky defies explanation.

As chance would have it, Tommy Docherty was at that Palace match, checking on a young Palace defender, Tommy Taylor, formerly of the mighty Leyton Orient.

With Allison across the road, the thought of getting Docherty in must have had the Old Trafford board salivating. Go for your quotes and go for them now. Manchester would never be out of the headlines. For Docherty, the appeal was two-fold. Managing a national team is huge on the pride side – to use the Yiddish, it gives you great *nachus*. It makes you glow. But it doesn't fulfil the basic need every real football person has to be involved in the game. To be really involved on a day-to-day basis. That essential desire they have to have a coronary every Saturday afternoon. National managers check out players. See how they're playing. National managers have reasonable blood pressure. The other thing is the eternal. United offered Doc £15,000 a year, twice as much as he was getting at Scotland. When Docherty said he'd walk to Old Trafford, it was probably because the Scottish FA wouldn't give him the expenses.

Going to Old Trafford also offers the chance to write yourself into the history books. Say you do better than Sir Matt. Wouldn't that be something?

Docherty knew that Sir Matt was the key to success. Wyatt Earp may have been a great sheriff, but at the end of the day he was still only an employee. As it turned out, he only crossed swords with the Great Man once. As he relates in Brian Clark's *Docherty: The Living Legend of Football*,

'During a club holiday in Spain, the chairman, Louis Edwards, threw a party in his room for the players and Docherty went along for a drink. The next day he was pulled to one side by Busby and warned of the dangers. "He told me that familiarity breeds contempt. I reminded him that he played golf every Sunday with several of the players and when he did I felt the same way. He didn't like what I said, I could tell, but he took my point."' A phrase containing the words 'three bags full' might have been more politic, but . . .

United's problem was the same one that Docherty had faced at Chelsea almost exactly ten years before. The team was run by a cartel of senior citizens, players who had done their bit and were essentially waiting for the gold watch. They were great players, but perhaps lacking the hunger. And when you're a Manchester United player, you need that hunger. It doesn't matter if you're playing in a crap team that's struggling for survival at the bottom of the league, you're still Manchester United and everybody just loves to beat Manchester United. Every match is, as they say, like a cup tie.

As the great and the good prepared to pack their bags, Docherty went shopping. In a three-week blitz, he spent £500,000 – a mighty sum – on four new players. If the problem was similar to Chelsea's, Docherty's first impulse solution was exactly the same: sign George Graham. Ten years before, he had cost £6,000 from Aston Villa. This time around, he was a bit more expensive and Arsenal received £125,000. 'George is the Gunther Netzer of British football,' said Docherty in a statement that explains why Tony Currie had to be invented. (Looking at Graham's managerial career, it's easy to see that he took as much from The Doc as he gave. In retrospect, it looks to have been a regular masterclass. A grim, disciplinarian Scot with a sharp line in self-protective wit, a man who gave and expected loyalty from his players, a man who believed in giving youth its head and wouldn't take any bullshit from anyone. Now who does that remind you of? We could, of course, add something about successful careers collapsing spectacularly, financial irregularities, controversial claims and counter-claims . . .)

Not even his mother would describe Doc's next signing as a British Gunther Netzer. Big Jim Holton came from Shrewsbury for £80,000 and was to football what – how can we best describe this? If Hollywood ever decided to make *The Manchester United Story*, the part of Big Jim Holton would be played by Fred Gwynne, aka Herman Munster. Followers of modern dance might understand it if I said think of Leigh Bowery dancing with Michael Clark.

'Jim Holton came off the field with cuts and bruises all over his knuckles, not from hitting people, but because his hands drag on the floor when he walks. We put bells on a football so that he would know where it was. Then we had complaints from Morris dancers saying he was kicking them all over the place.'

The shopping basket was completed by Alex Forsyth from Partick Thistle for £100,000 and Lou Macari from Celtic for £200,000. Paying so much for Macari might have seemed a gamble, but the odds were on him to succeed.

Just when it seemed that you had to be Scottish to get a game for United, Docherty bought two young Irish players, Mick Martin and the brilliant, if erratic, Gerry Daly. Daly was a United player through and through: brilliant, yet erratic, an all-too-familiar mixture of the sublime and the idiotic.

Of all the famous names to leave Old Trafford in Docherty's clear-out, none were more famous than Bobby Charlton or Denis Law. Sunday, 29 April 1973, was probably the best day ever to be a sub-editor in the sports department of a newspaper. The day before, both the Charlton brothers played their last game and Manchester United gave Denis Law a free transfer to Manchester City. Now, write a headline from that lot.

The crowd at Old Trafford probably didn't know what to say. One day they're watching Law, Charlton and the rest. The next day it's Big Jim. From Docherty's perspective, there was some logic to what he was doing, but up in the Stretford End? Sometimes you've really got to feel for football supporters. Grown men running around chasing a stupid ball.

Funny game, football. Bobby Charlton, the Greatest Living Englishman, had begun his career twenty years earlier against Charlton Athletic. It could only have been against Charlton Athletic. He'd done it all, seen it all. He'd had the ups and he'd had the downs. From the Busby Babes to the World Cup to the European Cup. If it was round and bounced, Bobby Charlton had done it.

'Bobby came to see me one day and told me he'd decided to retire. He asked my permission to inform the chairman and directors. It was a marvellous gesture from a magnificent servant of the club. I wish some of his team-mates had behaved like he did. But then, Bobby was man enough to accept the situation as it was.'

His final game – his 640th – was at Stamford Bridge on 30 April 1973. It was a game in keeping with the man and the times. Both teams provided a guard of honour as Sir Bob walked out onto the pitch. There was a presentation of a silver cigarette-box, a few handshakes, a wave to the 44,000 capacity crowd and that was that. Nothing frivolous for Lord Bob. United duly did their bit by losing 1–0.

Denis Law's exit was very different, but that's another story. Docherty's attitude to buying and selling players was as unpredictable as he was. When he took over at United, he bought George Graham. The 'elegant midfielder' helped them avoid relegation in that first season and then? Graham was swapped for Portsmouth's veteran Ron Davies. Davies never started a game for United. Very odd.

'Most of the disagreements between players and managers have been argued out in a healthy but surprisingly public fashion, yet his players are everything to Docherty. He's disciplined them, he's sacked them, he's sworn for them and been fined for it. He's publicly taken their side against the club board and been censured for it. He's worked so many of them so hard that they've left. Yet he's warm, instantly likeable and, one hopes, about to become a successful manager.' That could have been said about Docherty at any time in his career, the only clue to the era is the phrase 'one hopes'. So even in BBC-land it's before the 1980s. For those who need to know, it was said by Frank Bough in a news report on Chelsea on the eve of their 1967 FA Cup semi-final against Leeds.

Frank Bough was many things to many people, but soothsayer? Best to say that Docherty was his own man and, perhaps, he preferred it if the players were his own men, too. One senior Old Trafford figure who was cold-shouldered by The Doc had the temerity to ask why he hadn't been selected to play. 'Because the A team haven't had a match yet,' came the reply.

Of all the famous faces to leave Old Trafford in Docherty's clear-out, one was more famous than either Bobby Charlton or Denis Law. And it was a face that had 'grief' written all over it.

*'Tommy Docherty is the funniest, most two-faced, self-obsessed man I have ever met; and he is the reason that I finally, unequivocally, quit Manchester United. Tommy Docherty lied to me and that, to me, makes Tommy Docherty a liar. I came back to Manchester United because of him. I walked out on the club I loved, that had been my family, my life for eleven years, because of Tommy Docherty . . . People say to me, "Tommy Docherty is a lovable rogue, he's a character." He may be a lovable rogue, but character is something he does not have. I regret walking out on Manchester United. I don't regret for one moment walking out on Tommy Docherty. He lied to me.'*

(From *The Good, The Bad and the Bubbly*, by George Best and Ross Benson)

What was this heinous lie that Docherty told George? What was so terrible? The George Best story is too long and too convoluted and, most of all, too horrible to tell in great detail here, but . . .

Three days before Docherty took over at Old Trafford, on 22 December 1972, Best had announced his official retirement. The previous May he had announced he was quitting. He was twenty-six – the same age that Bjorn Borg made his equally sad decision to quit.

It's a rare occasion that you go against the judgement of history, but in the case of Best, it may be justified. Best was a shooting star, a bright light which dazzled, but burnt out. That's the way it is in life. It squeezes out the sparks. You either burn bright and fast or you glow slow, and our culture is littered with the corpses of the bright – Morrison, Rimbaud, Hendrix, Mozart, The Adverts . . .

Best's other mitigating argument is that he was the first. And he truly was. He was the first pop-star footballer, the first person to be subjected to all the temptations, yet he was still expected to be a top athlete in peak physical condition. Mortals can't do one thing as well as he did all of them.

Anyway, Busby wanted his boy back. Docherty also wanted him back. He had a dog of a team, and Best – in whatever shape – was a star, and would improve the team out of sight. Also, let's not forget Dochetry's love affair with the column inch. And Best came complete with column yards.

Eventually Best came back. He was – comparatively – fat and old and slow, but he came back, making his 'debut' on 15 October 1973 against Shamrock Rovers. By 12 January 1974, he was out again, this time for good. What had happened? 'He lied to me.'

Docherty and Busby felt that Best was so important to them that they said that he could, more or less, do things his way. He could train when he wanted, as long as he did the requisite hours. He would not be subject to the normal rules. Writing this, reading this, it seems an obvious recipe for disaster, giving Best his head. But so much had been tried, so many different ways, that all concerned were at their wits' end. They just wanted him back. Interestingly, he wasn't given his head as far as money was concerned. He was still on £150 a week – less than club captain Willie Morgan.

The inevitable happened. He didn't turn up for training. Crunch time was one fateful Saturday when United were playing Plymouth in the FA Cup. Best turned up at 2.30 p.m. for a 3 p.m. kick-off only to find that he'd been dropped. Well, *quelle surprise.*

'Plymouth?' said Best. 'You don't think I'm good enough to play against Plymouth?' But . . . but . . . but . . . 'Well, if that's the case, if you don't think I'm good enough to play against Plymouth, I'm off.' And so he was.

Docherty: 'He ruined things for himself, but he was a good lesson for any footballer who feels that he wants to perform more off the pitch than he does on. George was a great lesson to any footballer in danger of thinking of himself as a superstar off the pitch. I can't say if I'd handle George differently if I had the chance again. I don't know. It was a question of balancing the talent against the problems. In the end no one had the right to disrupt so many other people so much.' Cynics may feel free at this point to look at the line about wanting to perform more off the pitch than on, and smile that cynical smile.

'The only one George has really got to blame for finishing his career is himself. He was twenty-seven years of age, a genius of a player, he had the world at his feet and he walked out. The thing that annoyed me about Best was that he deprived so many people of seeing a true genius on a football pitch.'

Now, though, Docherty is indebted to Best (though he probably wouldn't admit it). Best has given him enough gag material for a thousand after-dinner speeches. 'We went to dinner last week, but he didn't turn up. He said he was launching a ship in Belfast but it was seven miles out at sea before he'd let go of the bottle.' You've heard them before and you'll hear them again.

Docherty's United staved off relegation. Just. But the executioner hadn't been sacked, he'd just nipped out for a bite to eat. A year later, he was back, and this time he was serious. Under anyone else, United would have been relegated. Under, say, Frank O'Farrell, they'd have lost 1–0 away to Coventry. Life with The Doc, though, is generally a bit more entertaining than that.

On the Chelsea FC centenary video, the narrator, Barry Davies, says of Docherty, 'Wherever he went in football he generated a new dynamism, an element of flair on the field and a feeling that something unforgettable might happen.' And so it was on 29 April 1974.

This is the scenario. United are playing City at Old Trafford. If they lose, they go down. With three minutes to go and with the score at 0–0, United look safe. Francis Lee breaks on the right; forced wide, he knocks – mishits, really – a ball into the United box. A group of players look at it and do the pinball shuffle. The loose ball rolls across the six-yard line and Denis Law, standing with his back to the goal, casually back-heels it. A reflex action which probably bypassed his brain entirely, it causes the ball to roll agonisingly into the net. It was to be the last time Law kicked a ball in League football. Colin Bell, his City team-mate remembers running up to him to congratulate the goal, seeing Law's face and backing off. 'He was absolutely sick.' A very big parrot. An enormous parrot. United, it seems, are relegated and Denis Law, one third of United's glorious triumvirate, did it.

The crowd crash on to the pitch, determined to have the match abandoned. Sir Matt Busby was to dignity what Blackpool was to rock. He made an announcement to the crowd, pleading with them to get off the pitch 'for the sake of the club'. The crowd – let's play the game and call it a mob – disagreed and stayed on the pitch, again, no doubt, for the sake of the club. The match was restarted and Law was immediately substituted, but then fighting broke out again. No one knew who was fighting, really. It didn't matter. Fires were started, one goalmouth was obscured by clouds of smoke. Thinking it was all over, the crowd came on to the pitch. It is now, said Dave Smith, the referee. The game was duly abandoned and United were duly relegated.

The Law back-heel was a wonderful moment, the sort of thing that reminds football fans why they are football fans. Every adolescent boy has had a fight with his girlfriend about football. Playing or watching, it doesn't matter. Oh, it's so stupid. Grown men running around chasing a stupid ball. I thought we were going to buy some shoes this afternoon. Grown men running around chasing a stupid ball. Why is it we can never have a lie-in on a Sunday morning? Grown men running around chasing a stupid ball. Sometimes the girls don't know but the little boys understand.

The funny thing, in the way that football is always a funny old game, was that the other matches played that Saturday afternoon made the result at Old Trafford irrelevant. Docherty went back to his office, got out his trusty atlas and looked around the England map. There were some nice small towns that had clubs in Division Two. There were some nice small towns that had clubs in Division Two that might need a new manager, someone with a bit of clout, someone who'd get them a bit of publicity. There was a knock at the door and The Doc, his stoicism ready, prepared to welcome in the Vote. At United, failure is tolerated like a dose of some horrid scratchy disease. Terminated with extreme prejudice. Instead there was a crate with a dozen bottles of champagne and a message to get on with the job of getting United back into the big league.

It's said that fortune favours the brave, and United were brave. Again, Docherty's answer to the crisis was exactly as it had been at Chelsea: throw in the kids. United, it seemed, were transformed overnight from a bunch of ageing has-beens resting on their laurels into a bunch of hungry young guns who were going for it. The reality was that the sweep wasn't total; rather, Docherty's skill was in making it seem so. Five of the team that was humiliated against Manchester City made it through to play in the FA Cup final against Liverpool two years later.

If there was a complete change around at Old Trafford – and there was – it wasn't so much the personnel. It was their attitude. One of The Doc's great gifts is that his teams have always mirrored his mouth: they've always been quick-witted, fast and entertaining.

This is something that George Graham forgot to take from The Doc Masterclass of football management. While Docherty believed that sabre-witted attack was the best form of defence, Graham thought that defence was the best form of defence. He also thought that defence was the best form of attack. But who are we to question these things? Tom won a couple of cups and picked up his Jack Nicklaus gag. George won everything and stayed at the Arsenal for a hundred years. There's a moral there somewhere, but it's not one that we'll go into here. If you cast your mind back to the beginning of this chapter, you'll remember that we're romantics.

'I sold a lot of them and gave a lot away because we weren't really good enough. Really, that's what was wrong. It was a team getting old together and they needed replacing.' United? It could have been, but it was Chelsea. There, Docherty overcame the loss of the incomparable Jimmy Greaves to build a team that was that most desirable of beasts, the small, highly-mobile, intelligent unit. His 'little diamonds'. Though he always made sure to credit his predecessors at Stamford Bridge for bringing the kids there in the first place – inventively, the press called them 'Drake's Ducklings' in the manner of Busby's Babes – it was Docherty who had the balls to say 'enough' and throw them all in after the (already doomed) team he inherited had been relegated.

The next season they bounced straight back – again, the comparison with United is too sweet to bear. At Chelsea, though, things were a little more dramatic. Under the old, baffling goal-average rules, they gained promotion by 0.401 of a goal, courtesy of a last-match-of-the-season 7–0 victory at home to Portsmouth. What's the fun in doing it the easy way?

The next season, he threw in Venables, a couple of Harrises, Murray, Butler and Bridges. Waiting in the wings was the jewel, Peter Osgood. 'Peter. What can I say? He had skill, two great feet, was great in the air, a marvellous heart . . . what more is there?' Not a lot. Looking back now, it's easy to remember Osgood as a ridiculous haircut bookended by two of the bushiest sideburns you ever did see. They weren't sideburns, they were sideboards. Big, veneered sideboards which probably contained a cocktail-cabinet or two.

If Docherty was two managers (the brain and the gob), Osgood was two players (the before and the after). The before was sublime. There's a piece of footage which shows the eighteen-year-old prodigy cutting through a Liverpool defence as if it wasn't there. Grace, balance and strength, he ran through them like a knife through butter. 'Osgood? He was in a different class. He lost a bit of pace when he broke his leg, but I thought he was world class. He liked a bevvy but he was great, no problem.'

As with so many of Docherty's careers, there's a huge What If? What if Osgood hadn't broken his leg? The What If? for Osgood doesn't bear thinking about. We're talking a large collection of caps, goals, legends. For Docherty? Chelsea would have, undoubtedly, been more successful, and success often covers up the grief. If Osgood hadn't broken his leg, it's no stretch of the imagination to say that The Doc may not have spent the year of the Summer of Love starting his collection of irons and putters by moving between three different clubs. Maybe, though, that other trait of Docherty's would have thrown a spanner in the works anyway. When Osgood broke his leg, Docherty just couldn't resist the temptation to go out and buy . . . Tony Hateley.

'My philosophy was to let the boys express themselves. We sparkled with wonderful, entertaining football, and the fans loved it and poured through the turnstiles to watch us.' Chelsea? It could have been, but actually that was United. Docherty may have been a gob-on-a-stick bore at times but, football-wise, he's always put his belief in entertaining football where his mouth is. Fortunately, there was room.

Whatever his faults and whatever his foibles, Docherty had a habit of creating great teams, often from little or nothing. Manchester United turned, within the space of one summer, from a bunch of lumbering, lazy has-beens into a thrilling team of verve and flair. With Steve Coppell on one side and Gordon Hill on the other, it was this team that was as responsible as any for finally banishing the nightmare vision of Sir Alf Ramsey's wingless wonders. At centre-forward was Stuart Pearson, he of the pigeon-stepped, arm-raised goal salute. The mercurial Gerry Daly was the perfect complementary midfielder – at least he was before he stepped on the toes of his equally mercurial boss. Martin Buchan was the Alan Hansen. The Greenhoff brothers fetched and carried well enough (they were good in a Steve Perryman sort of way, but reports that Brian got eighteen caps have to be discounted as some sort of sartorial deal). Lou Macari nipped and tucked. Sammy McIllroy. Jimmy Nicholl . . .

Sixty-six goals and a million fans later, United were back home. The match that clinched promotion, at home to Oldham, attracted 56,678 punters. The Second Division was never going to be big enough for them. The next year, they finished third, but the showcase was the FA Cup. At one stage, the semi-finals, it looked as though the headline writers would get an early Christmas. Everything was building up for a Crystal Palace v United final. Big Mal v The Doc. Sergio Leone was on stand-by. Ennio Morricone could've done the music. It would have been a treat.

Sadly, Southampton beat Palace. Even more sadly for Docherty, Southampton then beat United. There was a bit of interest by the appearance of two former Docherty diamonds, but Osgood was good a long time ago and McCalliog was also well past his sell-by date. Southampton were, in truth, a bog-standard Division Two team. Honest enough, you know. It might have been said before, but football, you know, is a funny old game. United were hotter than July with the bookies and lost 1–0. The next year they were back at Wembley, only this time they were the Southampton. The mighty Liverpool juggernaut was on course for a record-breaking League, Cup, European Cup treble. No one messed with Liverpool. United won 2–1.

'Our attitude was wrong and we lacked total commitment against Southampton last year, but it worked in our favour because we came into this match determined not to make the same mistakes against Liverpool. The pressure was on them because they were the favourites and you could see that several of their players had the treble on their minds. The taste of defeat last year was so bitter that none of our players wanted to experience it again. Now we can set our sights on the European Cup-Winners Cup.'

'We beat the best team in Europe,' said The Doc. 'I felt we could go on from there and take more honours.'

*'Who broke my heart?*
*You did, you did.*
*Shot through the heart*
*Just blame Cupid.*
*You think you're smart*
*Stupid, stupid.*
*Shoot that poison arrow through my heart.'*

It would have been as easy as ABC for Docherty to lead United to greater and greater triumphs – maybe even that elusive Championship. But the fates had other ideas.

Tommy, did you feel shafted by United?

'Yeah, I did. But it didn't really bother me. Did for about a fortnight.'

But they couldn't condone what you did.

'You look at what's happening today. With the chairman, Martin Edwards. He's in and out of more beds than Percy Thrower, yet I get the sack for falling in love with another woman.'

After West Bromwich Albion beat Preston North End in the 1954 FA Cup final, Tom Finney said this about Docherty: 'He is a great footballer and he could be a great manager one day. Mind you, he takes some understanding but wherever he goes and whatever he does, they will certainly know he has been there.'

Mary told Laurie that they were seeing each other. 'Ha,' laughed Laurie. 'Doc always takes the girls out.'

To those involved, it must have been a nightmare. But to the outside world, it was a joy. And if that sounds harsh, remember in the outside world, Mills & Boon are one of the biggest-selling publishers, ever.

Docherty: 'The crunch day was coming. Mary and I knew that it could not be avoided and that is why, despite Manchester United's glorious victory, I was the loneliest man at Wembley . . . It was the supreme moment of my soccer career, but in truth I was alone and miserable.'

At the FA Cup celebratory banquet, 'Mary wasn't that far from our table and she has since told me that she desperately wanted to come over and share my triumph. But she was with her husband and I was with my wife. It was agony, but there wasn't any way we could have been together for any length of time or our love would have shown.'

Mary: 'I love him. I know it sounds corny, but I do.'

Mary: 'When Tom propositioned me that first time I said no, but I was flattered that someone took an interest in me. It was nice to know that I wasn't past it.'

'We didn't book hotel rooms or borrow friends' flats or anything like that. We used to go on picnics into the Derbyshire hills. We would either sit in the car and listen to music or go for walks.'

'It's unfortunate the way things have turned out, but we could not go on living a lie.'

Just before the story broke, Docherty had gone to live with Mary at her mother's large eighteenth-century house in what sounds like almost hippie-ish commune bliss. There was Mary and Tommy living downstairs, while upstairs were Laurie and the Browns' kids. Mary's mum lived in another part of the house. Each night, Mary went upstairs, kissed the children, tucked them into bed and said goodnight to Laurie before returning downstairs to the arms of the waiting Doc. It's a lovely image, Docherty the Sergeant-Major living like some New Age crystal-gazer.

There's one other bizarre aspect that The Grateful Dead would approve of. Docherty said this later: 'I had been going out with Mary for nearly two years and I am convinced that no one at the club had known about us apart from Laurie Brown, who actually used to baby-sit for us.' Apart from Laurie Brown, who actually used to baby-sit for us. It warms the cockles.

It's easy to pick out quotes and see the humour in the situation, but at Old Trafford there was little in the way of laughter. People were upset, and despite chairman Louis Edwards' sympathetic shoulder, it couldn't last. Apart from anything, there was a Roman Catholic streak at Old Trafford that was as strong as the red of their jerseys. Sir Matt Busby wasn't nicknamed The Pope for nothing. It couldn't last.

It didn't help when Docherty appeared with what, to all the world, seemed like a black eye. Docherty, true to form, laughed it off with a reference to the Gillette blades he was advertising at the time. 'I've been having trouble with the razor-blades and this morning I shaved too high.' Gillette, too, laughed it off. They gave him the vote of confidence. Brown, meanwhile, was saying nothing. Pointing to his cut hand, he said, 'You can say I hit my hand on something unimportant.'

Docherty decided to take time out and went to visit some friends in the Lake District. In this whole bizarre episode, it seems almost normal that he drove up the motorway with the FA Cup trophy in the boot of his car. 'I'd promised to show it to my friends.' One 'clear the air' meeting and it was all over. There was some nonsense about selling Cup final tickets, but everyone knew what the real story was.

'Resign.'
'I won't resign.'
'Resign.'
'I won't resign. I haven't done anything wrong.'
'If you won't resign we'll have to sack you.'

It was like a scene from the surreal psycho-paranoia television show *The Prisoner* in reverse. All that was lacking was the giant white ball, but perhaps that wasn't missing at all. In *The Prisoner*, the 'hero', Number Six, spends his time wanting to find out who Number One is. Inevitably, Number One is the monster from the id. In Docherty's case, the giant white ball was the id monster, the something inside him that caused him to self-destruct every step along the way.

Looking back from this point, it all seems a million miles from the Docherty that started out; the archetypal young bruiser from Glasgow's rough, tough Gorbals area, the young Doc was anything but a mercurial ego monster. Armed with a short-back-and-sides that stood out in an era of short-back-and-sides, Tommy Docherty was a top player. A wing-half in the Dave Mackay mould, he was hard but fair. As far away as possible from his later image as a rent-a-gob managerial dilletante, Docherty was described by his Preston team-mate Tom Finney as 'a tremendous player, even on the training pitch. It was like having a juggernaut behind you in the team. He was a relentless competitor and a man to have on your side.' An early newspaper profile was more succinct: 'He's a short, tough, fairly ugly man. Speech heavily Scottish. Philosophy quite straightforward – success.' Fairly ugly man? And the press now is supposed to be too personal?

After 323 appearances at Deepdale, he found himself in an impossible position. Like a lion that's taken an intellectual decision to become a vegetarian but cannot contain his God-given desire to kill a Thompson's Gazelle, Docherty subjected himself to a terrible internal struggle as he sought to control the implosion impulse that had just awakened. 'Fight with the management,' he heard his inner self say. 'Leave after a row.'

He loved Preston and Preston loved him, but in 1958 he found he couldn't resist his natural impulse any longer. A 'club or country' argument developed and that was that. Docherty sacked himself. It was, I suppose, useful experience. In a gesture of desperate self-flagellation, he moved to Highbury. 'That'll show you,' the white Doc said to the black Doc.

Legend has it that on his Arsenal debut, the Highbury faithful were so startled by his incessant on-field yabbering and jabbering that they heckled him, requesting that he be quiet. Further legend has it (can't guess the source of these legends) that after Our Hero had laid on the first goal and scored the second, he left the field to applause both from the fans and his team-mates. It's a nice story, despite the obvious factual flaw – Arsenal scoring more than once . . .

By 1961, enough was enough and Docherty moved on. He had had, it seems, a bit of a barney with the Arsenal management. No, really, he did. They wanted to sell him, he didn't want to be sold. 'If I can't play for Arsenal, I'll hang up my boots. It's as simple as that,' he said in his usual placatory way. It was a ridiculous waste. He was thirty-one and at the peak of his playing powers, and yet it was over. Still, it wasn't as if it was a career without achievement. He'd attained twenty-five caps and, while at Arsenal, had been given a two-week ban by the FA for using abusive language to a referee.

Anyway, he went across town to Chelsea, first as player/coach and then as manager. He was thirty-two when Ted Drake was sacked and he took over with no experience to call his own, armed with only a haircut and an attitude that would've had to breathe in to get into Siberia. Even so, it was a bit odd. 'One day I was "Tommy", the next day it was "The Boss".'

At his job interview, Docherty recalls, 'Joe Mears, the Chelsea chairman, said that he knew nothing about football. He then pointed towards the other directors and said, "And this lot know even less".' Despite losing Jimmy Greaves, the greatest English footballer never to appear in a World Cup final in 1966, Docherty's 'little diamonds' flourished. It's ironic that a few weeks after Greavesie went to AC Milan, the minimum wage was lifted in England. Chelsea could've – would've – kept him, for Sir James was a little too young and a lot too English to cope with the big, wide world. Imagine a Chelsea team with Greaves, the Osgood, Venables and Bobby Tambling.

Though Docherty's Chelsea coffin took an astonishing eight years to build, it was only sealed by three nails. It goes without saying that Docherty used his own hammer.

In 1965 there was the Blackpool nail. 'I sent seven players home who'd been out on the booze and breaking the curfew.' Chelsea were going great guns and already had the League Cup under their belts. Though the ever-improbable treble had been lost, there was still the League and pride to play for, and Chelsea were up in Blackpool relaxing before an important match against Burnley.

'We were up there and I said that on Saturday and Sunday they could do what they wanted as far as I was concerned, and I told them on Monday night that they were mine now, and that I wanted them in on Tuesday at 10.30. But they couldn't do it. They went out Monday night and then went out Tuesday night when I'd told them not to.

'It was reported to me by the hotel porter that they'd been out at 3 a.m. and I obviously denied it. I told him that it was the rugby team that was also staying in the hotel and I said I'd prove it to him. So we got the keys to two rooms and went in and the players were lying there in bed looking as if they were asleep. Something didn't seem quite right, so I pulled the covers and they were lying there in their suits and ties. I don't know to this day whether they were on their way out or if they had just got back.

'Maybe I was too much the sergeant-major. Maybe I was far too strict in hindsight. And it wasn't as if they were living like hermits, you know what I mean? And it was the fourth time that it had happened and it became a case of them or me. Am I wasting my time? You've got to have rules, not stupid rules, but you've got to have them.'

Of the seven players, it was Terry Venables who bore the brunt of the run-in. Like Chuck Connors he was branded, though unlike Connors it was for something he had done. Docherty had checked Venables' room on the fateful night and had found it empty. Venables said that he'd been in Eddie McCreadie's room, which was a schoolboy error. Just before checking Venables' room – empty – he'd checked McCreadie's room. Empty.

'I never had a battle with Terry Venables. Terry was the captain at the time, a good player, and he was a lad who you had to be firm with, but he gave me very, very little trouble. But he was very popular with the lads, and quite rightly so. They listened to him and I felt that, as captain of the club, he should have been more responsible. He should've said, "Look, we've had a few nights out, let's play the game." He just said that he wasn't out, but he *had* been out. All the rest had admitted that they'd been out.

'It just became a matter of principle, if you like. If I hadn't taken action with those players at the time, it was a question of them or me. They were questioning my authority as manager, but a lot of the papers at the time slaughtered me for sending them home, for being too strict. But now they're saying we could do with a few more managers like that. I mean, if I had Vinnie Jones and that [Dennis] Wise, they'd be on their bike. They'd be off. I wouldn't tolerate their behaviour.'

Tom, if you had Vinnie Jones or that Wise do you really think they'd do all that they've done?

'Aye. True enough.'

In his autobiography, Venables (naturally enough) denies his guilt, but does own up to another occasion when he was caught singing 'Winter Wonderland' in a hotel ballroom when he was supposed to be sleeping.

He does, however, relate two Docherty stories that might expain the root reason for the two men falling out. Curiously, neither involves Venables. 'Tommy was giving us all a lecture on the need to be serious when he dived on Marvin Hinton and gave him a huge love-bite on his neck. "Go home and tell your wife Tommy Docherty gave you that, and see if she believes you," he said.'

The other story concerns the press conference after the home leg of their Fairs Cup tie against Barcelona had been called off. That, in itself, is a story. Chelsea were on a downer. Several key players were injured and, against a team like Barcelona, that was serious grief. So The Doc had an idea. He called in the fire brigade and they flooded the pitch with water. The next morning, the referee had no option but to call off the game. Barcelona had no idea what had happened.

Anyway, at the press conference, Docherty gave what is possibly one of the greatest press-conference quotes ever. Asked how bad the rain had been, he looked around, saw his chairman and said, 'It was so bad this morning that Mrs Mears couldn't even shave.' Then he walked out of the room. It's possible that reading this, you're having the same reaction as the assorted press lizards did then.

Football is like the army. A boys' club. And like any boys' club, there are leaders and followers, and, to quote *The Lord of the Flies*, neither Venables nor Docherty was ever going to be a Piggy. It was a classic 'this town's not big enough for the both of us' situation. Both comedians, both leaders and both arrogant. The difference was that Docherty was the boss. He was the one picking the team.

His second nail came on a tour of Bermuda in the summer of 1967, just

One shouts, the other thinks. Brian Clough and Peter Taylor back in the halcyon days of 1978 with Forest. Curiously, the relationship didn't last.

The coat, the raised fist, the cool confidence. Sadly, this picture of Huggy Bear was taken during a Palace game against (no disrespect) Aldershot. Curiously, the relationship didn't last.

Genial Uncle Joe and Big Mal, proof that love and hate are but different horns on the same goat. As long as they were pointing in the same direction, things were okay. Curiously, the relationship didn't last.

Manager of Manchester United Tommy Docherty with his assistant Pat Crerand (1973). Curiously, the relationship didn't last.

What's it going to be? A Glasgow kiss or a hug for the 'little diamonds'? Happily after 1967's FA Cup semi-final win over Leeds, it was the latter. Curiously, the relationship didn't last.

Still crazy . . . Tommy Docherty, manager of Altrincham, 1987. Curiously, the relationship didn't last.

Sam Longson (third left) introduces Clough and Taylor to the eager young pups of Derby, 1968. Clough and Longson were like father and son. Curiously, the relationship didn't last.

Big Brian and Big Shanks lead their teams out for the 1974 Charity Shield match at Wembley. For both men, the relationship didn't last. Curiously.

The Rebbe acknowledges his people after the 1974 Charity Shield. You'd have thought nothing could have soured the relationship between Shankly and Liverpool FC. Curiously . . .

Bill Shankly and an adoring fan congratulate each other on their choice of shirts. The relationship between Shanks and the fans was one that did last.

Big Jack with the 1968–69 Leeds United team. The curious thing with this photo is that it appears that Don Revie is smiling. It is, of course, wind.

Wor Jackie with his faithful sidekick Maurice Setters at the 1988 European Championships.

Wor Jackie with Paul McGrath, the Douglas Bader of British football.

Big Ron: hair by Velcro, mouth by anyone else, really.

after they'd been beaten in the FA Cup final by the mighty Spurs. 'It was nothing. We went there on a friendly tour and we were playing a match and were winning 7–0. Anyway, there was only a couple of minutes to go and the referee sent off Tony Hateley and Barry Lloyd. For nothing. I got up and asked the referee what the story was. It was blown out of all proportion.'

You can just imagine that, can't you. 'Excuse me, Mr Referee . . .' In *Docherty,* Brian Clark alleges that the reason for the grief was that Docherty's enquiry included the words 'you', 'back', 'swinging' and 'trees'. The referee reported it to the FA and Docherty was banned for a month.

Forgetting the racism for one moment, it's possible to feel a bit of sympathy. 'When you go on tour to these places, you're the big boys. Everyone wants to beat you. They don't realise that you're just there for an easy time and a bit of a break.'

Nails One and Two are rendered an irrelevance by Nail Three. Even if the first two hadn't happened, this one would've been enough.

The next nail was 'Because the chairman died. Joe Mears. I wouldn't work with the new chairman. He was a twat.'

He was actually a prat. Charles Pratt. Forget that. That's a cheap gag.

'If Joe was alive today I'd still be there because we got on so well. He'd have been there forever and ever amen. They hire and fire managers, you know, when you come into the job they're struggling and you build them a nice team, and they think they don't need you, they think they can do the job without you. I mean, it's happened to every manager. They won't give you the money to buy a couple of players and they sack you. Then they bring in a new manager and they give him the money they wouldn't give you.

'Look at Arsenal with respect to what happened to George Graham. It was on the cards that they were going to sack him yet they gave him £6 million to spend on new players. Now, Stewart Houston, who took over might not have fancied those players . . .'

It's a familiar managerial moan. The chairman. It was his fault. Docherty fell off the Bridge because of Docherty. He created a brilliant young team, but he also lost one. The list of players that went, or at least were asked to go, is impressive: Jim McCalliog, Barry Bridges, Eddie McCreadie, Bert Murray, Joe Facione, Peter Houseman, Terry Venables. And then Docherty sacked Dick Voss, the youth team boss.

Docherty's attitude to his players was like this: when goalkeeper Peter Bonetti asked for more money, Docherty responded by buying Alex Stepney for £50,000, a world-record fee for a goalkeeper. Then he told Bonetti he couldn't leave. As he said, 'I'm not here to be liked. A kind person comes in last. But I think I'm a fair man.'

By way of a slight sidetrack, has it ever occurred to you why there's Big Mal, Big Ron, Big Jack and The Doc? It bothered me a bit. Okay, Jack Charlton looks down on him, but it's not like Docherty is that small. Dudley Moore, he ain't. And if any other dimension other than height were the determining factor, then surely he'd be 'Big', up there with the rest of them. We're not talking analysis here, it's just curious. Anyway, a few days ago I was talking to a friend and he referred to 'Brush', someone he knew as a boy. 'Why Brush?' I asked casually. 'Because his name was Basil, obviously.' Obviously. Tommy Docherty could never have been Big Tom. But he was.

## Chapter 6

## COURTING TROUBLE

*'Sir, Mr Tommy Docherty tells us that football is full of liars, but is he to be believed?'*

Letter to *The Guardian*, 1979

TOMMY, YOU WERE TALKING ABOUT GEORGE GRAHAM. WAS ALL that business in the game when you were in the game?

'What business?'

The bungs. You know, the money

'No, there wasn't the money in the game in those days.'

There was still money. It might have been less money, but –

'A bloody lot less.'

Yes, but –

'Anyway, all those deals were done abroad, all those backhanders.'

But –

'There's been no, er, no *sleaze* with British players.'

So you mean –

'Most of the chairmen and directors used to do the deals; they'd always be involved in the deal. There was only the very strong managers who wouldn't have them.'

Does that mean –

'You've got to remember that in our day, the players were on £100 a week. I mean, I left Manchester United in 1977 and the highest wage was £300 and the highest transfer that I paid then was £200,000 on Lou Macari.'

Yes, but it's still money.

'I never signed any overseas players. It's only since the overseas players came over here . . .'

So you're saying –

'Look. It all started when the Yugoslavs came in here.'

The Yugoslavs? Yes, the Yugoslavs. They come here, take our bungs . . . The Yugoslavs. After all we've done for them. Bloody Yugoslavs. Let's leave that one for a moment. Tell us about Willie Morgan. What was the story there?

'Willie Morgan was a good player. I gave him his first six or so caps for Scotland. He was a good player. What an athlete! Brilliant, quick, worked hard, good crosser, a good pro. What happened was that I heard in the summer that he'd been injured. He'd been playing tennis and the ball had been smashed and it hit him right in the eye, and he got a torn retina in his eye. Anyway, he went into hospital and had an operation on his eye. And we bought Steve Coppell in the summer from Tranmere for £40,000. Willie never recovered. He was always good – his control never needed a second touch – but the doctor warned him that he might see things a little bit later. Anything on that side, where his damaged eye was, you don't adjust to it until your other eye catches it.

'Anyway, his form was all right but he was mistiming the ball, so I brought him in, had a chat with him and said, "I'm bringing in Coppell, give you a bit of a rest to recover your form." I didn't mention his eye, but he knew what I was talking about. So he wasn't happy playing in the reserves, which was understandable when you've been in the first team all your life. So he comes to see me and says, "I want a transfer." So I said, "Put it in writing." So he said, "I'm not putting it in writing," because in those days you lost 5 per cent of your transfer fee if you put it in writing.

'Now, he played golf. He always played golf with Sir Matt Busby – over the years they were great golfing pals – so I took it to the board and Sir Matt said, "You're right, Tommy. He's lost form." But I said, "I'd like to keep him, he's a great pro, a good lad, but maybe we should let him go." And he said, "Yes, you're right. The way young Coppell's come in." And we let him go very cheaply so that he could pick a few bob up for himself. We let him go for £30,000 to Burnley.

'He went to Burnley and it didn't work out. Burnley had the same problem with his eye, and they sold him to Bolton on a free. And it didn't happen for him there, and he appeared on the *Kick Off* programme on Granada on the Friday night (June 1977) after he left Bolton and he said, "Tommy Docherty's the worst manager I've ever had in my life." My solicitor said that was diabolical and I should sue. I wrote to Granada and asked for an apology. Granada wouldn't give me an apology. They said it was just Willie's opinion. So my solicitor said I should sue for defamation of character. They said, "You're not the best, but you're not the worst." So we sued them. I wouldn't have gone to court, but I was involved with Mary at the time and they dig up a lot of shit.'

But wasn't there a business with perjury and Denis Law and a whole lot of other stuff?

'Aah, one thing led to another. Footballers, they're like children. It was nothing to do with football. Sometimes with players, especially players who've been successful, they can't handle getting old. They go like children and scream and shout and cry. It cost me about £100,000 in costs, but they found me not guilty.'

The day that Docherty agreed to listen to the advice of his lawyer and sue for libel cost him a lot more than £100,000. Docherty claimed that Morgan's accusation had damaged his reputation as a football manager, but, at the end of the day, Docherty's legal action did far more damage. Never mind that the Mary Brown business had fatally deflated his love for soccer (or rather, for soccer people), this made people see him not so much as a manager, but more as a walking headline. While the gag about having more clubs than Jack Nicklaus didn't exactly lose its punchline, Doc's other staple – 'I've been in more courts than Perry Mason' – started to take precedence. And not without substance.

Mr Peter Bowsher QC, Docherty's brief, said that Morgan's claim had damaged Docherty's reputation as a 'skilled and fair-dealing manager'. Well, it would, wouldn't it. 'He's the worst manager I've ever had in my life.' Really, you're not going to put it on your CV, are you?

Bowsher said that Docherty was 'a controversial figure, but he is not averse to strong criticism as long as it is fair'. He said that when Docherty joined them, United had 'a lot of problems with ageing football stars'. He said that 'Mr Morgan was a brilliant star at his peak'.

Pause there for a moment and consider the 'brilliant star at his peak'. Lawyers. Love them.

Anyway, onwards. The QC said that Morgan had left United with 'a deep-seated grudge against the plaintiff. Within two months he had given an interview to a Sunday newspaper attacking Mr Docherty. His malice towards the plaintiff simply festered.'

The case developed into a whole catalogue of charges and counter-charges. There were so many allegations and denials going on that it was hard to keep up. More pointedly, there were so many allegations that it might have seemed natural for the regular punter to think, 'Oooh, I don't know. He seems a bit of a dodgy character, that Docherty.'

And every report on the latest alleged indiscretion came complete with the by now regulation punchline: Mary Brown. With the love angle complete, not only was Joe Punter hooked by the never-ending saga of The Doc, but so was his wife. Dodgy character, that Docherty. Run off with your money and your wife. Even *The Daily Telegraph* report of the day's events ended with the legend: 'The dismissal was in July 1977 when Docherty left his wife to live with Mrs Mary Brown, wife of the club's physiotherapist.' It's good that they mentioned that, really. We could've forgotten.

Back in court, Mr Bowsher referred to the 'dirty ditty' (you'll like this one) and said that Docherty denied singing it. He also denied the allegation that Docherty sold two £10 FA Cup-final tickets for £100. He said that Docherty also denied selling two hundred Cup-final tickets for £7,000 to a well-known tout, a contact of Lou Macari. He also denied that in 1974 Docherty accepted £1,000 from non-League Dunstable Town to induce George Best, then in dispute with the club, to play for them. Docherty denied that he was dismissed from his job at United for bringing the club into disrepute. Docherty also denied that he was involved in plans to scupper the Middle East peace talks.

The 'dirty ditty'? No, this is good. On 14 November 1978, *The Daily Mail* ran a story headlined TOMMY DOCHERTY SAYS: I DID NOT SING A DIRTY DITTY IN FRONT OF NUNS. In front of nuns! It just keeps getting better. The first paragraph of the story read:

'Derby's controversial soccer manager, Tommy Docherty, yesterday denied singing a dirty ditty at a Catholic sportsmen's dinner attended by nuns, priests and a bishop.' And a bishop! 'The denial came on the first day of fifty-year-old Docherty's libel action against former Scotland winger Willie Morgan and Granada TV over remarks Morgan made on the programme *Kick Off*.'

According to Morgan, the ditty went like this:

*Willie, Willie Morgan,*
*Willie Morgan on the wing*
*He's a* ****
*I'm going to sort him out*
*And he'll be on his way out*
*Before the end of the season.*

I wonder what that **** could be? What could scan? What could rhyme with 'out'? Lout? Pout? My personal favourite is trout. *Willie Morgan, he's a trout.*

But back to the allegations. The Dunstable/Best thing was dismissed fairly quickly. It seems that Docherty and Sir Matt Busby had agreed that anyone who wanted to hire out Best could do so for £1,000. This money would be split between the club and the player. Docherty told the court on the first day of the trial that he had gone to a police station with regard to this business, but he had gone voluntarily and the police had, in fact, paid him a visit a couple of months later, telling him to forget it.

The case had been bolstered by newspaper spills by Pat Crerand saying that he had witnessed Docherty receiving the dodgy money. Now, it could be argued by someone with either more legal qualifications or more money than me, that Crerand's opinion was coloured by the fact that Docherty had sacked him as United's assistant manager. It could be argued that Crerand was miffed that Docherty had described him as a 'disaster'. Docherty, in Crerand's version, was in the bath when he received the money, 'wearing nothing but a smile'. 'Naked' is such a great word to get in newspaper stories, don't you think?

The unfair dismissal claim was in reference to a libel action that Docherty had initiated against Louis Edwards the previous year, after a newspaper report stated that Edwards had said in connection with Docherty's successor, Dave Sexton, that 'We wanted a gentleman as well as a good football manager.'

Everything was going well when, on the third day of the action, Docherty dropped the case and was left with a costs bill of over £30,000. Why? Did he finally admit to himself that he was the worst manager that Willie Morgan had ever played under? Did he admit that he accepted the odd grand here or there? Did he finally own up to embarrassing some nuns, a few priests and a bishop? No. Docherty dropped the case because of Denis Law. It's one of the wonderful ironies of this business that it stopped when Law became involved.

In evidence given the previous day, it was alleged that Docherty, not long after his arrival at Old Trafford, had told Law that after ten years with the club he could have a free transfer. He said that being given a free transfer was akin to getting a golden handshake. He told the court that at one stage Law did not seem surprised or perturbed by the news. Later, when giving evidence, he said that Law had been 'disappointed and probably understandably so.' So he then told him that he wouldn't be putting him on the list.

The evidence said that the next day, Law was in Scotland and was watching the television. On it, he heard Docherty say that he had given him a free transfer.

On the third day, the defence lawyer, Mr Wilmers, said that 'No decent or competent manager would dream of treating a man like Law that way'. Docherty agreed, and agreed that this was 'a wrong thing to do'.

Docherty admitted that he denied this in court on day two. He had said then that he did not treat Law shabbily. Sensing blood, the brief went for the kill: 'Mr Docherty. Would you agree that a football manager must first of all have complete and utter probity?'

At this juncture, your heart's got to sink.

'It would be very nice to have such a complete . . .'

'That is not what I asked,' barked Wilmers. 'Answer the question, please, Mr Docherty.'

Have you ever seen a cat play with a spider? Johnny spider is a tricky enough geezer, but the cat just plays and teases, plays and teases, until it is good and ready to do what it was always going to do. I don't know if spiders sweat, but it's fair to say that Tommy Docherty does.

Again he tried bluffing an answer and again Wilmers slapped him down. Chop off one of his legs.

Finally, Docherty said, 'I'm not trying to be disrespectful, sir . . . not being clever, sir . . . but what does "probity" actually mean?'

The cat did not say anything like 'Well, Tom. Probity means XYZ.' No. The cat said, 'What exactly do you think the word "probity" means, Mr Docherty?'

It's reminiscent of the *Oz* trial of a few years earlier when the defence brief was trying to corner Felix Dennis, one of the defendants. He kept throwing these 'What exactly do you think the word "probity" means, Mr Docherty?' type questions at Dennis, and Dennis kept throwing them back. Finally, he went through his hypothesis and said, 'And that, Mr Dennis, is just about the size of it, isn't it?' Felix Dennis smiled and said, 'The size of what?' Exasperated, the defence brief gave up.

Docherty didn't have the confidence or the chutzpah to say that. Instead he said, 'Yes, it turned out that way.'

Mr Wilmers then said, 'You are simply not to be trusted when you say something – whether in the papers or under oath.' Docherty replied that he 'would disagree with that', but the damage had been done. You don't admit to telling a jury a pack of lies and continue with a libel case.

The court was adjourned and the hyenas came out for their lunch. Crerand said, 'I am disappointed that I was not called to give evidence because I could have said a lot more than I can now.' Law said, 'I was intending to make a full disclosure of the facts that I had kept to myself for the last five and a half years.'

From beginning to end, the whole thing was ridiculous. A folly that went horribly, horribly wrong. Docherty was the boss of the biggest club in the land. Okay, so he was considered in some quarters to be a maverick, a bit of a loose cannon. But he was respected and admired and well regarded. Under Docherty, United had reached two FA Cup finals (of which they'd won one), they'd finished third in the League, and their style of play was admired by all. Now at Derby County, Docherty was erasing the bad memories of how he left United and was building a top side again.

Willie Morgan was past his sell-by. He had nothing to lose. Docherty had everything to lose. More, even if the court had found in his favour, what could Docherty have hoped to gain? *Kick Off* was a small local programme and Morgan's comments carried no credence. What could The Doc have gained? A few bob from Morgan? This is nonsense. Docherty was on £25,000 at Derby. He was one of the highest-paid managers in the game. Ego is a terrible thing, and if anyone ever offers you one, politely decline.

The papers couldn't lose either. It was a familiar tabloid scenescape. They had their cake, they ate it and, when it was all finished, lo and behold, they found they had their cake still. A few exclusives beforehand, mass coverage of the trial, a few exclusives afterwards. And it was Docherty; he was always good value. Even as he was contemplating jail, he said: 'Well, I can always take charge of the prison team. After a few bad results, they'll probably send me on my way.'

By accepting his lawyer's advice and taking out the libel action, Docherty had voluntarily jumped into a pool of piranhas without even the comfort of water-wings. He was Gorbals-tough and media-smart. He could have probably out-manoeuvered John Wilmers on any other surface, but here in court? Here in court it was never a contest. From the minute Docherty entered the court, nervous and uncharacteristically submissive, it was never a contest.

On 4 October 1979, Perry Mason had another case. Docherty was asked to help the police with their enquiries concerning allegations regarding backhanders – bungs to you and me – paid out over the transfer of three Derby County players. Nine hours' worth of enquiries. Dramatically, the police played along with the tabloid feeding-frenzy. They said that they had secretly released Docherty out of the police station through a back door where he was believed to be hidden beneath a rug on the floor of a red car which sped away from the station. You can imagine the meal the papers made of that – and that the car was driven by Mary Brown. Football manager, police station, bungs, red car, lover who . . . It's a great story.

At the end of one tabloid report was tacked on the following: 'Mary Brown, the former wife of Manchester United's physiotherapist, who left her husband to live with Docherty, is expecting a baby. It is already overdue.' All that's missing is the vicar. No, sorry, the vicar wasn't missing. He was there, naked in the bath, trying to figure out where the trout came into it.

The Derby story concerned the transfers of Colin Todd, David Nish and Gerry Daly. There was also concern shown that Admiral, the Midlands-based sportswear firm, did not get the contract to do Derby's shirts. How, it was wondered, did the contract go to a French company? The implication was clear.

Docherty was cleared, but there was that distant whisper again: 'Oooh, I don't know. He seems a bit of a dodgy character, that Docherty.'

In July 1980, Docherty – now the manager of Queens Park Rangers – was charged by the Director of Public Prosecutions and had to stand trial for perjury. It might seem an irrelevance, but there's a bit of football talk that we can mention here. Don't worry – it ends with a legal action.

Just before this happened, Docherty was sacked from Queens Park Rangers. And just after he was sacked, he was reinstated. There was, as ever, a story.

Docherty was taking the train back from London to his home in Manchester when a gang of 'youths' started abusing him and Mary. He asked them if they would be so kind as to stop. They did. Then, as the train pulled into Stockport, just on the outskirts of Manchester, the youths attacked him, kicking him around the head and chest. The resulting injuries meant that he was out of the game for six weeks, and during these six weeks QPR dropped out of the promotion race. He also found himself heading back to court after charging his attackers with assault.

When he returned, the QPR chairman, Jim Gregory – himself a man not averse to the odd flash of a pressman's camera – said that he was terribly sorry, but it was the parting of the ways for them.

Docherty responded with a line that's since become a staple gag: 'Don't go. You're doing a good job.'

Following a protest by the players, he was reinstated. It was all football bullshit. The following year, 1980, he was sacked again, this time for good, after gabbing to the press when Manchester United wouldn't let him buy Andy Ritchie. 'This has nothing to do with results,' said Gregory. 'This has to do with the dignity of the club.' Anyway, enough football. The perjury business.

The perjury case went to court on 13 October 1981. Docherty – now manager of Preston North End – said that he'd been 'bullied' in court. The papers noted with interest that the controversial Doc was the partner of Mrs Mary Brown, the wife of Manchester United physiotherapist Laurie Brown. It's more interesting to wonder how many of Docherty's former players had sympathy with him at this point. Him pleading that he'd been bullied.

Denis Law gave evidence, saying that the news (of his free transfer) had come at a particularly bad time for him – his wife had been pregnant and he'd been in the middle of moving house. But it wasn't Docherty's qualities as a *mensch* that was under scrutiny here. If it had been, the outcome might have been different. Did he deliberately lie under oath? No, of course not.

The case lasted barely a week before being thrown out.

At the end of the day, after all the years of legal nonsenses and courtroom appearances, Docherty was found guilty of precisely nothing. Well, nothing bar being a bit stupid (in taking the Morgan case on) and a bit untrustworthy (he really didn't treat Denis Law very nicely at all). But actual guilt? No. No actual guilt. Still, the bill for all this was in excess of one Tony Hateley – just over £100,000.

*'If ever the game doesn't have room for him as a manager, I reckon he could make a living as a stand-up comedian.'*

Frank Taylor, journalist, 1978

*Chapter 7*

# RIDING ON THE CREST OF A SLUMP

*'Sometimes I feel that the media created Tommy Docherty. Had we left him alone, he might well have remained an adequate coach of impressionable youngsters. But we didn't. We nourished his ego, propagated his elderly jokes, publicised his dubious judgements and he became a "character".'*

Patrick Collins, journalist, *The Standard*

LET'S GET IT OUT OF THE WAY NOW. TOMMY DOCHERTY, HE had more clubs than Jack Nicklaus. There. That's what Tommy Docherty is. A geezer who got chucked out of a load of clubs, but lived to tell a gag about it.

After the Mary episode – you remember Mary, she was the wife of Manchester United physiotherapist Laurie Brown – Docherty went down. It was as if his interest had gone. Maybe he felt he'd achieved everything that he needed to achieve. Maybe (and no disrespect to his family) Mary filled a hole where football had been. Maybe the hunger just wasn't there any more. After all, the single-end Gorbals boy was a rich man now, minting it from after-dinner speeches, newspaper columns and media outings. Or maybe it was a simple combination of all these things.

'I don't regret the past. In the same circumstances with the same lady and with the same depth of love, I'd do it all again.'

Derby County were Docherty's last real shot at the big time. They'd been casting covetous eyes at Docherty long before he'd done the same to Mary Brown but, by the time he got there, Derby was a club in disarray. Still smarting from the legacy of Brian Clough, the club was skint and run by a gang of directors who wanted a Clough-like character minus the Clough and most of the character. They'd had Clough, they'd had Dave Mackay and now they had Colin Murphy. Murphy was a nice bloke, but he wasn't a Clough. The Derby board wanted someone strong and charismatic who they could control. They got Docherty. It was a marriage made in hell.

When he got there, he found a club in need. It's that familiar old scene that greets every new manager. Docherty looked around and said, 'There are Derby players who've been putting on weight during the matches. Thank God there haven't been any traffic wardens around or else they'd have been booked.' Again, there was the familiar flurry of buying and selling. It got so bad – or good – that it inspired another quip: 'I looked around before one of our matches and said "Good luck – whoever you are".'

Derby was a lost cause. Even aside from the courtroom shenanigans, Derby was a lost cause. The problems were typified by a ridiculous episode concerning the sale of Charlie George to Nottingham Forest. While the Derby board gave little import to the fact that Docherty didn't want or need George – he was transfer-listed – what did bother them was where he was headed to. Or rather, who he was headed to.

If Forest were riding on the crest of a wave, buying shelf space and silver polish like no one else, Derby were, to use yet another of Docherty's famed quips, 'riding on the crest of a slump'. The thought of selling someone to Forest, of helping Clough, was too much. With George in his side, who knows what he was going to win. No. It couldn't be done. The move was blocked.

As every schoolboy knows, a blockage here often releases pressure there – cause and effect – and so it was at Derby. On his way back from the George meeting, Docherty checked in his bag and saw that he was missing a sand wedge. Soon, he thought to himself, I'll need a caddie.

From here on in, Docherty was marking time, waiting to fulfil Frank Taylor's prediction about becoming a comedian. There was the Queens Park Rangers débâcle, a spell in Australia with Sydney Olympic – about which another manager cracked 'he's gone about two hundred years too late' – a few months at Preston North End, Wolves, and finally Altrincham.

Preston sacked him on 4 December 1981 after they found out he wanted to buy Big Jim Holton from Sheffield Wednesday. After going back to Australia, he returned to England and Wolves. That was in February 1985. By the time July came, he'd achieved little bar revamping an old gag he'd first used at Rotherham: 'I promised to take Wolves out of the Second Division and I did. I took them into the Third.'

Perhaps it's unfair to say that he achieved little at Wolves. He did come up with another two cracking gags and, to be fair, it's not bad in five months given the stress of having to pick the odd team now and then: 'With the luck that Wolves have had this season, if we were shipwrecked we'd get picked up by the *Titanic*.' No? Try this one: 'I took over at Wolves because I wasn't feeling too well and my doctor told me to keep as far away from football as possible. When I opened Wolves' trophy cabinet, two Japanese prisoners-of-war fell out.'

And that was that. Docherty going to Altrincham was like a bloke in his late-thirties buying a Triumph Spitfire. As you get older, these things look as if they'd be fun, but they're not. They're cold, they break down. 'The chairman said I'd have to go because we had a personality clash. I said to him, "You're joking. You haven't got any personality."' You've been a wonderful audience. Thank you and goodnight.

In some ways it seems a shame that the man who turned Drake's Ducklings into his Little Diamonds, the man who took Scotland to the edge of the promised land, the man who created the best Manchester United team since the European Cup should be reduced to a crack. A gag. But the thing is, the thing that keeps Docherty warm at night, is that it's *his* gag. Well, some of them are.

*On himself:* 'I may not be a good manager, but I'm great at interviews.'
'I was God's gift to the press, wasn't I? I used to start sounding off and they'd say, "Hold on, Tom. We can't get it all down." So I'd say the same outrageous things, only slower.' (1974)

'I've had a funny old career. I've said a lot of stupid things. I've made some bad decisions and I've been kicked in the arse more than enough times.' (1974)

'I'm not the best manager there is, yet. Possibly I'm too impulsive. Possibly I could be more understanding. Those things I'm going to try and change.' (1966)

*On Graeme Souness:* 'They serve a drink in Glasgow called a Souness. One half and you're off.'

*On the Aston Villa chairman:* 'Doug Ellis said to me, "I'm right behind you, Tom." I said I didn't want him behind me. I wanted him in front of me where I could see what he was doing.'

*On the directors:* 'I'm drinking from a cup today. I'd like a mug, but they're all in the boardroom.'

*On Malcolm Allison's Manchester City:* 'There are three types of Oxo cubes. Light-brown for chicken stock, dark-brown for beef stock and light-blue for laughing stock.'

*On Elton John:* 'Elton John has decided to rename Watford. He's going to call it Queen of the South. I hear he's just made a bid for an Italian football club. AC/DC Milan.'

*Banter with a rival manager:*
MANAGER: 'That boy doesn't know the meaning of the word defeat.'

DOCHERTY: 'He doesn't know the meaning of the words pass, tackle or shoot either.'
MANAGER: 'Half a million wouldn't buy him.'
DOCHERTY: 'And I'm one of them.'

*On Big Ron Atkinson (1):* 'Big Ron can't be here tonight because he's had a bit of an accident. He walked in front of an industrial magnet. He's due out of hospital in a couple of weeks.'

*On Big Ron Atkinson (2):* 'Remi Moses? Atkinson paid £500,000 for Remi Moses? You could buy the original Moses for half a million.'

*On Big Ron Atkinson (3):* 'Ron Atkinson sends his apologies for not being here, but he's had a bit of bad news. His hairdresser died . . . in 1948.'

*On neck-ache:* 'I can't watch Wimbledon, Watford or Sheffield Wednesday. Football wasn't meant to be run by two linesmen and air-traffic control.'

*On his television acting debut (1989):* 'When the television people asked me if I'd like to play a football manager in a play, I asked how long it would take. They said, "About ten days." "Good," I said, "that's about par for the course."'

*On a referee:* 'Thank God the referee and his linesmen were all out there together today, otherwise they could have spoiled three matches instead of one.'

*On Rotherham:* 'On the Sunday before Rotherham played Leicester in the FA Cup fifth round, I had the players down at the ground. I lined them up on the pitch and began introducing them to an old man in a bowler hat. The chairman came down and asked me what I was doing. I told him that I was getting the lads used to Wembley so that when they met the King they wouldn't be nervous. He pointed out that the Queen would be at Wembley. I said I know, but by the time we got there it would be the King again.'

*On George Best:* 'When anyone says that George Best was the greatest, I don't argue. The boy could play. But if I found another George Best on my staff I would – personally – help him pack his boots and show him the door.'

*On tactics (1976):* 'We don't discuss the opposition. I don't go and watch them and the players don't worry about them. Dossiers lead to confusion. By the time young players wade through pages of facts and figures, they go out onto the field baffled.'

*On managers (1979):* 'All managers are cheats, conmen and liars. In our world morals are different than in any other walk of life. The only way to keep going is by being a conman – it's the law of the land. We are hypocrites. We all go along to these meetings and agree to do things – and then don't do them. Clough and Taylor go their own way and I respect them for that. Sure, managers are honest some of the time, but then we turn them into plastic people. We have to. But I wouldn't want to do any other job and I don't mind taking kicks in the teeth.'

*On friendship (1983):* 'In some quarters I'm about as welcome as a whiff of bad breath. The way some people see it, a friend in need is a bloody pest .'

*Looking back (1984):* 'Whatever charisma I have will always overshadow what I might have achieved in the game. But people who think that I'm not serious enough don't really know me. If I didn't have a sense of humour I'd be dead by now. Of course I have been hurt. You laugh and joke and the pain goes away for an hour or so. But it comes back the next morning.'

*On football:* 'Football is a beautiful and an incurable disease. And it kills you in the end. But what a way to go.'

*On an old adversary:* 'Derek Dougan is to football what King Herod was to baby-sitting.'

*On regrets (1987):* 'I have no regrets. My life has been a mystery tour. Perhaps I should have been a travel agent. I've had low points, but just when you think you've had a raw deal you read of a kid dying of cancer and you realise that if you have your strength and health then you are a millionaire. So I am.'

*On players (general):* 'A lot of players are lacking in basic intelligence. There are a lot of players who think that manual labour is the Spanish president.'

*On Ray Wilkins:* 'He can't run, can't tackle and can't head a ball. The only time he goes forward is to toss the coin.'

*On the first sin he ever confessed in church:* 'I missed a penalty on Saturday, Father.'

*On being sacked by Preston:* 'They offered me a handshake of £10,000 to settle amicably. I said they'd have to be more amicable than that.'

*On a fellow manager:* 'Not so much a coach as a hearse.'

*On Ken Bates, Chelsea chairman:* 'He's looking well again after his charisma by-pass operation.'

*On agents:* 'They'd take 10 per cent of your ashes if they could.'

*On where he was born:* 'To those who have never lived in a single-end Gorbals tenement, all I can say is that Heaven has been kind to them.'

*On going to Australia:* 'English football is a rat race and the rats are winning.'

*On directors:* 'For a manager the ideal board should be made up of three men. Two dead and one dying.'

*On the press:* 'There's a place in the game for you people . . . but it hasn't been dug yet.'

Thinking about it, it does seem curious that Docherty didn't opt for a career on the stage.

## Chapter 8

# A RING OF AUTHENTICITY

*'All this talk about him not being fit to be a football manager. That's exactly what he's fit for.'*

Clive James on Tommy Docherty

AS THE 1970S TURNED INTO THE 1980S AND THATCHER TURNED Britain into a nation where solid earthy values had as much substance as the phosphorous shimmering on the surface of the sea, Ron Atkinson pupated and emerged as Big Ron.

Superbly constructed for the part, Big Ron was like Barbie's Ken – all man. Whatever criticisms can be levelled at him (Ron, not Ken), there's no doubt that he did what he did effectively. Part Tommy Docherty, part Malcolm Allison, he had the quips *and* the look. If the Natural History Museum ever decided to include a new exhibit, 'Homo Football Managerus', Big Ron'd be their man. Big Ron was the *Blue Peter* of football bosses. Today we're talking about football managers; here's one we made earlier.

It was like one of those window test advertisements that they loved back in the 1970s. The camera pans to a lab. A balding man with a large forehead in a white coat holding a bunsen burner turns round and he's talking in a sombre tone: '. . . The new, improved Big Ron comes in a kit form, which means that you can take him apart and put him back together, just as you please. Individual sections of the Big Ron can be cleaned and tanned as required. Scientists have proved that, after repeated contracts, the new, improved Big Ron will keep on going long after other Big managers have run out of gas. So go on, give your manager that ring of authenticity. Get Big Ron – Now!'

Ron also had an essential ingredient which Docherty (his predecessor at United) and Allison (his stylistic mentor) lacked: he was non-threatening. When The Doc flouted the moral code at Old Trafford, he was sent packing. When Big Ron did it, he survived. There were major differences in the two cases – Docherty's offence was seven years prior to Ron's and he involved someone else at the club – but the bottom line is still the bottom line: Ron survived. Maybe it's back to that Carolyn Cassady quote. Docherty didn't do anything wrong – who are we to encourage people to perpetuate their own unhappiness by staying in miserable relationships? – he just did it first. Atkinson didn't do anything wrong either, but he had the sense/luck to do it second.

From the Gucci shoes to the clothes – 'Double-breasted Scandinavian suits are the sort I go for' – to the Havana, Big Ron had the game down perfectly. He even had a nickname, BoJangles, because of his jewellery. As for the quips, here's his favourite (we know it's his favourite because he carries it around and shows it to people like a picture of his grandchild): 'I make it a rule never to comment on referees. And I'm not going to break my rule for that tosser.' Here's another: He's at United and at the post-match press conference when Ron Saunders, the Aston Villa manager, walks in. 'Giving the boys the usual load of rubbish, Ron?' Big Ron, quick as a flash, retorts, 'Yes Ron. I was just telling them what a good manager you are.'

If Mal was born Big, Ron was Big by design. His own. Maybe it was his background as a sales rep for a builders' merchant that did it. He understood that, in the age of the media manager, it was necessary to sell yourself. It's a curious thing that Mal's natural Biggism ultimately worked against him, while Ron's worked for him. Perhaps it's just a question of control. Ron could turn it on and switch it off. As a Mancunian journalist said at the time of his arrival at Old Trafford, 'He was a bit posey. He'd light a big cigar, puff out the smoke and then put it down somewhere and forget it.' By the time he was packing his bags, Ron was quite happy to junk the BoJangles image as wholeheartedly as he'd once embraced it. 'That's all crap,' he said referring to the Champagne Charlie bit. 'I've never owned a Rolex watch or smoked more than seven cigars in my life.' He counted, then.

'After a match, he'd give the press champagne. He'd pour champagne into people's glasses and happily chat away with them,' said Bryan Robson, his faithful adjutant at West Brom and Manchester United. 'Everyone drank his champagne and he'd drink orange juice and pretend it was Buck's Fizz.' Are we missing something, or is that the saddest thing? If it's true that 'I've never consciously built up any kind of image' as he's said, then it goes some way to answering the age-old question of what the other 90 per cent of our brain, our subconscious, does.

'My favourite drink is tea, and there's more chance of me being regarded as a tea-aholic than an alcoholic.' A comment like that takes you back to Boy George saying that he prefers tea to sex and then being photographed in every nightclub in town. Still, it's a useful ruse to get the conversation going.

Atkinson the image was the perfect Essex Man. Working-class boy made good: he had cash – loadsamoney – and flaunted it as the measure of his success. He was the lottery winner who buys a flash suit and a flash car and a blonde. He bought it and we bought him. He's been successful partly because he, more than any other Big manager, has understood the meaning of image and the power that it has. In fairness, it should be pointed out that maybe he's been successful because he's been successful. As he's fond of pointing out, he was the most successful manager of Manchester United since Sir Matt Busby. 'I never finished lower than fourth, won two FA Cups and nearly won the title, but I was still judged a failure.' *Nearly.* It's nearly such a good word. 'I don't know whether or not people there were waiting for me to fall flat on my face because they resented my so-called lifestyle. And, frankly, I don't care whether people think I am flash or not.'

Both measures of success were enough to impress a man called Jesus, impress him enough to soon offer Ron a two-year contract worth half a million pounds. An offer he couldn't refuse. First, though, Ron had to flirt around a bit.

After he'd been sent packing by United for nearly being their most successful manager since the last nearly successful one, Atkinson did what jilted lovers have been doing since before the dawn of history. He went back to his first love, the faithful maid who'd never stopped loving him, even after he had run off with Martin Edwards. Ron had been back at West Bromwich just over a year when he heard the call of Jesus and, once again, gave the Hawthorns faithful the old line: 'I'm just popping out for some Factor 5. I might be some time.'

It was particularly hard on West Brom. Ron had been out of the game for eleven months when they came calling and, though he was making a decent living as a football pundit, there's only so many times Brian Moore can call you 'Football manager, Ron Atkinson' when really it should be 'Unemployed football manager, Ron Atkinson' before it gets embarrassing. He was grateful for that first game against Shrewsbury. Grateful enough to return with a quip: 'Well, I've had to swap my Merc for a BMW, I'm down to my last thirty-seven suits and I'm drinking non-vintage champagne.' Very, very stylish. A BMW? It reminds you of Docherty's quote about him nicking the wrong bits of Allison. Can you imagine Big Mal in a Beamer, that status symbol for the upwardly mobile first-time house-buying post-yuppie yuppie? Shame the Albion weren't still offering that Jaguar 3.4.

In football, as in most other spheres, sentiment comes before a fall and half a million pounds was an awful lot of fall. 'In an ideal world, I would have stayed at The Hawthorns another couple of years and helped them into Division One on a sound footing. In reality, though, these lucrative offers do not come up when you want them. They come up when they come up. I have been very, very happy here but anyone who knows me well will tell you that it has always been one of my ambitions to manage a continental club.' And anyone who knows me well will tell you that it has always been one of my ambitions to earn half a million pounds in two years.

As he was waiting in the departure lounge, drinking his freshly squeezed Buck's Fizz (you never know who might be watching) and pondering the recent revolution in wallet design, Ron wondered about this Jesus geezer. Curious name, even for a continental. Little did Ron know that Jesus was so-called because his mother had a habit of exclaiming, 'Jeezus! Did you really do that?'

Jesus was, in fact, Jesus Gil, president of Atletico Madrid, a man for whom the phrase 'megalomaniac nightmare' was invented. 'Raging Bull', as he was known, had been at Madrid sixteen months – three managers ago – when Ron arrived, and nineteen months when he went.

Just as a hungry journalist with a column to fill is meat and drink for the character manager, so in turn the character manager is a tasty morsel for the character director. In the food chain, everyone eats but no one eats the director. 'Sacking a manager is as big an event in my life as drinking a glass of beer. I'd hire twenty managers a year if I wanted to. A hundred if necessary,' he said after dismissing Ron after ninety-six days.

In those ninety-six days, Big Ron had taken Atletico from eighteenth in the league to third. Second would have been better. Still, when you win your first game 6–1, there's only one way you can go. The irony was that it was the very reason that Big Ron was hired that got him the sack. His Bigness. Jeez reckoned that Ron was enjoying the good life a little too much. He thought that it was getting in the way of the football.

'I have never been so flaming mad. Villa on the beach, my foot. They put us in the poxiest hotel imaginable. I had the smallest car of my life in Madrid. A Peugeot. A small Peugeot. And my apartment was nothing elaborate. I've never had a happier period, but the president was barmy. When I was sacked, the most respected radio commentator in Spain called it the greatest injustice in the history of Spanish football.'

Well, lucky old Spanish football if that was the greatest injustice it's ever had to face. And, shortly after, Ron did indeed find himself a happier period: the day the pay-off cheque came in.

Over the centuries whole civilisations have found that you don't mess with Jesus. What chance did Ron stand? If it was any consolation, things didn't improve down Madrid way. 'I see Atletico just sacked another manager before the season has even started. He must have had a bad photo-call,' Ron observed in 1990.

'I'm concerned about ambition and for any ambitious manager the place to be is Division One. I look upon it as a challenge for which I am fully equipped to accept.'

Ron Atkinson first unleashed Big Ron on his suspecting public in 1978 when, after taking them out of Division Four as champions, he left Cambridge United to manage West Bromwich Albion. It was there he made his reputation and set the standard that was to hold him in good stead for the rest of his career. With a team that included the late (great) Laurie Cunningham, Cyrille Regis, Tony Brown, John Wile, Derek Statham and Alastair Robertson, West Brom set the game alight by playing fast, joyous football that sparkled as much as their manager's fingers. In his first year in charge there, the statistical record spoke for itself: played 53, won 30, drew 16, lost 7. Goals for 96, goals against 45. There was an FA Cup semi-final, too, where WBA were beaten by the eventual winners, Ipswich.

The statistics might have had their own eloquence, but the manager wasn't taking any chances. Headlines like 'TORA! TORA! TORA! –THAT'S OUR NEW CLUB MOTTO!' flowed quicker than the soccer. The back pages loved him. So did the critics. 'Atkinson is one of those football managers who impresses, initially, through presence as much as presence of mind,' said David Lacey in *The Guardian*.

Ron tasted life in the Big league and liked it. And why not? After a career scrabbling around in the lower reaches of football, to be a headline-maker must have been sweetness itself. As a midfielder who looked as if he belonged on a rugby pitch, Ron had spent most of his playing career with Oxford United and had been the cornerstone of their dramatic rise out of the Southern League and into the real world. 'The Tank', he was called. Maybe if his playing career had been a little more sparkling, he wouldn't have felt the need to compensate later when he was successful.

'When I was seventeen and on the Villa ground-staff, I bought myself a car, a Ford Anglia. Paid £34 for it. I used to drive to training in it and some mornings I'd see Jackie Sewell and Peter McParland standing at the bus-stop. Now they were real big-time; I mean, Sewell held the British transfer record and McParland had won the Cup for Villa practically on his own. "Jump in," I used to say. "And mind the upholstery." They might have thought I was a real flash bugger, but they never said a word.' It was just an idea.

Big Ron's still compensating. He's always structured his training sessions around competitive five-a-sides, partly to inspire the team to new levels of fitness, but more importantly so that he can play himself. His eagerness to play the game is legendary – 'It's the highlight of his week' is a common enough comment – which is curious until you remember his inauspicious playing career.

hrew himself into those games. He was the centre of the action and
s injured or ill – which was extremely rare – we wouldn't play, it was
le as that. I don't think he could bear to watch us play football if he
't join in.' Needless to say, he took the penalties. 'He absolutely loved
it. He placed the ball very deliberately, then walked back with a swagger and
crashed it in. He never failed. If the goalie saved it then he had moved too
soon and it would have to be retaken.' We can all take the piss out of Big
Ron, his ego and those five-a-side games. Only that was Liverpool stalwart
Phil Thompson talking about the late Bill Shankly. And who's going to take
the piss out of Shanks? So maybe we shouldn't be so cynical. Maybe it's just
a man who loves football playing football.

'Pressures? What pressures? Perhaps I'm wrong, I don't know. Perhaps I
enjoy things too much.' The zenith of this period was a dazzling 5–3 victory
at Old Trafford. No wonder there was no pressure. There was something
else that Albion became known for – their Three Degrees. The name is a
giveaway.

For a working-class sport, British football in the 1970s was riddled with
a racism of the most ridiculous variety. Black players, it was said, lacked
'bottle'. They couldn't compete. They lacked the appetite for the physical
aspect of the game. It is to Atkinson's eternal credit that he turned this
nonsense on its head. Inheriting Cunningham and Regis, Atkinson went
back to Cambridge and bought Brendan Batson to complete the set. 'I don't
care if a player's black or white or green with purple spots. If he can do a
job for me, he's in the team.' It was, at the time, a brave thing to do. Regis
says now, 'Looking back, it must have taken some courage to sign the third
black player. Three black players in one team, there was no such thing at the
time. It was unique.' Whatever other –isms Big Ron may have bought into,
racism wasn't, and still isn't, one of them. Sexism, though. That's a different
matter.

Examples of his sexism are rife. When he arrived at Sheffield Wednesday
he was interviewed by *Sunday Times* journalist Sue Mott. 'Can we expect
less of the long ball game now at Hillsborough?' she asked him. 'Blimey,' he
replied. 'You're the first bird I've met with an FA coaching badge.'

'I can't stand women talking about football,' he said famously. 'I don't
know why, but it grates on me. They shouldn't interfere.' Or, as he said in
1989, 'Women should be in the kitchen, the discotheque and the boutique,
but not in football.' The discotheque? The boutique? These words existed
in 1989? Backing up his view is one of his best, most familiar stories. He's
manager of Aston Villa. 'I'm at the ground one day when Terry Cooper
walks in. He's managing them at the time and he's got this young girl,
Karren Brady, with him who's just been made managing director of

Birmingham City, God help us. She's very pleasant and she says what a nice ground it is and what a good team we've got and how I must be really proud of them all, but particularly proud of my son who's playing so well. Now this throws me a bit, and I say, "My son?" very casual. And she says, "I've seen a lot of good reports about your Dalian." Now that's what I mean about women and football.'

It was the inspirational Albion side that really attracted United in 1981. Dave Sexton was a good coach but, like a dog to its owner, his United team had started to resemble his outlook. Steve Coppell, a thrilling winger in Docherty's day, had become a sensible midfield support. Ray Wilkins had lost all interest in being butch and had discovered the joys of the five-yard pass to a colleague in whispering range. United were nothing if not United and they needed a bit of flair and *joie de vivre*. Old Trafford was, as Sir Bobby Charlton said, 'a theatre of dreams' and United needed a minimum of 36,000 paying dreamers every week to stay in the black. More, they needed to recapture the joy of the Docherty era, preferably, though, without the ear-ache. Big Ron'd sort it out. No one mentioned that he was fourth choice after Bobby Robson, Ron Saunders and Lawrie McMenemy.

Ron? As Tommy Docherty said all those years before, he'd have walked to Old Trafford. If Ron had never had a go at United, he'd never have been able to look His Bigness in the face again. It was a marriage made in the print room. At his first press conference there, Ron set out his stall. 'Gentlemen, you can have my home number, but please remember not to call during *The Sweeney*.' Such chumminess.

His arrival at Old Trafford was difficult for some United fans to cope with. For years they'd taken the piss out of City and Allison and the flash. Now they had a flash of their own. Supporters never took to him in the way that they took to Docherty. While The Doc was a rogue, likeable enough, but undoubtedly a rogue, Atkinson seemed just flash. A showboating showman. It's no coincidence that towards the end of his reign at Old Trafford, he was making a conscious effort to tone things down. Out went a few of the rings and he started wearing sun block under the tanning machine. But as he glittered less, so did United.

Things started pretty well, though. Things started, naturally enough, with the jangle of cash registers. Players came (Stapleton, John Gidman and Remi Moses – nicknamed 'Dogshit' by Atkinson 'because he gets everywhere') and players went. Money generally went. The glittering star was Bryan Robson (aka 'Captain Marvel' © Bobby Robson). Robson had followed Ron to Manchester from West Brom and was the ultimate macho all-action player. Put him and Jean-Claude Van Damme in a room together and you'd be pushed to tell them apart. Still, this sort of player is an invaluable addition to any side. (It's rumoured that Van Damme gets $5 million per movie now. Make of that what you will.)

There's a story that Bill Shankly was in Big Ron's office when the question of buying Bryan Robson came up. Ron knew that he wanted him and Ron knew that he'd have to pay. 'How much should I be willing to pay?' he asked as if to no one in particular. Shankly got the drift. 'Give them every penny they're asking.' Sound advice from The Man, as always.

There was only one problem with Robson. He was – how shall we say? – prone to the odd knock. He'd pull a hamstring picking up the phone. (That he'd approached the phone flying both feet first through the air in a manic frenzy didn't help matters). Robson and his injuries became such a standing joke that he received the ultimate accolade – a Spitting Image puppet. It'd sneeze and an arm would fall off.

Ironically, if Robson was United's greatest strength, he was also their biggest liability. If Robson hadn't been so injury-prone, there's a chance that Big Ron might have produced the goods. But he was and he didn't. Robson missed nine games in the 1982–83 season, nine again the following year, and ten in the next. In that 1984–85 season, United won thirty-one of the first thirty-three possible points and looked to have things sewn up by November. The Championship was on its way, surely, and a place in the sun beckoned for Big Ron. Move over Sir Matt, I'm coming on through. Then disaster struck. Someone phoned Bryan Robson . . .

Word was that Robson, knowing that the World Cup was around the corner, refused to be operated on. If this is true, it means that Atkinson and chairman Martin Edwards acquiesced – a ridiculous state of affairs. Player-power is all very well, but putting the self above the team? And the manager and chairman agreeing? Very odd. Still, it's only a rumour.

What was more than a rumour was the, by now, *de rigueur* domestic strife. There's something about Manchester United and this bizarre love-triangle deal. Perhaps it's the preponderance of Catholics at the place. The story broke in classic style: a splash headline in *The Sunday People*: 'I SHARED RON WITH HIS YOUNG MISTRESS'. The story led, 'The stricken wife of love-triangle soccer boss Ron Atkinson spoke last night of an amazing sex pact she made in a desperate attempt to hang on to her husband.' It seems that 'honey blonde Margaret, 45' found herself on the wrong side of Ron's revolving door looking at 'blonde mistress, Maggie, 35, a part-time fashion party hostess'. A part-time fashion party hostess? Tell that to your careers adviser.

As her twenty-four-year marriage was collapsing, Margaret said, 'This affair is the worst-kept secret in football. Nobody can believe he has been so foolish. He is destroying himself and I have told him so. But Ron won't listen to advice. As far as he's concerned, he is God, and there is nobody around who's big enough to tell him what to do.'

Ron might have been on the ropes, but he wasn't out. He took the stick from his wife and put it in his gag memory bank, ready to use later. His chance came many years later. When Wednesday were playing Coventry in 1990, he bumped into his old striker, Cyrille Regis. Since leaving Ron's charge, Regis had become a born-again merchant. 'I just bumped into Cyrille and I said, "What's all this crap about you just finding God? You worked with him at West Brom for four years."' Now take my wife . . .

Back on the marriage-go-round, the tabloids were serving up a comical side-dish. 'Margaret Atkinson offered to let the other woman, Maggie Harrison, have her husband during the day if Maggie would send him home to her at night. But Maggie rejected the deal. "I'm madly in love with him and I'm not sharing him with anyone – not even his wife."'

Beneath all the stories – secret holidays on 'the sunshine island of Majorca', revealing see-through crocheted tops, the 'ROMEO RON'S AWAY GAMES WITH MAGGIE' headlines – was a story as old as time. Middle-aged man dumps wife in favour of younger, blonder model. Man in the spotlight at public institution stares in the mirror one day and lingers too long at the hairline. Tries to check his willy but can't see because his stomach's in the way. Obviously he's not getting old, must be the wife. Bang goes the testosterone overload and his relationship breaks down. It's always sad, whether it's sadness for the death of a relationship or sadness for the death of dignity. United chairman Martin Edwards said, 'This is a private matter. It doesn't concern the club.' How often have we heard that, only to have it reneged upon later? Edwards, though, stuck to his position, possibly because he believed, possibly because he didn't want another Docherty.

There was another *de rigueur* case, but one that only came to light many years later. The splash headline on the front of *The Sunday Mirror* read BIG RON TRANSFER DEAL SENSATION. In a cute juxtaposition, it shared the front page with a bare-buttocked tease for a different inside story. ADULTERY – IS YOUR MARRIAGE SAFE? The story – the transfer story – concerned the transfer of Peter Barnes from Coventry City to Manchester United in 1985 and the question of a 'missing' £11,000.

Nothing was proven and the words, hidden away on the inside of the paper, revealed that the deal was nothing to do with Big Ron at all. Barnes may, or may not, have paid £11,000 to persons unknown, but Big Ron certainly paid for having a Big name. BIG RON TRANSFER DEAL SENSATION. Great front-page story.

The story? The story as reported in *The Sunday Mirror* (and we aren't alleging anything here, we're just reporting what they said, okay?) was this. Barnes was represented by a Mr Fix-It called Brian Hassell and Hassell was trying to 'interest' clubs in his merchandise, Barnes. But, though he was only twenty-eight, Barnes was perceived as being past his sell-by and, when Hassell put the word out, the phones didn't start ringing. Then the idea came up that wouldn't it be great if Barnes went to his dream team, Manchester United. Hassell contacted Big Ron. Ron said that he wasn't interested. (Now comes the allegations bit which we aren't alleging.) Barnes told *The Sunday Mirror* that 'Brian Hassell told me I would have to pay £11,000 to Ron Atkinson if my transfer was to go ahead'. 'Investigative' calls were made to Big Ron. 'I know absolutely nothing about that. As far as I'm concerned it's a load of rubbish.' Who said anything about Mandy Rice-Davies?

The five-page spread contained all the usual Champagne-Charlie-BoJangles-huge-house-in-the-country stuff. There are two ways of looking at it. First, you can say that bungs – and we're absolutely certainly not implying that there was anything bungesque here – have been going on since time began, and to deny it is to play the ostrich. A little sweetener here, a 'thank you' gift there . . . The other thing you can say is this. Who'd be a tabloid journalist?

That last lost Championship was enough for United. Atkinson nearly hadn't done badly, but he nearly hadn't done well either. When he was sacked, United were fourth from the bottom with three wins in thirteen matches and that's just not good enough. Players went and players came, but those that came were not the full shilling: Alan Brazil, Terry Gibson, Peter Davenport. Players who made Remi Moses look like a Manchester United footballer. Ron was asked by a major shareholder (the piper) what was happening. 'We needed major surgery,' Big Ron said. The major shareholder replied in classic Ronese: 'The next time we need surgery, would it be possible to have it done on the NHS?'

Partly it was his fault, but partly it was United's. When they sold Mark Hughes to Barcelona, they gave notice where their real priorities were. Football was no longer just a sport, it was a business, and £2.5 million was good business. Good business business but bad football business. But perhaps even then Hughes was seen as part of the Atkinson era . . . Desperately, Ron pawned his rings, sobered up his suits and toned down his tan. Anything to get himself off the feature pages and back to the back. I'm a real football manager. Ifs and perhapses.

Ron hadn't helped his cause by being photographed coming out of a 'top London nightclub'. It's curious, isn't it, how the word 'shot' is sometimes used when describing photographs. Maybe he caused his own downfall the day he signed an 'exclusive' contract with *The Sun*. It might have meant that *The Sun* was on his side, but what about the other papers? While the knives were being sharpened, there were plenty of vultures around to feed on the corpse. There's nothing the tabloid press likes more than a flash bastard down on his luck. Not for the first time in this story, the name Boy George comes to mind – bet Big Boutique Ron would just love that association.

It's the classic tabloid game where the hunter becomes the hunted. The victims never learn because, by that time, they are ink junkies and they need their daily fix. Doesn't matter if it's I SHARED RON WITH HIS YOUNG MISTRESS, BIG RON TRANSFER DEAL SENSATION or ATKINSON MUST GO. As long as there's the name and a picture, it'll do. Who cares if they're ripping your life to shreds and giving you a one-way ticket to the dole queue. There'll always be another paper, another exclusive. My fall from grace, that kind of thing. (Incidentally, being shot in a top London nightclub is never bad news. An unemployed moral vacuum I may be, but I'm still a bloody sophisticate – all right?)

Ifs and perhapses. If there hadn't have been a ban on English clubs in Europe perhaps United wouldn't have been so myopically desperate for that £2.5 million . . . Then again, if Brighton's Gordon Smith hadn't bottled it in the 1983 FA Cup final . . . Ifs schmifs. Big Ron was gone.

If Big Ron has had a Big Success, then it's got to be Aston Villa. West Brom (first time around) made him, United was the flash and Madrid was the cash, but it was at Villa that Ron the Football Manager and Big Ron the Quipmobile finally merged.

Big Ron was at Sheffield Wednesday when Villa's own character, chairman 'Deadly' Doug Ellis, made contact. Ron had turned Wednesday around, changing them from a sad Wimbledon lookalike outfit playing neckache football into a characteristically neat passing team. Ever since the West Brom team of the late 1970s, Ron's saving grace has been his belief in attacking football. 'The criterion I always use to judge my teams is this: do I enjoy watching them?'

Even when he was a ground-staff boy at Wolves in the mid-1950s, and Stan Cullis's prototype long-ball team were taking on all-comers, Ron never lost his faith. After they had beaten – on television – the top Hungarian side, Honved, Wolves were declared 'Champions of the World' in that Little Englander way so beloved on this fair isle. Ron smiled quietly to himself. 'Had Cullis not ordered me and my mates to water the pitch, Honved would have won about 10–0.'

At Wednesday, he proved his belief in the science of pure football by breaking the bank, paying West Brom £750,000 for Carlton Palmer.

Obviously a manager who knew what he was doing, then. Carlton Palmer 'is the worst finisher since Devon Loch. When he's in a clear shooting position, he's under orders to do one thing: pass.' £750,000 for a quip.

Ron's time at Wednesday also yielded another well-worn quip: 'We were terrible, scandalous. We were so bad that I was up there on my feet, shouting "Atkinson Out, Atkinson Out!" with the rest of them.'

The rumour-mill went into overdrive and there were declarations of loyalty, betrayal and more loyalty flying around like it was a deal involving a football manager. Finally, loyalty won the day. 'I realised that I must be barmy to even think of leaving here. I could have walked out but there was no way I was going to do that after the brilliant way I've been treated here. I have worked for some of the biggest clubs in the business but never a better one than Wednesday.' No, no. Not that sort of loyalty. This sort of loyalty: 'Leaving Wednesday has been the biggest wrench in my career,' he said, five days later. The Villa deal was said to be worth £750,000 over three years. It seems that chairmen aren't the only ones who can give the vote of confidence. In that curious way where the Fates demonstrate their sense of humour, Villa were drawn against Wednesday in the first match of the new season.

Still, at least Big Ron had a genuine reason for his leaving. 'I have been living out of a suitcase for almost five years and it wears you down. Wednesday have bent over backwards to accommodate me, but I did not feel that commuting four hours every day was something I could do for another two or three years.' The tabloids enjoyed it: THE MRS MADE ME DO IT was *The Sun*'s headline. While at Wednesday, he also turned down an approach by Marseille because of the travelling. 'I told them that just because they're building the Channel Tunnel, it just wouldn't be possible for me to drive back from Marseilles every night.'

The question might arise in your mind now that there is an answer to commuting. Why didn't Big Ron just move house?

Ron and Maggie had moved into a real dream home, a fourteen-room Gatsby-type effort just outside Birmingham. 'I arranged the colour scheme and furnishings of the entire house to match the dog,' joked Maggie in a 'Room of My Own' feature in one of the Sunday supplements. Maggie's haven is the kitchen. 'Ron doesn't spend much time there – his cooking stretches to cheese on toast – so I wanted the decor to suit me. The colours are cream and pink with marbled design flooring, with matching *en suite* breakfast-room.'

Well, it's fair game. Put yourself up for these features and you're asking for it. Still, why do I feel like I'm taking the piss out of someone with a speech impediment? 'The tree-lined gravel driveway leads to a splendid portico with a panelled front door. This opens into a hallway with a grand sweeping staircase . . . The master bedroom has a bay window leading onto a semi-circular balcony overlooking their acre of grounds with swimming-pool, rock-garden and perfectly manicured flowerbeds . . .' Sounds lush. It probably jangles when there's a strong wind. The dog, incidentally, was a peach-coloured Lhasa-Apso called, naturally enough, Rambo.

It's great image. A friend comes round for drinks, Buck's Fizz perhaps, *chez* Atkinson. He's not been there before and, mindful of his guest, Ron asks, 'You all right with dogs?' 'Yeah, fine,' the guest says, wondering what type of dog a man like Big Ron has. And why the need to ask if I'm all right with them? Ron smiles and calls, 'Rambo, here, boy!' The guest sees his life flash before his eyes. Rambo! A Rhodesian Ridgeback Rottweiller cross? Ron cannot contain himself and laughs a mighty laugh as the peach-coloured cottonball wad yaps its way into the room.

Meanwhile, back at a different Villa, Big Ron created another top side. Paul McGrath, Ray Houghton, Steve Staunton, Tony Daley and his Dalian namesake up front with Dean Saunders, a record £2.3 million buy. 'If I'd had him with the group I had at United – the Robsons, the Strachans, the Olsens and the Stapletons – we'd have won everything going, including the Ashes. He's the best natural finisher I've ever worked with.' There was also a sense of solidity with the likes of Earl Barrett and Kevin Richardson. In all this ramble about Atkinson and his attitude, taking the piss out of everything from his 'style' to his dog, there's one thing that's relevant here that makes everything else forgivable. He played Tony Daley's haircut.

The highpoint of Ron's time at Villa Park came in 1994 when he won the Coca-Cola (*née* League) Cup against, sweetly, United. Alex Ferguson's whinge machine had been going for an unprecedented domestic treble and looked odds-on. But Big Ron pulled off a top tactical coup and, on the day, the Cup only ever looked like going one way. The League title slipped away again, but flash, fast, entertaining teams like his rarely win Championships. The League's a marathon not a sprint, you may have heard.

Having just risen, Villa started to fade. Suddenly the team seemed old. McGrath was thirty-four, Houghton thirty-two, Saunders thirty-one. Results started going against them. Confidence dropped. It was a familiar scenario with familiar quips: 'I feel ashamed to be the manager of a team like that. You heard that booing at the end? Well, I started it.' More. A match at Coventry yielded: 'At least we were consistent – useless in defence, useless in midfield, crap up front.' When they were beaten by Trabzonspor of Turkey, Deadly Doug phoned Ron. 'I've got faith in you. Stay and get it right.' He then put the phone down, picked it up again and called the removal men. It's doubtful that many tears were shed over at West Brom or Sheffield Wednesday.

When Aston Villa sacked him in February 1995, Ron knew that he wouldn't be hanging around for long and, sure enough, in stepped Coventry City with an offer no unemployed man would refuse. Two and a half years at £500,000 is enough to jingle anyone's jangle. But Coventry City? It's not exactly Manchester United, is it? Well, no, it isn't, but take away the rings, strip away the tan, throw away the Scandinavian double-breasted suits and Big Ron is revealed as Ron Atkinson, football man. Football runs through his life. 'I'd rather play a one-two with Maradona than with Madonna . . . I'm more interested in Johann Cruyff than Joan Collins.' Well, aren't we all.

For Ron, that's the important thing – football. The money sounds impressive, but money is the least of his problems. When he left Villa, he received a £200,000 handshake. No, Ron's back in the Premier Division and that's enough to keep him happy.

As for Coventry, the appeal is as the appeal always was. 'Ron will give Coventry a sense of style and charisma,' said City's chairman, Bryan Richardson, a man who had sacked six managers in the previous five years. 'He will give us a lift in terms of presence.' So what if he's got to swap the BMW for a Ford and drink Chardonnay instead of non-vintage champagne.

Everything that goes around comes around and Big Ron is nothing if not the bounce-back type. He's now fifty-six – the oldest manager in the Premier Division – and is the last of a dying breed. The old jangles might not jingle as they once did, but he's still there, and that's the important thing. While the others take the piss, Ron just gets on with it.

Tommy Docherty: 'In Manchester we call him Kruger Ron.'

Malcolm Allison: 'He's the worst manager in Europe – Fat Ron. When I was manager of Bristol Rovers I was in the house and the phone went. I picked the phone. The fella said to me, "Mal, you seen the Cup draw?" I said, "No." He said, "It's Big Mal against Big Ron." I said, "No, it's Old Mal against Fat Ron."'

Kruger Ron. Fat Ron. Employed Ron. Of all the 'character' managers of the 1970s and 1980s, only Big Ron is left. Docherty and Allison are doing the roadshow shuffle, Clough is, well, Clough is elsewhere, and John Bond is tending the garden.

'I always admired managers like Malcolm Allison and John Bond – people who believed in doing things with a smile on their face. That's all it was with me, really. I'd invite the press round for a talk, crack open a few bottles of champagne and they'd go away and write about me like I was some kind of flashy character. It all started out as a bit of fun. Then it all started to be taken too seriously. They'd write that I wore expensive Gucci shoes when I didn't even know where to buy the bloody things. So I play it down a bit these days. Also, I'm fortunate that I've reached a stage in life where I don't give a bugger what people write about me as long as it's not slanderous.'

Big Ron is the perfect example of someone who creates a public face and then finds that it's taken as the real one. First, he likes it. Likes the attention, likes the ego. Then he finds that it's a bit limiting, just being known in this way, so he tries to change. But the media, the public, won't let him. It's almost the classic pop parable of the teen star who wants to go serious. The Ferrero Rocher/Babycham chic aside, it's hard not to like the man. When he got the nod from Old Trafford and became manager of Manchester United, he had a sun-bed installed in his office. Just to wind people up.

## Chapter 9

# REVENGE OF THE UGLY DUCKLING

*'The North-East, Tyneside, Geordieland – it's more than just an area of England, it's almost a country. In that peculiarly English way, it has been separated by a culture, an economy and (as near as dammit) a language. It's not just a class thing, though that's the cornerstone of the differences. There's a certain, yet indefinable, gulf between, say, Tyneside and London. Let's call it racism. Yet, for Charlton, being a Geordie wasn't the only defining factor. As the* Sunday Times *journalist Chris Lightbown wrote, "Part of the reason that England has never understood Charlton is that he is not an Englishman, but a Geordie. Moreover, as the son of a miner, he is a member of two groups many English people tend to see as quaint but necessary. Curiously, this is a view the English also tend to take of the Irish." Jack knows he's not always right, but he believes he's never wrong.'*

Johnny Giles

IT'S AUGUST 1985 AND JACK CHARLTON'S NEWCASTLE UNITED are at home to Sheffield United. The sun is shining, the birds are singing and everything is going well. The game ends in a 1–1 draw, nothing remarkable, but it's a pre-season friendly and it's there so that players can stretch their legs, not break them. It would seem, on the face of it, a perfect scenario. But by the time the dust has settled on that Saturday evening, Charlton has gone. He's told chairman Stan Seymour that he's resigning. He's had enough. He's out. 'I need that like a hole in the head.'

Big Jack Charlton. Son of Ashington. Professional Geordie. Manager of Newcastle United, the job he was born to. The job that was, in many ways, his destiny. Big Jack Charlton, nephew of Jackie Milburn, walks out as manager of Newcastle United. Needs it like a hole in the head.

It's a decision that seems a few streets down the road from curious; it seems bizarre.

Look. In 1983, after six years of hard graft, after giving Sheffield Wednesday the by-now routine kiss-of-life and putting them back where they belong, he's decided that he's had enough. He decides to quit. No, make that he decides to leave. Big Jack would never quit. Anyway, he's gone. After thirty years in the game, he's richer than a rich person and he's bored with this caper. There are bags full of small, furry and gilly creatures out there just dying to meet him and, really, it's no contest.

After walking out on Wednesday, Jack took time out from football. He killed a few deer and perched on the riverbank and assassinated a few fish for a television series – he probably did more of the same when the cameras weren't running, too – but, basically, he was out of football. He said that there were only two jobs that would tempt him back: Leeds and Newcastle. Then, as chance would have it, Newcastle approached him and made him an offer he couldn't refuse. In truth, Newcastle couldn't have made him any other type of offer. Yet fourteen months after taking the job, a week before the start of a new season with all the hopes and opportunities that that brings, he walks. He's out. Needs it like a hole in the head. Unlike the deer, he had a choice. There's not a great deal of logic to it and perhaps that's the logic.

Stories of Jack's life are united by two common punchlines, both of which basically say the same thing. There's the one that goes 'That'll do fine for me. I'll stay here,' and there's the one that goes 'That's my lot then. I'm off.' I know my mind, I'm stating my mind, I'm doing my mind.

Jack Charlton has been a success for so long that he's simply forgotten that there are other possibilities. He's also been touched with enough tragedy to be able to differentiate between what's important and what's really important, between the stuff that's worth fighting for (honesty, loyalty, dignity, independence) and the stuff that's not worth fighting for (everything else). Calling Charlton a maverick is perhaps wrong. True, he does march to the beat of a different drummer, but unlike most true mavericks, he's made sure that the drums are his. Paid for. In full.

There's not a lot about Big Jack that's not, in retrospect, entirely predictable, entirely in character. Walking out of his dream job when he was manager of Newcastle United? At the time it might have inspired a few miles of newsprint, but in retrospect? He's just fifty, he's at the zenith of a glittering career that would have King Midas scratching his head, and suddenly 'I need that like a hole in the head'.

There are a million apocryphal stories knocking around about Jack Charlton and, like most apocryphal tales, they're probably all true. The fishing one, usually attributed to Chris Waddle, is probably the key to the Newcastle decision. It's 1984 and Newcastle United are training. Jack is standing around giving the lads a team talk when a car pulls up. The window winds down. 'Jackie, Jackie. There's troot in the Tweed.' Big Jack stops talking, jumps into the car. End of training session.

It's a top story but what are the implications? That Big Jack has a pathological hatred of trout and feels compelled to hunt and kill them at every opportunity? Well, yes. But it tells us something more. Look at it this way. What does it say to a Division One footballer – a top level, highly paid, ego-strutting professional – when his boss is more interested in a fish than in him? Then we hear (surprise) that there was unrest between some of the senior players – i.e., the most famous, most ego-laden – and Charlton. By the time the 1984–85 season was approaching and the fans were shouting 'Sack Jack, Sack Jack' and 'Charlton must go' in a pre-season friendly, you could see why Big Jack was worried about his ongoing cranial ventilation situation. Really, there's trout in the Tweed and he's getting this grief. For £35,000 a year.

On closer examination, there were a number of reasons for his dissatisfaction with the way that things had been going. Chris Waddle had just been sold to Spurs for the relatively paltry sum of £590,000. This was a player Big Jack rated. When he joined Newcastle and saw Waddle for the first time, he said that he thought that in some areas of his game, Waddle was a better player than Pelé. It's one of those 'ten years ahead of his time' type comments that are liable to become millstones for the unfortunate genius involved, but Jack meant it. And the League tribunal, the body that fixes disputed transfer fees, had decided that Spurs should pay £590,000 for Waddle.

The Newcastle fans were similarly upset, and they weren't placated by Big Jack's idea of a replacement – Alan Davies, a £50,000 buy from Manchester United. He said that 'I have always felt that Newcastle have used the chequebook too readily. A couple of bad results and they were looking elsewhere for new players. I'm careful when I spend a club's money – I spend it like it was my own because I believe that managers should have a sense of responsibility,' but the fans didn't buy it.

Charlton tried to sign Eric Gates from Ipswich for £150,000, but Gates couldn't agree personal terms (i.e. he wasn't offered enough money) and chose instead to go to arch-rivals Sunderland. That didn't make anyone happy, either. The final straw as far as the fans were concerned was news that local hero Peter Beardsley had not agreed to sign a new contract. In retrospect, in the light of what happened to Liam Brady – another deity in shorts – under Charlton with Ireland, the Beardsley situation is easily understood, but to the Newcastle faithful in 1985, it was madness.

The episode undermined not his confidence – heaven forbid – but his faith in football. Everywhere he looked, he saw maximum disrespect. From the authorities, from the players, from the fans. When the chants of 'Sack Jack' went up, is it any wonder he picked up Maurice Setters, his trusty steed, and walked? 'That's my lot then. I'm off.'

Another classic story concerns the way Jack chose his local pub in Dublin. Think about it. He's just arrived in Ireland, the new manager of the Republic's football team. The new English manager of the Republic's football team. It's an alien land. His knowledge of Irish football is so poor that for his first match – another great apocryphal Charlton story – he let the team physio, Mick Byrne, choose the team. What would you do? Find somewhere friendly, somewhere warm to the idea of football. Maybe somewhere recommended by one of the players (or Mick Byrne, perhaps). Somewhere sympathetic.

So Big Jack's driving around Dublin with a friend. He sees somewhere on the hard, northern edge of town, lost in the sort of area where the buses don't stop and the locals eat their croissants without butter. This'll do. His friend, hoping it's a joke, says that if they're lucky they might have their car wheels stolen. The pub, Hill 16, is a temple to the art of serious drinking. The walls are covered with old sepia pictures of the heroes of the April 1916 uprising and the only references to football come prefixed with the word Gaelic. In short, it's not the sort of place where a loud, proud Englishman with soccer on his mind would be likely to be found. Maybe he'd have been a more unlikely figure if he'd have been wearing army fatigues and was pontificating about the joys of ribbed condoms. Maybe.

Still, Big Jack wanders into Hill 16. 'That'll do fine for me. I'll stay here.' The great, apocryphal part of the story says that not long after he arrived, Big Jack was so popular that his picture was up on the wall behind the bar and he had to lay down some rules. 'I'll buy you all a pint. I'll even sing you a song, but after that I'm just another bloke at the bar.'

'I'm the local lad made good. I appreciate the finer things in life but I will always remember where I came from'

A northern pit town, Ashington sounds like the classic 'we were poor but happy' role model for Monty Python's famous 'We were so poor we lived in a cardboard box' sketch. 'In our time it was a red letter day in Ashington when we heard that a ball with red leather casing had arrived in town. I bet there was never more than three or four of them there at any one time. Ever. That's gospel. We used to roll our dad's pit socks up into a ball and play with it. Going to school I would always try to get an old tennis ball and dribble that back and forth to meself.' Socks? They had socks? Bloody welfare state.

By the time he was fifteen, Charlton decided that the life of a mole was not for him. 'I left school at fifteen and started working down the pit – on the bank, not underground. I enjoyed that. It meant I could still set out rabbit snares while I was at work. But after my sixteen-week training which qualified me to work underground, I was taken down a pit to work with my father as a hanger-on and knocker-off. The big haulage tubs would come up one way full of coal. You pulled them round a bend, knocked them off their haulage rope, hung them on another haulage rope and sent them back the other way. I said to the guy in charge, "Am I going to be here on my own all day?" And he said yes. Then I said, "Is this all I'm going to do?" And he said, "Too bloody right." There was no way I was putting up with that. I went up to the manager's office and resigned.'

He applied for two jobs and both offered him interviews, as luck would have it, on the same day. In retrospect, there was never much chance of him passing up the chance of a trial at Leeds United in favour of an interview to become a policeman. A policeman. Thinking about Big Jack now as a policeman and you think of Chief Constable of Northumberland or some such. A powerful patriarch in the manner of a rational James Anderton. But then? Standing in line, in uniform, taking 'Yes sir, no sir' orders? It makes about as much sense as the thought of him becoming the most popular man in Ireland this side of the Pope. No. It was always going to be Leeds. His Uncle Jimmy was on the books there when he went up. Big Jack, you see, had round DNA. Football was in his genes and they fitted him perfectly.

Jack Charlton came from a footballing dynasty. Cissie, his mother and a matriarch in the grand old tradition, was a Milburn. Her dad, Tanner Milburn, was a goalkeeper and Wor Jackie's brother. Their father was a professional. Of her four brothers, four of them went on to become professional players. And then there was Jack's brother, Bobby. Becoming a footballer was like going into the family business.

Despite being older than his brother by twenty-eight months and taller than him by a good few yards, Jack was always in Bobby's shadow. Undeniably a genius, Bobby was to football scouts what the Pied Piper was to rats. At one time, there were eighteen clubs in the hunt for Bobby and one, apparently, was so keen that it said it would double the best offer Bobby got – regardless. Bobby passed his eleven-plus. Jack, needless to say, didn't.

To most mortals, it sounds like a recipe for sibling disaster, but Ma Charlton had other ideas and Big Jack was given special orders to look after Little Bob. 'My mother always told me to look after the little one. I had to take him with me everywhere I went and I moaned like hell about it. Later, when we played against each other in League football, I remember she was still telling me to lay off him. But it didn't really matter because I couldn't catch him even then.

'But I could never be jealous of Our Kid. Never. He was different to me, another creature. We always knew he would be great. Everyone in Ashington knew it. He could play. I could only stop people playing. I was a clogger. He was a footballer. I knew that. I had to work.'

Bobby was Our Kid but never Our Mate. Blood brothers but never soul brothers, their relationship has cooled to the extent that now they don't even talk. In all probability, it's not that they don't talk, it's more that they'd have nothing in common to talk about. Same family, same business, nothing in common. It's a familiar enough scenario, I guess.

Even on that sunny day in 1966, when every Englishman became, for an afternoon at least, an honorary Little Englander, the love thing never happened. Shortly after the crowd had come onto the pitch, thinking it was all over, Jack looked at Bob, Bob looked at Jack and they smiled. Then they nodded. Shirts wringing wet with the sweat of a nation that had just won the World Cup, beating the Germans for God's sake, there was no hug, no embrace, just a nod.

Despite Jack's protestations that Bobby 'changed' after the Munich air crash which decimated the Busby Babes in 1958 – 'He was never the same lad afterwards' – even the most distant outsider can see that a Grand Canyon of thought and attitude stretches between them.

On the one hand, there's straight-talking Big Jack, all blood and guts and loyal honesty. Big Jack, fisherman. A gob on a stick. Then there's Bobby the reserved English gent. A *Boys' Own* hero, quiet and dignified to the exclusion of all else. Put it this way, Big Jack could be Wor Jack, Bobby couldn't. Bobby could be a Sir.

Perhaps it's simply that the good and the great can always inspire people's admiration and respect. But gaining their love, that's a different thing. Talent can only go so far. Jack's gift is that he's good but he isn't great. Everything about him is touchable. While Bobby was off doing his Kenneth More as Douglas Bader, Jack got by at second-rate, Second Division Leeds United, a nondescript team living in a rugby town. Well, it was for the first ten years of his time there anyway.

None of this should distract us from the fact that Jack had a great career. Jack the footballer was the classic example of someone who knew what he did and did what he knew. He was a stopper. He may never have been a great player, but he was always a great footballer. Check out his statistics. By the time he bid farewell against Southampton on 28 April 1973, he had played 629 League games in his twenty-two years with Leeds (773 including Cup matches), scored 67 goals, and won every domestic honour the game had to offer. He was capped 35 times for England, making his debut against Scotland at Wembley in April 1965, at the age of thirty, and scored six goals for his country. In 1967, the clogger was voted Footballer of the Year, the year, incidentally, after it had been won by England's Greatest Footballer. For the record, he received 43 bookings and was sent off eight times.

'Jackie, Jackie. There's troot in the Tweed.'

It's another great Charltonism that he's more interested in carp than *catenaccio*. For the most part this has probably done as much as anything to endear him to his ever-adoring public, though it hit a bit of a rough patch in January 1984, when he was in the headlines after *Jack's Game*, a ten-part series for Channel 4 made when he was between jobs (after he'd quit Sheffield Wednesday and before he joined Newcastle United) showed film of him shooting a stag. Fish, it seems, are okay to kill, cute furry deer are not.

He's a Wild West hero with a touch of the old John Waynes – a man's gotta do – imbued with the spirit of the countryside where men are men and animals are shot to prove it. To outsiders, it's a strange illogical place full of people who claim that they love animals, and then demonstrate this by spending their time killing them. It's a place where the 'animal-lovers' say that they understand how the countryside works and prove it by spilling blood. It's a place where people extol the 'traditional' values, like family, community and honesty. Yet they spend their time decimating families and destroying communities.

'I fish and shoot to relax and some folk find that odd. They would say nothing if I spent my time playing golf.' It's a justifiable argument and one that says as much about the class-obsessed nature of English society than it does about Jack, yet . . . I don't know. How many golfers are there that shoot, murder or maim their clubs for the sheer sporting hell of it? How many orphan golf clubs are there?

It's arguable that Jack might not be in the position he's in today if it wasn't for his fisherman persona. It had, in the public eye, created a three-dimensional figure where there might otherwise only be the cardboard cut-out silhouette of an ex-footballer. The television series, the pictures, the image, it's all high-profile stuff and does nothing to harm his career.

For many years, he managed quite happily to run the two interests side by side. When Charlton was manager of Middlesbrough, he used to 'employ' the club's apprentices to act as beaters. (For the uninitiated, beaters are used by people who shoot game birds. The way it works is this: the birds are sitting in the undergrowth, minding their own business, feeding their young or whatever, and the beaters come along, literally beating the ground and scaring the birds into taking flight. Once the birds are airborne, the noble savage hunters pick them off with their guns.)

In 1982, when he was manager of Sheffield Wednesday, Charlton said, 'If I were presented with an ultimatum – any one of hunting, fishing, shooting or staying in football – then, to be fair, at this stage of my life, I'd choose fishing. The only trouble is, there's no pay for fishing so that's why I'm a football manager. I tell you, the day I caught my very first salmon I remember every detail to this day much more vividly with a clear picture than England's World Cup final win at Wembley in 1966.'

While it would be a braver man than this one to say 'bollocks', it does seem a little odd, to say the least. The only thing that makes you appreciate that that statement is for real is the fact that shortly after he said it, Big Jack walked out on Wednesday and went fishing. For a year.

So there was Jack Charlton, a successful footballer, a successful manager, a successful coach, a successful media star, a television presenter, a pundit, a talking head. But all of this paled into near insignificance in February 1986 when a grey puff of smoke emerged from the Merrion Square headquarters of the Football Association of Ireland in Dublin. When he took over as manager of Ireland he transcended all this. Jack Charlton became, in that instant, a legend.

The story of how this gruff Ashington lad came to be the manager of the Republic of Ireland team has been told before. Still, it's a good story.

This is how it ended. Peter Byrne, a journalist on *The Irish Press*, wrote: 'If it is not overstating the case to suggest that the FAI now finds itself with a manager it does not want . . . the end product is that a bitterly divided Association now finds itself committed to a manager who was, possibly, even more surprised than they were to discover that he had headed the poll on the fifth ballot.' Other Irish journalists followed the same line. The only dissenting voice was that of Eamon Dunphy, a former player for Millwall and Ireland and now a columnist on *The Sunday Tribune*.

Dunphy is – how shall we say? – a mercurial figure. After hanging up his boots, he turned his hand to journalism and found a power unlike anything he'd known before. He has the unenviable talent of getting up people's noses – and it's a talent he's nurtured. After all, there's no better way for a writer to stay in demand than to be controversial. Sentences that start with 'The only dissenting voice was' tend to finish with the words 'that of Eamon Dunphy' with a curious regularity.

There are two ways to look at Dunphy. Either he's the lone gunman out to clean up the town, a principled man who'll speak the truth and say what has to be said, regardless of the cost to his personal popularity. Or he's a self-interested ego-driven publicity-seeker who goes out of his way to find cause that'll get people talking – about him. Polemicist or not – it's always hard to tell. Either way, you get a picture by-line.

To look at Jack and the Ireland job, it's perhaps useful to first look at how he found himself as boss of Middlesbrough in the early 1970s, his first foray into the world of football managership.

It's 1973 and Jack was lurking deep in the national psyche, somewhere between a footballing figure and a national icon. He was the funny-looking World Cup hero who'd made his bigger splash in 1970. First, he was chastised by the media for admitting to having a 'little black book' in which he kept the names of those players whom he was going to get. 'I will make them suffer before I pack this game in. If I can kick them four yards over the touchline I will.' In reality, this was little more than a macho bluff. The facts just don't lead to any other conclusion. Compared to the likes of Giles and Bremner, Jack was a pussycat. He was disapproving of that side of Revie's team. Anyway, Ian Hutchinson never lost his legs. Anyone who doubted the bluff side of the black book story should have just asked themselves one question: would Big John Wayne have carried one? A man's gotta do what a man's gotta do. He doesn't write it down and do it later when no one's watching.

But 1970 was important for Charlton's image for another reason. Left out of the World Cup equation by Sir Alf (he felt aggrieved, but it was the right decision. He was thirty-five and the heat of Mexico was no place for his ageing legs), he'd been picked for the very first ITV pundits panel. The panel. It was one of those inspired ideas that television throws up every decade or so. Get a fistful of big mouths to rabbit – controversially, of course – about the game. Joined at the hip and shooting from the lip, Big Mal was there alongside Big Jack. It was compulsive viewing.

A high-profile son of the North-East who was guaranteed column inches and, therefore, gate receipts, Big Jack was the perfect choice for Middlesbrough. A sleeping giant, Middlesbrough needed not so much the kiss of life but a soppy great snog. Possibly the last time that the club had made a real splash was when they broke the British transfer record, buying Alf Common from Sunderland in 1905. Anyway, so they asked Jack. Each side of the equation – Jack and the 'Boro board – prepared for the interview in their own ways. When the day came Jack hit them with a list of demands. While the board were protesting that this was an interview, that they were the ones doing the deciding, Big Jack walked out saying that he'd wait for ten minutes. They should make up their minds by then. That year, Middlesbrough won the Division Two Championship by a record fifteen points, beating the division's record number of points won set by Leeds in 1964.

(As a curious historical footnote, much the same thing happened to Middlesbrough in the 1994–95 season. Dozing away in the mid-waters of

Division One (Division Two to those who live there), Middlesbrough asked Bryan Robson – another high-profile son of the North-East – to come to the rescue. Again, it worked for them. Odds on Robson nicking off to Manchester United and Middlesbrough going coma within three years.)

It was the same when Jack joined Newcastle. 'I said I would take the job but that I must be completely in charge of everything. I might not interfere with the commercial manager, but if I think I should interfere with them I will. And if the secretary and me have a row, then I will win or I'll leave.'

Jack also set out his stall as regarding his status. As he said in March 1974, 'I don't think it's necessary to have a contract. I enjoy doing the job without one. Contracts are not necessary in football. I'm not looking for security in this job, but to fulfilling ambitions in the game.' In 1977, when he was in charge of Sheffield Wednesday, another coma chameleon, he elaborated: 'I've been a fortunate lad, really. A bloody-minded bighead perhaps, but fortunate. I had a good playing career, had a good testimonial and made money outside the game, all of which left me financially independent. I'm not in the game for the money alone and this [not having a contract] gives me the freedom to do the job the way I want to do it. It also keeps me on my toes.' Clever Jack knows that it keeps everyone else on their toes too.

The Republic of Ireland was one of those teams that sportswriters love to call a 'Cinderella' side. They can look good, but only at certain times of day. To the casual observer of the English leagues, the mystery about the Republic was that it wasn't a top team, challenging for trophies. The players they've had over the years, some of them could have walked into the England side if they'd have had English grandmothers. Liam Brady, John Giles, Frank Stapleton, Mark Lawrenson, David O'Leary, Gerry Daly, Kevin Sheedy, Chris Houghton . . .

Jack's predecessor was Eoin Hand, a one-time player in the Leyton Orient mould. He turned out and no one expected much else. It was something to do. As a manager, the best (and the worst) thing that could be said of Hand was that he was nice. He lacked the necessary gravitas to, for example, tell Liam Brady what to do. Frank Stapleton later said that 'I think he felt a little bit overawed'. Ireland was still in the grip of what Giles, the team manager in the early 1970s, called 'the idea of being champions of the moral victory'.

It all went horribly wrong for Hand in the build-up to the 1986 World Cup. Not only did they not qualify, they didn't qualify with style. Their lacklustre campaign was something England would have been proud of, and it ended with a 4–1 defeat at home to Denmark. True, the Danes were a top team and were on the verge of becoming the new Holland, but still. Of the 15,000 who turned up to see the game, maybe three were Irish. Worse, news filtered through that Northern Ireland had drawn 0–0 with England at Wembley and had qualified for their second World Cup in a row. It became obvious to the FAI that it was time to sound the bugle and call for the cavalry.

So, okay. There's Jack, fishing for troot on the Tweed, and, miles away in Dublin, there's a group of suited and booted officials looking for a charismatic leader. A marriage made in heaven? In retrospect, yes. But at the time, to the officials? No. Their idea of an Irish Moses was genial Bob Paisley, the legendary former boss of the mighty Liverpool. Paisley was officially the most successful manager of all time, and during his nine years at the top at Anfield, Liverpool had won everything, everything from the Division One Championship to the Eurovision Song Contest. If Paisley's Liverpool entered it, Paisley's Liverpool won it. But the idea of him rekindling his career with a part-time acceptance of the Republic? To Paisley, the idea was something akin to a pensioner's relationship with his allotment.

What should have been quite a simple operation turned into a ridiculous political farce. It was like watching the Labour Party select a new leader when it should have been more like the Tories. Different camps, different ideas, power groups, conflicts of interests, people playing interests off against each other – it was all there. An advert went out with the only stipulation being that the new manager must speak English. The field sufficiently narrowed, four names emerged: former Celtic star Billy McNeill, the Manchester City manager who had just finished putting the team back together again after the successive gale storms that were Malcolm Allison and John Bond had all but destroyed it; the eternal John Giles; Liam Tuohy, manager of the Irish youth team; and Big Jack. McNeill was initially favoured, largely because he was Scottish, a Celt. But City chairman Peter Swales blocked the move. It was now that the name of Paisley first came into play.

Without getting too involved into the politicking that went on, the basic idea seems to have been to use the others as beards and then push Paisley into view at the eleventh hour. He needed ten votes to get the gig, but beards were being grown and shaved quicker than anyone knew. Assured of the magic ten, Paisley got nine votes. Who reneged? No one knows, but speculation is rife that it was Lee Harvey Oswald. It was that kind of deal. By the time the dust settled, the troot had bit. The FAI found themselves having voted in Big Jack whilst having absolutely no idea whether or not he'd accept.

All of which takes us back to Eamon Dunphy. The week after the vote had taken place (Jack had accepted: 'That'll do fine for me. I'll stay here') there was a press conference. Everything went well and Jack gave a good account of himself. His years in front of the cameras and his alter-career as an accomplished after-dinner speaker gave him a confidence that had the audience eating out of his hand. He even gave out his home telephone number to all present – he'd learned the lesson of Don Revie. Towards the end of the conference, Peter Byrne addressed Don Casey, top man in the FAI and head political honcho. What, Byrne asked, was the story of how Big Jack had come to be elected? What was the truth about Bob Paisley? Cue Dunphy.

Seeing as it's Dunphy's story, let's let Dunphy tell it. 'Byrne and I were hardly friends, yet I felt compelled to offer a modicum of support. Byrne was absolutely within his rights on an issue of acute public interest. When I argued this with Charlton, Byrne was let off the hook. I replaced him on it. Big Jack now gave me the treatment: "I know you . . . you're a troublemaker." I insisted that journalists had rights which he could not proscribe, and anyway this argument was not with him or his appointment, but with the boys in blazers beside him. My conciliatory tone did not mollify Jack. Sensing that the mood in the room favoured him, he made to rise with the words "Do you want to settle this outside?". I declined. The assembled élite of Dublin journalism then did something quite remarkable. There was a burst of applause, like a wave. It engulfed the room. They were applauding him. The Charlton era had begun.'

Listening to this account, you can't help but feel that there's something missing: John Ford shouting 'Cut!'.

On accepting the position, Charlton said that he wasn't taking it for the money. 'I don't need the money. I made a good living as a player and was successful in my business interests. And my friends will tell you that I'd much rather smoke their fags than my own.' He said that he would take whatever Eoin Hand had been on. When they told him that the figure was about IR £15,000 a year, 'I told them that I wanted a bit fucking more than that. I got a bit more, but not much.'

Money and Jack is like Morecambe and Wise. One doesn't work without the other. Quite aside from his footballing career, he's made a fortune from television, PR advertising and his after-dinner speeches, where his appearance fee is £3,500. Apparently, at one of these speeches, a friend recently told him, 'Jack, you can't take it with you.' To which Charlton's answer was the inevitable 'Has anyone ever come back to confirm that?'. On the eve of the Italia '90 World Cup, he was asked what it meant to him, to which he apocryphally replied 'What? Financially?'.

Since taking over the Irish team, he has come under fire for two things: the policy of recruiting non-Irish Irishmen and the team's style of play.

The first criticism – the so-called 'granny rule' – is probably borne out of envy more than anything else. Article 18 of FIFA's consitution says: 'Anyone who is a naturalised citizen of a country in virtue of that country's laws shall be eligible to play for a national or representative team of that country.' Ireland's citizenship laws are, perhaps, more liberal than any other country in the world. No matter where you are born, if you've a parent or a grandparent who is an Irish citizen then so are you.

Shay Brennan, who played for Manchester United in the 1960s, is widely thought to be the first 'Englishman' to play for Ireland. All Charlton has done is apply the rule – rigorously. Prior to the 1990 World Cup, the joke went around that FAI stood for Find Any Irishman. But the reality is this: if you can choose, you're always going to pick the best players. Playing the game sometimes involves playing the game.

The other criticism is more personal to Charlton, and it should be remembered that Jack only ever played under two managers: Revie and Sir Alf Ramsey. Two more dour pragmatists you couldn't hope to avoid. Even when England won the World Cup, their style of play was criticised. It's not hard to see why Big Jack isn't that bothered by criticism.

As footballers, there's really very little to connect Mick McCarthy and David O'Leary. They're both centre-halves, they both wear shorts, and . . .? If they were pugilists, you'd call O'Leary a boxer and McCarthy a fighter. O'Leary, despite his Arsenal connection, may be the more cultured player, the more refined artiste. McCarthy, though, is a Jack man through and through. 'My record for juggling is sixty kicks without it hitting the ground,' he said once, before adding 'but that was with a centre-forward.' Not for him any of this 'I've always been Irish, really' nonsense. A gruff, straight-talking Northerner, McCarthy was proud to play for Ireland, but he saw it as an opportunity to represent the land of his father, not the land of himself. There's a story McCarthy tells about how, when he was making his debut for the Republic against Poland, he couldn't distinguish between the two national anthems. 'I'd never ever heard the national anthem and, to be fair, they both sounded similar. I said that jovially as well. But it's awful when you look at things in black and white: they look totally different, they look out of context. Somebody was making the point that if you had an Irish Setter you could play for Ireland. Well, yeah, when the national anthems were played I didn't actually know which was which. My dad didn't go around the house playing the national anthem.'

Elsewhere such honesty might be seen as politically naïve and embarrassing. Not here. Little did McCarthy know, but his gruff honesty had just earned him a place in Big Jack's team and in his heart. There's a story that goes like this: In 1987, Ireland were playing Bulgaria in Sofia. As usual, before the match the band played the two national anthems. As the band finished the first, the Republic's 'Soldier's Song', Jack turned around to one of his assistants and said, 'I hope ours doesn't last as long as that.' Again, maybe true, maybe not. Take your choice, but here's a clue. The Republic played in Sofia on 1 April.

By contrast, O'Leary – one of the most 'cultured' defenders of his era – found himself in exile. Not long after Jack arrived, the Irish team was booked to play a minor tournament in Iceland. Curiously left out of the squad, O'Leary arranged to go on holiday with his family instead. The inevitable happened. Circumstances forced Jack to decide that he needed O'Leary after all. The call went out but O'Leary had arranged to go on holiday with his family. And that, as far as Jack was concerned, was that. Less than 100 per cent commitment. As a postscript, Jack was, as ever, vindicated. Ireland won the tournament, the first time in their history that they'd ever won anything, and they never looked back. There's another postscript. In the Italia '90 World Cup, Ireland were playing Romania for a place in the quarter-finals. Vertigo time. The game was drawn. Extra time. The extra time was drawn. Penalties. All were taken and everything depended on one last shot. Packie Bonner saved the Romanian effort. Now for the Irish try. Up stepped . . . David O'Leary. Surely if he scored all would be forgiven. He shot true and straight, the net duly bulged, but Big Jack never did give him cause to sell his condo on Elba.

As Tom Humphries writes in *The Legend of Jack Charlton*, 'In the days when both Giles and Brady ran the midfield together there was a popular joke which had to be performed in the voice of any well-known commentator. "Giles is looking for the crossfield ball, beautiful, and Brady takes possession from Giles, moving into space wide on the right, pauses, looks up, plays the pass to Stapleton. Stapleton beats one, beats another, rounds the goalkeeper, he's through. Stapleton has to score, oh yes, and the ball is played safely back by Stapleton to Giles in midfield. Giles looks for Brady . . .".'

OK, so it's a joke, but even so. It's a joke that would have Big Jack reaching for the oxygen mask, not rolling in the aisles.

'We are working to the same principles now as we did the first day I took over. Ours is basically a hustling game. We prefer to play the ball in behind people, aiming to turn them all the time. The idea is to go towards the corner flags first, which draws the sweeper out and then move the ball in from there. When I was playing, the only time I was totally uncomfortable was when the ball disappeared over my head toward the corner flag and I had to turn and chase.'

One thing that Jack learnt from Sir Alf is a recognition that in English football what was good wasn't as important as what was effective. Thus, David O'Leary might be a better ball-player than Mick McCarthy, but Mick McCarthy is a ballsier player than David O'Leary. To some purists, it's an odd logic, but it's a logic that has taken Ireland to unknown heights.

Charlton's Ireland are not the Wimbledon that everybody seems at such pains to compare them to. Then again, neither are Wimbledon, but that's a different story. The two teams are united by a common attitude, a common 'us against them' spirit, a common 'little man' chip.

The same attitude that inspires Wimbledon to get out their ghetto-blasters inspired a furore in 1990 when Jack published his diary of the Italy World Cup campaign. It showed that he encouraged his team to sing IRA rebel songs to inspire the players. 'We play Irish rebel songs on the coach-ride; then, as we approach the stadium, one of our men puts on a tape of "Sean South of Garryowen". That's the kind of stuff that raises the temperature.' It didn't help matters that he was referring to a match at Lansdowne Road against England.

After conceding that the Irish style might be self-defeating in the USA, Big Jack said, 'Closing the opposition down, not giving them time or room to see what they want to do . . . but that's the way we play and that's that. We've been playing too much of the football the pundits say we should be playing. We can do that as well as most. But we're better at our own way than anybody.' But it's all bluster and hoodwink. When it comes to the crunch, Jack's Ireland do the right thing. It might not please all of the people all of the time but, for the most part, it works.

The arch pragmatist, Jack isn't ruled by fear; he's ruled by common bloody sense. You do what you do with no fancy frills. Once, when he was doing the TV pundit bit, he told the truth – albeit mischievously (it was a TV pundit's job, remember): England were playing Finland and they were 2–1 up. But it was a dull game. A typical England international at Wembley – you know the kind. The crowd were baying for substitute attackers to be put on, to try and liven the thing up. Jack said, yes, they should make a substitution. They should put on an extra defender. He said that it was a dull night; they might as well protect the only good thing about it and win. It's the managerial truth, not the punter's truth. The difference between getting paid and paying. And it's a truth that's served Jack well.

In April 1994, the Republic beat Holland, inflicting on them their first defeat in ten games. Dick Advocaat, the Dutch manager, said, 'We have to learn from their patience.' The Dutch learning patience from the Irish? You couldn't take that many coals to Newcastle if you tried.

Andy Townsend, Jack's Charltonesque midfield runner, is in no doubt.

'Just look at the record of the country since he took over if you want proof of his success. Anyone who underestimates Jack could not be further off the mark. He is very shrewd tactically and knows the style of play all over the continent.'

Big names meant little to Big Jack. Neither did big reputations and neither did big egos. You've got to remember that there are few players who can pull rank with Jack in terms of achievement on the pitch. The Giraffe might not have been the most skilful player in the world, but there's the twenty-two years in the game, the six hundred-odd matches, the thirty-five caps, a World Cup winners medal . . . Some fancy-dan tap-dancer is going to tell him what to do?

Alf Ramsey once told Charlton that he would happily leave out the most brilliant player in the world if that player wasn't willing to follow his plan, if he wouldn't do as he was told. Anyone who doubted Jack's commitment to that idea shouldn't have.

Back in the days when Big Jack was bossing Newcastle, he'd been greeted with a rare feeling of hope. He said, 'I always felt that I was the logical choice [to manage Newcastle]. I always felt that I would manage this club one day.' The fans seemed to agree, and responded by buying £80,000 worth of advance season-tickets.

When he showed that he was willing to sacrifice Chris Waddle, things changed. Worse, as far as the fans were concerned, he said he was glad that Kevin Keegan had left and that he'd ostracised Keegan's adjutant, Terry McDermott. Keegan had been the Messiah to the Geordie faithful, galvanising the team, galvanising the whole area. In the two years that he was there, the frog had turned into a prince and Newcastle were back in Division One. On Tyneside, no one doubted who had done the kissing. Big Jack wasn't writing a manifesto for the Popularity Party when he said, 'There's a great feeling of relief in the dressing-room that Kevin's gone, great player though he was. He dominated the whole place, everything revolved around him. Now the other players have a chance to blossom and show what they're made of. The players never mention him and neither do I.' And, as for his mate McDermott, 'As for his mate, McDermott, he's been offered £600 a week to play for Newcastle and he's still not satisfied. He's not training with us and the sooner he leaves the better.'

Likewise Liam Brady. If Charlton is a near deity in Ireland these days, Brady in the 1980s wasn't far off. The fulcrum of Arsenal's three Irish stars (Frank Stapleton and David O'Leary being the others), Brady was a delight. Delicate and divinely skilled, he danced and jigged around the pitch in a way that must have had Highbury's marble foundations quaking. Something between pride and fury. In the late-1980s, in the days when

Jack was still mortal, he pulled off Brady at half-time in a friendly against West Germany. Big Jack could have criticised the Pope's haircut and got less flak. But a man's gotta do. 'I am paid to win matches. I like Liam and have great respect for his ability and reputation, but he wasn't doing what was expected and it was necessary to make a change.' What was it that Ramsey said again?

'I have my ideas and they are firmly fixed. The one place we cannot put the ball at risk in is the midfield. We cannot match the Europeans in that sort of build-up. I simply don't want the ball put at risk in areas where we are immediately vulnerable to counter-attacks. The team must never be stretched when we press forward and that also means the goalkeeper. I have tried to pin down a pattern of play which is simple to follow. We have to get behind defenders, turn them and then compete. We are good at that. We have to play behind them, not in front of them.' Jack said that in 1987 and he's never really deviated from that path.

The secret of Big Jack isn't really that hard to see. It goes back to his pre-Revie days at Leeds, back to his youth, back to his childhood. Jack was never afflicted by success. As a kid and as a player, he was rarely Jack Charlton, but always Bobby's brother.

As Humphries says, 'He never quite experienced the giddiness of being young and successful with the football world at his feet. Jack Charlton indeed isn't a man whom one would lightly accuse of ever having experienced giddiness.'

Being born into football was one thing, but for Jack the side-effect was that making it was never, perhaps, the achievement it might have been in other families. When Wor Jackie's your uncle and Bobby Stardust is your brother, you making it to Second Division Leeds United is hardly going to make the dinner-table conversation rattle.

Possessing a pragmatism such as his doesn't preclude the odd daydream into the world of giddiness. Tom Humphries tells of Jack's almost paternal attitude to three of his young charges during the 1994 World Cup in America. 'It was interesting to watch Charlton at press conferences standing at the back of the room as three of his young prodigies, Jason McAteer, Phil Babb and Gary Kelly, performed for the media. Jack would watch them intently, all the while his eyes flicking from his players to the media, wondering at the sheer lightness of it all. The lightness of being that had eluded Charlton as a young footballer. He would encourage the three in their enjoyment of the tournament, prompting them to buy masks and wigs for press conferences and permitting them to enjoy a remarkable amount of media coverage. The three amigos became a strange media phenomenon during the World Cup, indulged in their enjoyment by Charlton. "Ohh look, it's Bobbee Charlton!" roared Phil Babb excitedly one morning as Charlton strode into the press interview room. The media erupted. Charlton permitted himself a broad, almost paternal, smile. So that's what it would have been like. That's how it was for Bobby.'

It's a touching image and we can forgive Humphries the gushing sentiment of that final sentence. It wasn't like that in Bobby's day. And even if it were, if Bobby had taken the piss out of Matt Busby in public, he'd have had his balls chewed off. Still.

Fifteen years after first joining them, Leeds and Big Jack finally won a trophy. In 1967, they beat Arsenal in the final of the League Cup. (That they won by a single goal, that that goal was scored after a goalmouth scramble following a corner and that they were condemned after the match for their dull 'method play' is one of those strange, almost spooky, events that, for lovers of the art of football, prove that there is indeed a God. One-nil to the Arsenal indeed).

More, that scrambled goal was scored by Charlton. Column inches turned into column feet as various pundits mouthed off about the questionable moral legality of the tactic of putting Big Jack on the goal-line. Words like 'soccer' and 'cheat' were applied in tandem. Leeds' stall was set out as soon as they were promoted to Division One in 1964. Revie had revolutionised the club after the abolition of the minimum wage in 1961 and had produced a fitter, faster, more physical team than anyone had seen before. In 1963, Revie signed John Giles from Manchester United and it was Giles, more than anyone else, who epitomised the Leeds way.

Blessed with a natural footballing brain, Giles was skill itself. Sublime, sometimes. When he was good he was very, very good, but when he was bad . . . There's a famous story told in Rob Steen's *The Mavericks* about Giles and the great Frank Worthington. 'I was playing for Leicester one day,' said Worthington, 'and we were beating Leeds 1–0. I was down by the corner flag, hemmed in by Johnny Giles, so I flipped the ball over my shoulder and over his head. He just turned to me and said in a very cold, calculating matter-of-fact sort of way: "If you ever take the piss out of me or Leeds United again, I'll break your legs."' The sad thing about the story is not (only) that it's true, but that Giles had the skill to respond to Worthington in the proper way. As he said later, 'To do it [the 'tackle'] properly you have to have the nerve, the timing and above-average skill. You pretend to play the ball in tackling situations but instead leave your boot in so the opponent connects with your boot.' Now you can see the truth about Big Jack's Little Black Book.

Revie, far from condemning such activity, positively encouraged it. And the more that he and his Leeds team were criticised – no, they were more than criticised, they were hated – the more they dug in. Revie surrounded himself and his boys with a forcefield of pure paranoia. His methods began to reflect this too, as he force-fed his players the now infamous dossiers, detailed studies on that week's opponents. Even in the 1970s, when they dressed themselves in all that poncey nonsense – little numbers strapped to the tops of their socks! – they were hated. It's surprising that Leeds never morphed into the Leeds in the manner of the Arsenal.

This, then, was the environment that Jack found success with. And even then, even when success finally came knocking, Big Jack found himself out on a limb, considerably older than his contemporaries and of a different mindset. Age, obviously, had something to do with it, but also Munich had imbued Jack with a deep sense of mortality. A sense of priorities.

In everybody's life there are many defining moments, and Big Jack's aren't that hard to see. First was the time when he was invited to apply for the vacant managership of England. Check that. Invited to apply. Not only was he not accepted, he never received a reply. No 'We'll keep your name on file in case a suitable vacancy appears'. Nothing. England, with all its stuffiness and protocol and stiff upper-lips rejected Big Jack without having the grace actually to reject him. The selection board simply didn't bother to reply. For a man who ate loyalty and honesty for breakfast, this was horrible. And for it to have come from the England heirarchy. In a typically Charltonesque piece of play, the record has now been set straight. He wouldn't want the job now even if it were offered to him.

The second moment occurred in 1985 when Wales were playing Scotland at Cardiff in a qualifying match for the World Cup. 'It was one of the saddest days of my life. I was watching the game when Jock [Stein, the Scotland manager] had a heart attack. He was a very good friend. I had known him for years and he was a great man. How can you believe what Bill Shankly said about football being more important than life or death when you have seen someone die at a match? The game isn't that vital.'

It was a day that raised a fear of mortality which had existed in Jack ever since Munich. That fear came to the surface again in 1992 when he had to have a brain-scan after doctors feared that he had a tumour. The tests proved negative, yet the shock which had hung over him never really disappeared. 'When something like that happens, you really have to take stock of your life. Football means a lot to me, but there are things that I hold dearer: my wife, my family, my friends.' It's a happy-ever-after story and, true to the Wayne in him, Jack said: 'When I was given the all-clear it was a case of saying, "Right. I'm okay. Let's get on with life again." That's what I did and I haven't really thought that much about it since.'

Dismissing Jack as a bumbling anti-aesthete is a national game that still goes on in some sections of the worldy-wise media. And it still hurts. Responding to a 1989 tabloid article, he said, 'It hurt me, all that stuff about sitting on river-banks instead of concentrating on the job, turning up late and being more interested in fishing and shooting than football. They forget that I took the Ireland job on the understanding that the management of a national team can only be part-time employment. What can you gain from sitting behind a desk making and waiting for telephone calls, going from game to game watching players you already know about?'

Part of this part-time ethic is his attitude towards his players. 'I don't want the players to get bored with me or me with them. There are rooms booked for them if they want to sight-see or visit relatives, but I don't expect them in Dublin before big games until two days before we play. From then on, they are with me.' Another of the lessons learnt from Revie. Like 'People are always asking me about the other team. I couldn't tell you about the other team. It's us I worry about.'

There was the time that Ireland played Egypt during the 1990 World Cup. Jack was asked at a press conference what he thought of them. 'There was the boy with the beard, the dark lad in midfield, the keeper, the little dark lad who played centre-midfield, the very coloured boy and the boy who played up front – Hassan? Hussain?' Dossiers, schmossiers.

It's all a scam, of course. Deep inside there, buried beneath all the troot jokes, and beneath the bitterness that when Leeds started their ill-fated and, quite honestly, ridiculous experiment of passing the managership one-by-one to former players from the 'golden' Revie era (Clarke 1980–82; Gray 1982–85; Bremner 1985–88) they decided to bypass the one man who had proven himself at managerial level, there lies a germ of pure truth. The man who was jokingly dismissed as 'The Giraffe' had a footballing brain second to only a very few. Clarke. Gray. Bremner. No disrespect, but we're talking insults here. Premier Division.

'I have always been the one who took a different direction to what took place under Don Revie at Leeds. I looked in different directions. I don't think Gilesy, Billy Bremner or Eddie Gray had ever looked in different directions. And I've suffered for it a lot because people have got this idea that I don't know about football, that all I know about is motivation, humping the balls up, chasin' fuckin' this. A lot of crap. I am the only staff coach that Elland Road has ever produced apart from Freddie Goodwin. I was a staff coach by the age of twenty-six, twenty-seven; that's an appointment by the FA by people who look at you.'

His gift, says Townsend, is that 'he talks the language of the players. He knows how players think and what they want. He says it's okay to go and have a beer and all he asks is that players act sensibly. Basically, he treats you like men. And if he has a problem with someone, he'll tell them. Straight talking, face to face. He doesn't pull punches and everybody gets treated the same.' And he cares.

He was fined about £8,000 and charged with 'unsporting conduct' after the match against Mexico when he voiced his opinion of the fact that substitute John Aldridge was made to wait about five minutes before being allowed to go on. FIFA said that he had been verbally abusing the referee and the linesman and that that 'could not be tolerated'. Jack said he was merely yelling at the players, 'attempting to get things sorted out'. FIFA responded with typical bureaucratic understatement: 'Jack Charlton is a funny guy.' Charlton, for his turn, felt that he was being punished for the critical campaign he had been waging against the officials regarding their policy of not letting players have access to water during matches.

When he was at Newcastle, after all the Keegans and Beardsleys and Waddles, there was one player Jack helped. A player not so much trouble as troubled. The club secretary, Ena Hunter, relates a tale of how the trainer wanted to get rid of a young player. 'Jack said he would deal with it. So he called the lad into his office. After about ten minutes, he came out and said, "Ena. I don't know what to do. He's crying his eyes out in there." In the end the boy came out with his place at the club intact and with an improved contract.' God knows what Gazza said to Big Jack. Similarly Paul McGrath. With Manchester United he became a news item. With Ireland, he was diligence itself.

Charlton is famed for his malapropisms. They could be malapropisms, or they could just be Big Jack having a gas. For example, he took his players to Orlando earlier than necessary so that they could get 'alcoholised'. You or I might have used the word acclimatised. It may have been more accurate, but it wouldn't have been as funny.

Similarly, he cannot remember players' names, and calls Liam Brady 'Ian'. Again, who cares if it's true. It's funny and you can get too literal with these things. Talking about Ronald Coleman instead of Ronald Koeman.

When Jack took over from Hand as the Irish boss, the players were all shocked. 'His record of walking out if he wasn't absolutely happy was well known and the state of soccer in Ireland at the time was very different to how it is now,' says Niall Quinn. 'Gaelic football and hurley were the top games, but now kids are buying soccer strips and there's even a Manchester United shop in Dublin.'

Andy Townsend concurs: 'They are now talking about ten-year plans in Ireland. It wasn't that long ago that there were four or five thousand at Lansdowne Road. Now our games are invariably sell-outs. We've beaten

Holland and Germany away and we were the only team to beat Italy over ninety minutes in the last World Cup. The interest in the game in Ireland now is tremendous. Success breeds success and you can see new players coming through all the time. A lot of that is down to Jack.'

And Jack himself knows it too. 'Boys who never gave much thought to the game are now enthusiasts. They buy football magazines, talk about great players and dream about stardom for themselves. This is how a game develops and Irish football will always be in great debt to this team.'

Football is big in Ireland now, no mistake. Prior to the 1994 World Cup, Big Jack was promoting Shredded Wheat, Guinness, the Bank of Ireland, shops, milk, and himself. General Motors, the team's sponsors, have doubled their market share in Ireland since linking up with them. Honest, straight-talking cars. It's a winning formula. And it's said that Irish hotel bosses frame Charlton's cheques rather than cash them.

When Jack took over the Ireland job, he used to joke that it was his initials that confused the authorities. Some joke. 'Charlton is now so big in Ireland,' says Quinn, 'it's outrageous.' And the feeling's reciprocal. 'Once you've experienced the warmth of the Irish, once they have taken you to their hearts, you want to make sure that things will always be that way. I'd hate to go into a pub and have somebody say something really nasty to me. I don't want to fall out with the Irish. Everybody here calls me Jack. People consider me theirs.' Coming from the man who walked out on Newcastle, this is big.

The players, too. Quinn: 'I'm more in awe of him than I've ever been of anyone before. I can't really describe why, it's just that he has a wonderful attitude. He puts smiles on faces. He doesn't operate from some coaching book, he works from his character.

'He's got a deep aura but he's also down on the level of the players. Football can be the last thing on his mind, but there's always the respect. I can honestly say that I'd call him a friend – and how many managers could you say that about? – but I've still not got anywhere near him. I'm into horses and my family's a farming family and I'm delighted that he talks to me about it and takes an interest.

'The only time I've really seen him angry is when that book [Paul Rowan's *The Team That Jack Built*] came out. He was furious that they'd printed all the swearing and cursing as part of his conversation. Okay, he swears at times, everybody does, but he's revered in Ireland by really young kids and he was horrified that they'd see him swearing.

'Ireland seems to be tailor-made for him. He's taken for what he does here. He's not dissected in newspaper articles like he would be if he was in England. But then, at the moment, he's respected by the Irish press. If it starts going wrong, you don't know what might happen.'

When anyone's in the middle of a love affair, it's hard to see what could harm it. And ever since Jack's rebels beat England at Stuttgart in the opening game of the 1988 European Championships, the love affair has just got deeper and deeper. In July 1990, the readers of *The Irish Press* newspaper campaigned for the national stadium to be renamed Charlton Park. Along with Mother Teresa and Nelson Mandela, Jack Charlton is now a Freeman of the City of Dublin. But if anything ever did happen . . . what then?

Actually, we do know what then. And so do the troot. 'That'll do for me. I'm off.'

# Chapter 10

## SUPERCALIFRAGILISTICESPIALIDOCIOUS

*There's a scene in Mary Poppins where Mary takes the kids to see Bert who's doing a pavement chalk painting. He's smiling (or 'smoiling' as Dick Van Dyke has it) as he's working, whistling and singing and being happy. All around him, the suits are marching along, going about their business. Bert tells the kids that they can be loike him and have joy in their hearts. All they've got to do is believe. Mary tuts and gives one of her perfectly reasonable incomprehensible lectures, but relents as always to Bert's charms. They all hold hands and jump . . . into the picture. Suddenly, they're in a magical land where anything is possible and they all sing a song about a little leap of faith.*

ON 25 APRIL 1979, NOTTINGHAM FOREST WERE IN THE DEPARTURE lounge of a major international airport, waiting to board a plane to Germany to play the second leg of their European Cup semi-final against Cologne. It had been a brave journey, a magical ride – that Forest were there at all seemed just another testament to football's unending tendency to make the improbable possible and the impossible probable – but now it was surely coming to an end. Cologne had lacerated Forest in the first leg with their counter-attacks and powerhouse midfield play and were unlucky in coming away with only a 3–3 draw. But with away goals counting double and the prospect of them having their best player, Flöhe, fit again, it might have seemed to the cash-strapped Forest board that throwing in the towel and saving the air fares was the logical thing to do. Logic. What did the Greeks ever know about football?

When they appointed the mercurial Brian Clough and his faithful librettist Peter Taylor, the Nottingham city elders must have had a suspicion that things would happen – things generally did when those two were around – but what? That was in the lap of the Fates, and when Clough and Taylor joined Forest, the Fates weren't smiling, they were in hysterics.

On their first night in charge, Clough and Taylor looked out of their office window and, seeing a clear blue sky, decided to go for a stroll around the ground. As they sat under the goalposts, gazing out over their field of dreams, Clough sat mesmerised as his old talismanic partner rabbited on, regaling him with his tales of what they would do, who they would buy, what they could only achieve. It was a beautiful evening and, after drinking their fill of the night, they both drifted off into a hazy slumber. Then, in the dead of night, something strange happened. There was an almost imperceptible flash, and in front of them appeared a ghostly vision who told them that they could have anything they wanted. The only proviso was that at the stroke of midnight, things would be returned to normal. Thinking it some kind of joke, Clough looked suspiciously at the vision and said, 'Eh, young man. So you're a miracle-worker then, are you? Okay. Work a miracle. We've got a fat, chain-smoking winger who's addicted to chips. If you can do something with him, I'll give you an exclusive interview.' The vision smiled gently and sprinkled some sparkling dust on the winger. There was a puff of smoke and the winger turned into John Robertson. Clough was speechless.

On a personal note, I can bear witness to the workings of the spectral presence at Forest. When I was younger, so much younger than today, I used to go to watch the mighty Orient play. Now, they had a young, ginger-haired lad playing for them who, even in the less than stately surrounds of Brisbane Road, seemed like a bottle of house red. Years later, he turned into Ian 'Bomber' Bowyer. Of his performance in that first Cologne match, Clough said, 'His contribution, at left-back, in midfield and in attack, was magnificent.' With Bowyer, as with Robertson, Kenny Burns, Larry Lloyd and Frank Clark, it wasn't so much a case of the ugly duckling as the invasion of the body-snatchers.

Just press the pause button a minute on this unlikely episode of *The Twilight Zone* and go back to 14 May 1977. It's the last Saturday of the 1976–77 season and the Division Two promotion race is all but settled. Wolves and Chelsea are up and it looks likely that Bolton will join them. All they've got to do is raise a smile against Wolves and *they're* hardly going to be breaking a leg, are they? Really, they've already won the title. Playing no part in this non-drama are fourth-placed Nottingham Forest. They're on holiday in Spain. But then Wolves beat Bolton and Forest are up.

Despite the messianic presence of Clough and Taylor, no one expected much of Forest. No one was too sure whether the old partnership was as potent as it had been at Derby – that was, after all, a long time ago now – and, anyway, things were different now. Division One was basically Liverpool and a few others. Even so, Forest up there? It was like setting up an Oxfam shop in Savile Row. As Clough said later, 'No one gave us a cat in hell's chance of winning a raffle let alone the title.' In retrospect, that's a curious phrase for Clough to have used. A raffle is luck-dependent, no?

Luck schmuck. Luck had nothing to do with it. Bolstered by the arrival of Peter Shilton in goal, they clinched the Championship with five matches left to play and finished seven points clear of the runners-up, Liverpool. And remember, this was in the two-points-for-a-win era. Their total of sixty-four points had been bettered by only four post-war champions. 'Seasy. With a motley collection of workaholics like Bowyer, John McGovern and Archie Gemmill, reformed hooligans like Burns and moderate club players like Peter Withe, Forest out-Liverpooled Liverpool and took the art of eleven individuals playing as one to a new dimension. To call upon the spooks again, perhaps it was no coincidence that it was in Nottingham that the cry of 'One for all and all for one' became so successful. It was a maxim that ran through the whole team, from Shilton through to the front pair of Withe and the efficient Tony Woodcock. The only exception was the enigma that was John Robertson.

Further salt was rubbed into Liverpool's wounds when Forest beat them in the final of the 1978 League Cup with what Clough distressingly called 'his reserve team' – Shilton, Gemmill and centre-half David Needham were ineligible. After only a year, the cat had run off with all hell's cream.

The following season, Liverpool had their chance of revenge on the biggest stage of all. In the first round of the European Cup, Forest, the League Champions, were drawn against Liverpool, the Cup-holders. Liverpool had won their opening five matches, while Forest were in disarray. They'd sold Withe and had made a big song and dance about not being able to find a replacement. His stand-in, a young rookie called Garry Birtles, was some reserve no one had heard of. Oh, woe is Forest. You can guess the rest. Forest won the two-leg tie 2–0 and Birtles scored. He's acclaimed a 'revelation', a 'sensation', the 'find of the season'. And, just in case it needs pointing out, this was against Bob Paisley's Liverpool, the most successful British club side ever, not some Mickey Mouse bunch of Swedes from some seaport. Lucky old Clough and Taylor. They sell Withe and then, at the eleventh hour, find Birtles waiting in the wings. Lucky?

Clough and Taylor didn't rely so much on luck as on a strange kind of alchemic psychology. Martin O'Neill gives a good example of this. In their first match in the big league, the players are sitting in the dressing-room at Goodison Park, nervous and, as usual, left to their own devices. Peter Taylor walked in and, instead of the more obvious 'Do this, don't do that' team talk, proceeded to let rip with a ten-minute stand-up comedy routine which had the players still laughing as they went out onto the pitch. Relaxed, they won 3–1.

Another example of this psychological unorthodoxy occurred just before the League Cup final the following year. The Forest team arrived at their hotel at 9.30 p.m. the night before the match and expected just to book in and go to bed, so as to be ready for their big day. Not a bit of it. The players were ordered to go into the lounge bar whereupon a waiter appeared carrying a dozen bottles of champagne. Archie Gemmill complained and asked to go to bed. 'No one leaves until this lot's finished,' said Clough. John O'Hare, looking for a way out, said that he didn't like champagne; he prefered bitter. Clough ordered a dozen pints of bitter. For three hours, the players were regaled by Clough and Taylor with tales of their past. By the time their hangovers had started to wear off, they were a goal down. They recovered.

While we're here . . . Immediately before the 1980 European Cup final against Hamburg, Clough took the players to Cala Millor in Majorca (where Taylor had a summer place) for a week. 'We did bugger all for a week. The Germans were rehearsing corner-kicks and set-pieces. We were busy doing nothing.' Forest won 1–0. Lucky? No. It doesn't happen like that. It really doesn't.

Under Clough and Taylor, Forest had gained promotion to Division One, won the League Championship and the League Cup in their first season there, and were now in the semi-final of the European Cup. To outsiders, it seemed as if Forest were in some way protected, as if they'd signed some kind of Faustian pact. If the outsiders suspected it, the insiders knew it. Clough and Taylor had not forgotten their first night at the City Ground. But now, as they were waiting for that plane out to Cologne, the hands of the clock were ticking ominously towards the 12 and the fairy godmother was sitting in the departure lounge, drumming her fingers and looking at her watch.

There was only one way this episode of *The Twilight Zone* could have ended. Clough blagged some injury-time from the good fairy, Forest went to Cologne and won 1–0. The winner, needless to say, was scored by Ian Bowyer. In the final, they beat Malmo, a Mickey Mouse bunch of Swedes from some seaport.

Sometimes in life you come across people who, regardless of their chosen field, are something beyond inspirational. It's nothing to do with what they achieve or what they do, though that obviously helps them get recognised. In, for example, something like politics, the internationally famous are easy to call: Gandhi. Golda Meir. Jesus Christ. But that's just the sort of recognition that winning the fame game gives. It's the effect, not the cause. Special people are everywhere, it's just a matter of how they carry themselves. And no, it's not a case of 'Oh, we're all special in our own special ways'. Sorry, but we're not. We're all people, all creatures and as such we're all valuable. But special? No. That's a space reserved for the few. Take Nelson Mandela. An obvious example perhaps, but consider what he's achieved, what he's been through, what he's inspired. Looking at people like that, it's easy to question their basic humanity. Listen, to the likes of me and you, getting up, having breakfast, reading the paper and making some more coffee is, near as dammit, a full-time job. When would there be time to overthrow the oppressors and free the people? And when would you have time to take Maxwell C. Wolf for a walk? Maybe these people delegate more. Get someone else to drink the coffee. That'd be a job. Nelson calls you into his office. Drink this coffee for me, I've got to liberate the people now.

Special can be good or bad, heroic or evil, mad or sane. It is often insane. As Dennis Hopper says of Mickey Rourke's Motorcycle Boy in Coppola's *Rumblefish*, 'Even the most primitive societies have an innate respect for the insane.' By the youth he's idolised, by the authorities he's hated. But none dispute his power.

> *'Hi. It's Cloughie here,*
> *When the team you support loses a game,*
> *Don't look around for someone to blame,*
> *It's the toss of the coin,*
> *It's the luck of the draw,*
> *Football's a game,*
> *It's not making war.'*

(The first verse of Brian Clough's 1980 pop single 'You Can't Win 'Em All')

If the back page is a soap opera – and who ever doubted that it was? – then Clough had himself firmly cast as the hero. Not everybody was of the same opinion, but then he always made sure that he had two votes more than everyone else. But heroes need villains, and our particular soap had no trouble in finding the perfect candidate for that role. Don Revie took on the part as if he'd been studying long and hard at Lee Strasberg's Method School. He even had his own gimmick: he was miserable. Don Revie wasn't merely sad or unhappy or pissed off, he was miserable. Sour, bitter and miserable. In the land of very miserable people, he'd have stood out as being miserable. Whenever he was pictured he looked miserable, whenever he spoke he sounded miserable. If there'd been an Olympic event, the miserableathon, Revie would have been able to cover his lounge walls with gold medals. As it was, there was no Olympic event, so the Football

Association did the next best thing. They appointed him manager of England.

Revie produced a bunch of dull England performances from a dull England team – well, there's a thing – and contrived to make the Ramsey years seem entertaining. In 1977, after a 0–0 draw against Uruguay (what could have been a more fitting last match?) Revie did the only thing a man like him could do; he ran off to Arabia for £350,000 – tax-free. The reason cited was money, and no doubt that played a part. But, more important, Revie realised that Arabia was probably the only place where they'd have appreciated his sense of humour. When he went, everyone tutted and breathed a sigh of relief.

And 1977 was also the year that Forest won promotion to Divison One. Though little was expected of the club, a lot was expected of Clough. It may have been nearly five years since one of his teams had won anything – there was the Anglo-Scottish Cup won earlier that year, but it's not something you'd cite as a reason for becoming England manager – he was, what you might call, good value. But aside from any footballing criteria, he would have been the perfect antidote to the Revie era. English soccer had become dull and predictable. Liverpool were winning everything in sight (bar the Anglo-Scottish Cup, of course) and Bob Paisley might have been the greatest manager English soccer had ever seen, but he wasn't God's gift to the back-page lizards. Apart from a few jokers in the pack like Docherty and Allison, things were grim. Thank God Cloughie was back.

He was immediately hailed as the People's Choice. Newspaper poll after newspaper poll 'proved' that Clough was the man the people wanted to succeed Revie. It could, of course, be argued that the people's thoughts were directed by those very newspapers which commissioned them, for in the story-hungry world of journalism there was never any doubt that Clough (and Taylor) was the hack's choice. Everyone knew that they'd get better stories with Clough than with virtually anyone else. Of those who could have challenged him on the quote front – Hitler and Napoleon immediately spring to mind – only Groucho Marx was still alive.

But, really. My mother had a better chance of becoming England manager than Clough and her record was nowhere near as good as his. True, she'd been unlucky with injuries . . . Faced with the thankless task of filling the vacancy, the FA took the only course open to them. They gave the job to Ron Greenwood.

Clough later said, 'If the post of England manager had been filled on the basis of outstanding achievement in soccer, then Ron Greenwood would not even have had a smell,' and, of course, it was true. At West Ham, Greenwood had encouraged attractive football, nice football, but his teams

Richard Gere takes charge of Crystal Palace.

Happy days. Tommy, Stu and Lou celebrate winning the 1977 FA Cup final.

Emlyn Hughes and Ray Clemence at Bill Shankly's funeral.

Why, Gordon Smith, why? Big Ron celebrates winning the 1983 FA Cup final
with Big Butch.

Big Ron, in his guise as manager of Aston Villa, pensive after thinking up another gag.

We're on the road to nowhere . . . Big Mal after missing the last bus.

And now the end is near, and so I reach the final curtain. Brian Clough's last game at Forest, 1 May 1993. They lost 2–0 to Sheffield United. Says it all, really.

The eagle has landed. Wor Jackie meets adoring fans. Curiously, the relationship has lasted.

never stood a cat in hell's chance of winning a raffle, let alone a trophy. But he was the Establishment boy and, in the notional democracy that is England, the Establishment always chooses the Establishment boy. The Old Boy Network refers not only to school-ties, it relates to values and ideas as well. Greenwood fitted; Clough would have been an embarrassment. Not one of us. So maybe he'd have won something? He might even have been able to choose his best goalkeeper between Peter Shilton and Ray Clemence, something Greenwood never managed.

There was one other thing about Greenwood that appealed to Sir Harold Thompson and the other streetwise urchins who comprised the FA: he'd effectively retired. He was no longer boss of West Ham, he was general manager. He'd been West Ham manager from 1961 to 1974, during which time they'd won the FA Cup in 1964, the European Cup-Winners Cup in 1965, and, er, that's it. Stuff the injuries, my mum should have applied.

In fairness to the Carlton Club cobwebs, Clough probably would have been the embarrassment they'd feared. Diplomacy was never one of his strong suits. In 1970, after Derby County lost a UEFA Cup semi-final tie to Juventus, he referred to their boss as 'that car salesman' (technically true: Agnelli owned Fiat) and ranted to the assembled journalists '. . . and you can tell those fucking cheating Italian bastards . . .' (He actually had good cause. A *Sunday Times* investigation reported that the referee had been approached with a bribe, and the Juventus substitute, Helmut Haller, did seem to be unnaturally friendly with the officials). His methodology probably wouldn't have suited the suits either. It's the night before the crunch qualifying match for the World Cup and the players are gathered at the hotel. They are ordered to the lounge whereupon Clough and Taylor produce a dozen bottles of champagne . . . They'd have loved that up at Lancaster Gate.

'My being in charge at Leeds was like Brezhnev becoming Prime Minister of a Tory government.'

There was another thing that put off the powers-that-be. Leeds. For forty-four fateful days at the start of the 1974–75 season, Brian Clough was manager of Leeds. It was, to say the least, a curious place to find him, for if there was one team he hated, it was Leeds.

'I had thrown a few barbs at them over the years and I meant every single one, but I thought the slate could be wiped clean on both sides. How could I know they would be so sensitive? They hadn't conveyed much sensitivity on the field. I thought that was something that Don had erased from their lives.'

To Clough, Revie was 'that man', a reviled character who created a team of cheats. To the 'cheats' in question, Clough was a lippy bastard who needed putting in his place. If a dating agency had set them up, both parties could have claimed damages. What made it worse for Clough was that he had no Taylor by his side. He had stayed down south in Brighton.

What Clough hadn't counted on was that everybody hated Leeds to such an extent that they had developed a deeply felt sense of Arsenalitis: us against the world. In their defence, it was largely true. Clough set out his stall in his first meeting with the players. He started in cracking style. Textbook, it was. 'Gentlemen. The first thing you can do for me is throw your medals and your pots and pans in the dustbin because you've never won anything fairly. You've done it by cheating.' Love at first sight is not really a phrase that is applicable to this situation.

'Like some turbulent priest, Brian Clough descended on Elland Road determined to drive out the spirit of Don Revie and all his works.'

The Leeds FC Official Club History.

Still, it wasn't all bad for Cloughie. As he later said, 'When I became financially secure courtesy of the Leeds chairman, I was the best in the business. I was much better than I am now, honest. When they sacked me Leeds gave me a blue Mercedes and £25,000 and paid the tax. All my worries about pensions and bringing up the kids were over. They took that burden off my shoulders and then I became a very good manager.'

The rat-pack weren't interested in any of this, and something needed to be done to placate the public and the press. The answer lay in the very niceness that was at the core of Greenwood. He didn't really want to offend anyone and wanted to give everyone a chance to play. His plan was to create a kind of management by committee where each tier of the structure had its own boss. Typically, it was only *The Daily Mail,* that monkey to the Establishment organ, which supported this move. 'It may well be remembered if and when English football flourishes again that it was Greenwood who made the courageous and visionary decision to offer places to the major personalities who were rivals for his own job.' Wash your minds out, you sad, cynical cases who are thinking that Greenwood possibly did this because he didn't have the confidence or personality to do it all himself.

In his autobiography, Greenwood outlined his philosophy. In England's first match in the qualifiers for the World Cup, he asked his back-up team to write down what they thought his team against Italy should be. Everyone bar one complied. Clough, the stroppy bastard, thought the manager should be capable of picking his own team.

Clough and Taylor were given the task of looking after the England youth team. It's a classic management tactic. You need to make a public display, so you hold out what looks like an olive branch but which is, on closer inspection, an insult. Then you sit back and wait for the reaction. The reaction comes and then you, the aggrieved party, can justifiably sack or reject the person you didn't want there in the first place. If anyone complains – well, we tried. It was his fault.

In Tony Francis's excellent book, *Clough: A Biography*, Peter Taylor throws some light on those days. 'The job didn't excite us, but to have refused it there and then would have looked bad. It might have ruined any future chances. Ron was genuine enough about it, but what an insult by the FA.' Still, it was accepted in the spirit with which it was given. 'When we heard there was an international youth tournament in the Canary Islands, we suddenly fancied the job. Four days in Las Palmas sounded too good to miss. We had a day off after the final and I managed to wake Brian at about 8.30 in the morning. I'd ordered a taxi and told him we were going to get a November suntan. We missed breakfast and fell asleep on a deserted beach. When we woke up we were surrounded by nudists. We thought we were still dreaming and Brian persuaded me to stay all day. That was the highlight of managing the England youth team.'

Two other incidents during that trip sealed their fate. The first came just as our dynamic duo were about to give the youthsters their first team talk. They walked into the changing-room to find Professor Frank O'Gorman and John Bayliss, a doctor and an administrator, preparing things. Cutting up lemons. Clough explained that their presence wasn't required and asked them to leave. That was bad enough, but the other incident was almost heresy. England won the tournament.

Soon enough, there as an 'FA probe' into Clough's neglect of the England youth team. 'What can you do with a man who says he wants to be manager of the youth team and then fails to put in a single working day with them?' wondered Sir Harold.

You can only guess at what Clough really thought of being handed the youth portfolio. Maybe he truly did want it like he always maintained. Maybe he was just saying that to be diplomatic. There's another possibility. Clough might have turned down the big job had it been offered. Admittedly, it's unlikely, but consider it. It would have meant a big drop in salary and he'd have had to button his lip. Clough was nothing if not a good socialist. Imagine the childlike glee in the Establishment offering you the top job and you turning the Establishment down. Still, that's conjecture. When it was Greenwood's turn to step down, Clough's moment had passed.

He won two European Cups and a League Championship at Forest, and was obviously even more unsuitable for the job than before. He was still what he was. And the FA was still what it was. Bobby Robson, the Ipswich manager, got the job.

'One of the main reasons that I never became the England manager was because the Football Association thought I would take them over and run the show. They were dead right.'

If it was a surprise to him when Greenwood got the nod, it shouldn't have been. After all, it wasn't the first time that England had rejected him, for if Clough the Manager can be considered a success, then Clough the Player was something else. Between 1956 and 1963, he scored 251 goals in 274 games, an average of 0.9 goal per game. It's a phenomenal record, bettered only by Dixie Deans, who scored 283 goals in 300 games. Clough was a striker in the Greaves mould – fast, direct and ruthlessly efficient. He knew what he was good at and wasn't backward in coming forward in saying so. Like his hairstyle, his views haven't changed; they were just sharper when he was younger.

Despite his astonishing goal-scoring record, he was repeatedly passed over by his country, possibly because he was playing in Division Two for unfashionable North-East clubs Middlesbrough and Sunderland. But the public (read press) clamour got too much and finally, in 1959, he got his chance. His first game, against Wales at Cardiff, was a goalless wash-out. In the second, Sweden beat England 3–2 at Wembley. That Sweden had reached the World Cup final, losing only to Brazil, passed over everyone. When Johnny Foreigner comes to Wembley, it's expected that he's put in his place; 1959 might have been post-Hungary, but we still had a bloody Empire. If this self-deluding racism still exists today, back then it was rife. As ever, defeat brings on self-reflection and, as ever, self-reflection quickly turns into the much more satisfactory hunt for the scapegoat. As the spotlight was circling the team, looking for that elusive goat, a young, skinny twenty-four-year-old approached the England manager, Walter Winterbottom and emitted a strange, nasal whine. 'Eh, young man. How can I play centre-forward alongside Charlton and Greaves when we're all going for the same ball? You'll have to drop either Greaves or Charlton.' The dogs were called off and the hunt was over. The scapegoat had been found.

It's a wonderful image. Cloughie telling Walter Winterbottom, the last of the great gentleman managers, that he'd have to drop Greaves or Charlton. It's doubtful whether Winterbottom ever recovered.

Before he had a chance to redeem himself, it was all over. It's three years later, Boxing Day 1962, and Britain is knee-deep in snow. Really, they shouldn't have played, but Sunderland were pushing hard for promotion and didn't want to lose momentum. It was decided to go ahead with the game against Bury. Clough, all sharp eyes and razor quiff, was lurking around the Bury box, waiting for his chance. A mistimed back-pass and the young striker sniffed blood. He ran into the Bury box, focusing on the net. The Bury goalkeeper ran out of the box, focusing on the ball . . . You could have heard the crack a mile away. As he lay there in the slushy mud, knees broken and legs a mess, Clough's primal instinct took over. He looked up and, like a fatally wounded gazelle trying to reach cover, tried to crawl towards the loose ball . . .

*'If he'd have been out of work any longer, he'd have gone to pot. He was a no-hoper: jobless, boozing heavily and on his way out.'*

Peter Taylor

So there's a famous old Jewish joke. Husband: 'I make all the important decisions in the house. What the government should do about the exchange rate, who to recognise as an independent state, how to counter global warming. All the other things – where to send the kids to school, where to live, what to eat – my wife decides.' It's a great gag, playing on the essential matriarchal nature of Judaism. It's also a gag that Clough has claimed as his own. 'Women run everything. The only thing I have done within my house in the last twenty years is to recognise Angola as a free state.' Fortunately for Clough and the reason why he's been so successful is that, in his case, not only is it true, it's doubly true. Let's put it another way. It's said that behind every great man is a great woman. Clough had two.

Peter Taylor first saw Brian Clough when they were at Middlesbrough together. Like Tony Randall and Jack Klugman, they were the perfect odd couple. Clough was young and a supremely gifted striker. Taylor was six years older and a supremely average reserve-team goalkeeper. The one thing they had in common was they they both thought that the lack of sunshine was something to do with young Cloughie wearing trousers. 'Bobby Charlton used to wind up for his thunderbolts. You could see them coming a mile off. You had no warning with Brian. It was phenomenal. There's been nothing like it since,' Taylor said later. Taylor knocked his own career on the head as he became Clough's mentor, guru, agent and PR man. As a couple, they became inseparable, and what that must have done for their popularity rating in the dressing-room, you can ponder. Just imagine the mouthy (would-be) star striker backed up by the reserve-team goalkeeper. Signing a protest petition to the manager was the least the other players could have done.

On 27 October 1965, Clough took over at Hartlepool. On his very first day there, he sold centre-half Alan Fox to Bradford City. He'd never seen him play but, you know, people sometimes get caught up with details, don't you think? It was a warning shot of what was to come. Nobody should take anything for granted. 'Things that other managers find hard work are no problem to me.'

When Clough was offered the job of managing Hartlepool at the tender age of thirty – he was the youngest manager in the League – the first thing he did was phone Taylor and ask him to come too. It wasn't such a tempting offer – to borrow a well-travelled line, many people thought that their full name was Hartlepool Nil – but the chance to work again with Cloughie was too good to pass up. Together they worked a near miracle there, taking the 'Pool from eighteenth in Division Four right up to the nose-bleed zone of eighth.

Just as he timed his runs into the box when he was a player – perfectly – so he timed his assault on managership. As Shankly had shown, managers were no longer simply managers, they were 'personalities' and Clough, who recognised what a tasty morsel a sound-bite was to a hungry hack, was the personality manager *par excellence*. When he became a manager, he said, 'Age doesn't matter. It's what you know about football that matters and I know I'm better than the five hundred managers who have been sacked since the war. If they'd have known anything about the game they wouldn't have lost their jobs.' It was easy.

And, all the time, Clough was sharpening his PR skills. While he organised raffles and lotteries to get a few bob for the team (raising enough to buy some new floodlights) and drove the team bus when they were skint, he made sure that there was a local pressman on hand to see it all happen. Just as the name of Hartlepool got around, so did the name of Clough.

'Carry on playing like this and you lot will get me the sack,' Clough told his Derby team after they'd been held to a 2–2 draw at home to Manchester United on the opening day of the 1971–72 season. It was a wind-up. Everything was a wind-up. He'd been there four years and before the fifth was out, Derby County would be knee-deep in vertigo – and League Champions, an achievement the players found out about sitting round a pool in Majorca. While they'd been there, Leeds had been busy back in England getting beaten . . . The only way.

When they arrived at Derby, there were player revolts because they thought their new bosses were too young. The management team responded in typical fashion, and soon only three of the original twenty-eight staff remained – Kevin Hector, Ron Webster and Alan Durban. Derby swept through Division Two like Clough and Taylor swept through Derby.

It was a whirlwind romance, building a team around the rock that was Dave Mackay. A year older than Clough and a stone overweight, Mackay thought they were mad. But Taylor – it was his brainwave – knew what he was doing. 'We don't want your legs, just your brains and your mouth. Let the young lads do the running.'

This was Taylor at his best, scouring the lower divisions and reserve sides for hidden talent – and finding it. John O'Hare was Clough's only signing. All the others were Taylor-made. Roy McFarland, Alan Hinton – the John Robertson of the team – Willie Carlin and John McGovern, the quintessential Clough boy who followed his man from Hartlepool to wherever he was told to go. McGovern was the prototype Bowyer, an honest, industrious player who was guaranteed to do the job, was there at the beginning and was there – near enough – at the end. Solid.

Their methods were unorthodox, with Clough, in particular, taking a cavalier attitude towards coaching. 'Coaching is for kids. If a player can't trap a ball and pass it by the time he's in the team, he shouldn't be there in the first place. I told Roy McFarland to go and get his bloody hair cut – that's coaching at the top level.'

Mackay apart – Clough might be many things, but stupid isn't one of them – the managers would physically and psychologically take the team apart and put them back together again. Talking about the opposition was discouraged and instructions, such as they were, would be limited to a line dropped here, a word there. Training sessions would often just consist of Clough practising his volleying. Not that he needed the practice; by common consent he was the best striker at the club.

Their attitude found its natural outlet off the field. Signing players, they enjoyed toying with convention. O'Hare was signed on a Sunday, something frowned upon by the powers. McFarland found himself so besieged by Clough and Taylor that, in desperation, he turned to his father for help. 'If they want you that much, son, you'd better go with them.' The best one was when they signed Scotland international Archie Gemmill. Neither Gemmill nor his wife were over-impressed by Clough – by now he was a familiar face on the box – but Clough wasn't one to be put off. He went to the Gemmill household, talked his way into staying the night on the sofa while the Gemmills 'talked it over', did the washing-up while they were sleeping and did the business over breakfast.

Some of it, though, went horribly wrong. Ian Storey-Moore was signed from Notts Forest for £200,000 and paraded at the Baseball Ground in his crisp new Derby shirt. Only he hadn't been signed at all. Manchester United had signed him – or near as dammit had – and Clough was just trying to throw a spanner in the works. That pantomime cost Derby a £5,000 fine.

Worse was to come after their first season in Division One. Finishing fourth, they were eligible for a place in Europe. But a joint Football Association/Football League enquiry opened a can of financial worms that was to lead to a £10,000 fine and a Euro ban. Illegal cash payments, wastepaper bins full of folding, iffy, petty cash. 'I can't pretend we were innocent. Perhaps Brian and I were a bit cavalier at times,' said Taylor.

Still, relations between chairman Sam Longson and Clough were good – good enough for Longson to give Clough a bag of Derby shares and a £5,000 pay rise. Taylor got nothing and it was the first of many thin ends that went into an ever-widening wedge driven between them.

In a typewritten letter – dead personal – delivered on 16 October 1973, Clough was told by Sam Longson to 'stop engaging yourself in literary work by writing articles in the press and other publications and entering into commitments with the radio and television media'. If he dared disobey, Clough was told, they'd 'act with some reluctance but without hesitation'. Clough and Taylor had four years left of their contracts, worth about £100,000. But the ego, as they say, had landed.

'Thank you for your letter which was delivered to me today. I have studied it carefully and have come to the conclusion that this, coupled with the other events of the past three months, leaves me with no alternative course of action.' Taylor, naturally enough, thought likewise.

'Suddenly the board were not as big at the golf club as they used to be. People were saying to them "Who's running Derby? You or Clough?". In the old days when we were in Division Two they used to say "Clough, of course. That's what we pay him for." But recently everybody knows the answer before they ask the question.'

Down at the golf club, they also found it hard to defend Clough canvassing for the Labour Party, giving free tickets to picketing miners, docking players' wages for regular Oxfam contributions.

That he was a brilliant manager no one doubted, but that side of him had, by 1973, become submerged underneath a cartoon cut-out that was all mouth and little else. He did things football managers weren't supposed to do. He lent his name to causes that were, in the eyes of his employers, outside his jurisdiction. That they were good causes – the striking miners, for example – did nothing to dissuade Longson and his golf club cronies that he was overstepping the mark. Worse, he started a flirtatious dalliance with politics that was to see him approached by both Stretford and Lough-borough constituencies – Labour – with offers that, unfortunately, he did refuse. It's particularly sad that he didn't take on Stretford because the incumbent there was Winston Churchill MP. Now that would have been an interesting debate. Later, in 1979, Clough put his energies into helping

Philip Whitehead get elected in Derby. Canvassing, persuading, this was much more his forte. Can you imagine him in the House? 'Eh, young man . . .'

The Derby honeymoon had to end. Clough's profile was getting too big and what Longson at first tolerated was now simply too much. Clough had become more than just a football manager. In many ways he was, like Harold Wilson or Ted Heath, locked in a time-warp created by Mike Yarwood. The difference was that while Wilson never actually said 'the pound in your pocket' and Heath never did the shoulder shuffle in full naval twat regalia, Clough did pepper his conversation with 'Eh, young man'.

His whiney nasal tones of the period are still, twenty years later, stock fodder for young impressionists everywhere. The experts' expert, he had an opinion for everything and anything. He even had an opinion about his opinion. Even now, who can forget his expert analysis of England's 1974 World Cup qualifier against Poland. There was this goalkeeper they had, Jan Tomaszewski. 'No trouble, the man's a clown.'

'I shout my opinion. I yell my contempt. I mean every word of it. But when you talk like that you are a target. I've got to be a winner or they'll cut me to shreds.'

There was one thing the Clough mouth was right about. Asked about their success after winning the Championship, he said sweetly and succinctly, 'What we have is talent, that's all.'

# Chapter 11

## ROSEBUD

*'Once when we were in Jersey we were out shopping and spotted a cap with "Big Head" written on the front. We got it and handed it to him as a joke. He never took it off. He must have loved it because he has called himself Old Big Head from that day on.'*

John Robertson

WHATEVER YOU THOUGHT OF HER, YOU CAN'T DENY MARGARET Thatcher her place in history. She was, without doubt, an iconoclast. She was the first British political leader to take power in its purest sense – she didn't become leader, *she took power*. She ruled by fear, having a clear idea of her objectives and how to achieve them. Anyone who disagreed with her ideas or her methodology was banished to the political badlands but, after the initial bloodbath, there were very few dissenters. She didn't care what other people thought of her, she didn't care whose nose she put out of joint, just so long as she got her own way. She had a force of presence that simply blew away those who stood in her path and acted in ways that seemed to be illogical; but you can't dispute that, for an unnatural period of time, she achieved her ends.

So much so that she created a seemingly impregnable power base. People wanted to be on her side for two, equally valid, reasons. Firstly, she was a 'winner' and all the world loves a winner. Second, there were no half measures. If you weren't with her, you were against her, and if you were against her, you were out. Debating other people's points of view was never one of her major hobbies.

But in the end it was her very power that destroyed her. She had created so many enemies along the way, brewed so much nauseous poison, that it was only a question of time before they consumed her. As soon as a chink in her armour appeared, evils flowed in and out and within seconds, relatively speaking, the Tory Party antibodies – hatreds – engulfed her and rendered her harmless.

She was, of course, mad all along.

Maybe Caligula would have been a better comparison. But in comparing Brian Clough with other dictators, the temptation to choose Margaret Thatcher is just too great to resist. Let's call it being mischievous. Still, we shan't go on about Thatcher any more than we have to – children may be reading.

Now, here's a game for all the family. Read the following story – it's another of Lee Chapman's – and substitute the words 'Clough' and 'Jemson' with those of 'Thatcher' and 'Brittan'.

More than most players, Nigel Jemson had a strange father-son relationship with Clough. Maybe it was in the name. Maybe it was that Jemson had come to Forest with the singular blessing of Brian's greengrocer. Whatever. 'It was half-time in a reserve match and the manager was far from pleased with his strikers. All the players were sitting with their heads bowed down low. Nigel Jemson was young and still learning and had been having various disagreements with the coaches. Cloughie went over to him, stood directly in front of him and commanded Jemson to stand up. Nigel stood up. "Have you ever been hit in the stomach, son?" said Clough. As soon as Nigel said no, a forceful blow was delivered to his midriff. Nigel doubled up in pain and let out an agonised groan. "Now you have, son," said Clough as he turned and walked away. See!'

Barking behaviour, but symptomatic of a power gone mad. For those who've never been afflicted with absolute power, just think for a minute what a delicious game it must be. A friend shocked me one day by telling me that, for two years, he'd been a police cadet. He said that his favourite duty was sitting in with the motorway cops, watching them drive along at 70 mph, keeping everyone in line. Then, he said, the fun really started. They'd drop their speed to 65 mph. To 60. To 55. And all the time the other cars would drop their speed accordingly. No one would overtake them and the cops would piss themselves, watching all that horsepower being controlled by twitching sphincters . . .

Reading the Jemson tale, my mind flicked back to a time many years ago when I was small and the world was so much bigger. There was a bully at my primary school called Irvine – I won't reveal his surname, just in case he's learnt to read. Like all bullies, he was what he was because he got away with it. (He got away with it because he used to kick the shit out of anyone who questioned his authority, but that's a different story.) Anyway, he used to take great delight in 'joining in' our playground football games. He didn't like football, he wasn't any good at it, he just used to like seeing us cower. Tackle him? I might have only been about eight years old, but there are some things you learn young. And one of those things is just how quickly someone can score a hat-trick. The thought of Irvine and those far-off days of uncomplicated innocence occurred as I was reading another Clough story.

The Forest players were on an end-of-season break in Majorca. A group of them were hanging around on the beach, sunbathing, and then . . . 'We spotted the manager and his entourage coming our way and, when he asked to join us, all conversation stopped. Clough sat down, pulled out a paperback and began to read. This went on for fifteen minutes before he got up and said "Thank you for your company, lads" and then walked off with the staff in tow.'

It's a double-edged sword, this power caper. Yes, it's a great game, and yes, you can achieve results, but think how lonely it is. After he scored his hat-trick, Irvine got bored and went off, leaving us in peace. We got on with playing our game, being sociable. He went off by himself to score a hat-trick somewhere else, with only a sycophantic acolyte or two for company.

There's so much . . . *bollocks* surrounding the Clough legend. One of the biggest is that he's a 'Rolls-Royce socialist'. What does that mean? I don't know – I've never bought a Rolls-Royce – but is there a clause in the purchase agreement that says you cannot vote Labour any more? It's nonsense. Where lives this idea that to have a sense of social morals means that you must be poor, grey and miserable to be a caring soul? Where does it say that as soon as you get a few bob you must, by rights, become a Tory? That kind of cynical thinking is simply sad. It's what you do, not how much money you've got, that counts; it's what you are, not what you can afford to buy. Clough acted through deeds: he gave out free tickets to striking miners, he encouraged players to make regular payments to charity. In February 1979, he refused to talk to any jounalists apart from the twenty-seven who were sacked from the Nottingham *Evening Post* for taking part in a recent strike and withdrew his column in *The Daily Express*.

Where it gets mixed up is that, even here, Clough is a bag of contradictions. The *Guardian* reader who sells an exclusive column to *The Sun*. And what was a man of such principles doing having a column in *The Daily Express*?

But when it comes to people in need, Clough generally comes good – as long as they aren't playing for him. Jimmy Greaves tells a story that sums up the 'good-hearted Bri': 'Back in 1979, when my drink problem was first brought to the public spotlight, I was trying to scratch a living as a freelance journalist. I received a call from Cloughie out of the blue. "Eh, young man. Get yourself off your arse and get up here now. I shall give you an exclusive interview for nowt and you can sell it to Fleet Street for a handsome fee."' Nice.

'The other day I took my son and Roy Keane to visit a children's spastics home. They can't talk, move, walk. We lit the place up, but they lit us up also. When I came out I felt a million dollars. Then I went home to baby-sit and thought how lucky I was. So when somebody in the crowd shouts to me "What do you do every day in the week?", that's what I do. I visit the spastics. I go to board meetings and miners' rallies. I watch the youth side, and I teach deaf children to speak.'

The late, great Jock Stein talked of Clough's 'rage for perfection', but in his later post-Taylor years Brian Clough didn't so much rage as bark. The early unorthodoxies became a curious blend of affectation and dare: let's see what we can get away with this time. Enquiries as to the reasoning behind some of his notions were met, invariably, with a swift 'bugger off!'. Even at Forest, when the players implored his son Nigel to find out what the hell he'd been going on about in that training session, the answer was the same.

*'On our return from training, one of the players would go to the physio's fridge and take out a box of ice-lollies — one for each player. They were bought in by Clough from his newsagent.'*

Lee Chapman on life at Forest

Some of the stories make you wonder if, when he left, Taylor ran off with the Clough marbles. There are tales of him waiting outside the toilets in the training-ground, checking to see if players had washed their hands. In his biography, *More Than a Match*, Lee Chapman tells two Clough stories at opposite ends of the spectrum. The first concerns Chapman's one-time Forest team mate, Gary Megson.

'I had been with Megson at Sheffield Wednesday and knew he had a long-standing habit of making himself sick before a game and again at half-time. Just after he joined Forest, we played a friendly at Dundee, and at half-time Megson started going through his ritual. Clough heard the noise and demanded to know what was going on. "Why are you being sick?" he asked. "I'm always sick at half-time," Megson replied. "Not in my dressing-room you're not." Megson never played a first-team match again.'

Clough explained it away to the press by saying, 'When Gary Megson learns to trap and kick a ball, I'll play him.' So what is that? Was he trying to publicly humiliate Megson into doing something about his vomiting? Save him the indignity of having his eating-disorder made public? Or was he simply being nasty because someone was doing something he didn't approve of? As with everything about Clough, the correct answer is probably 'Yes'. Yes to everything. Yes, he's the sensitive patriarch. Yes, he's the bully-boy scumbag.

The other story is more typical of the post-Taylor Clough. He's got Forest full-back Gary Charles in his office and they're 'negotiating' a new contract.

'So how much do you think you're worth?'

'Er . . .'

'Tell me, son. Do you like vegetables?'

'Yes.'

'Which ones?'

'Er . . .'

'Do you like cabbage?'

'It's all right.'

'What about sprouts? Do you like sprouts?'

'Yes, I like them.'

'Well, then. Do yourself a favour. Go to the greengrocer and buy yourself a big bag of sprouts.'

End of discussion.

So you're a rich, gifted, pampered, fêted young idol and there's your boss treating you at best like a child, at worst like an idiot. Yet you stay loyal and you stay respectful and you stay. Why? It's the oldest question and it's a damn good one. Why?

Maybe it was all to do with his legendary powers of motivation. After all, is he not known for taking moderate players and getting them European Cup winners medals? 'I want to be number one in my industry for management not for motivation. I couldn't motivate a bee to sting if it didn't have the equipment. I couldn't motivate a snake to bite you if it didn't have teeth. You can only bring out of people what they are capable of giving. Two of the greatest myths circulating right now are that Heinz beans are the best and that I can get more out of men than they have inside them.'

Clough might have treated his players like children, like idiots, yet rarely will any of them speak against him. As Roy McFarland said, 'Most of the players who have worked with him will not have a word said against him, but that doesn't mean that they all liked him. The point was that they respected him and they nearly all had some sort of medal to show for their time with him.'

Larry Lloyd: 'He once fined Kenny Burns for making a bad pass. He sent one of his coaches off the bench to the office to type it up so that he could give it to him at half-time.'

Martin O'Neill: 'I've seen big men hide in corridors to avoid him. He was egocentric, sometimes a bully, often impossible. But I wouldn't have missed a moment of it because, as a manager, he was magical.'

Trevor Francis: 'He made me Britain's first million-pound footballer, but for my first game he stuck me in the A team playing on a local park in front of about twenty people. Even then I got a rollicking from him for not wearing shin-pads.'

Teddy Sheringham: 'The experiences I had were strange, but unique. I don't know if I could go through it again, but it was worth it. If any player had asked me whether to sign for Clough or not, without a doubt I'd have said "Go".'

Dissent came from a familiar source: 'I told him that I didn't like flying which was why I had a reputation for missing planes. He said, "Do what I do. Get pissed on scotch and then get some valium down you." And we both did. But Clough was never my cup of tea. The only time he was all right was when he was asleep. He refused to let me play in John Robertson's testimonial, wouldn't tell my why and we had a big row. Afterwards I stormed off back to London instead of going to play for Forest in the European Cup final against Hamburg. I never played for Forest again.' That was Stan Bowles.

The other weird thing about Clough, the maniacal autocrat, is that he managed to do something most parents dream about. He took his son – the 'number 9' – into the family business and made a success of it. 'My problem is how long do you give your son before you leave him out when he's not doing his job? His primary job is to score goals. It's what he gets paid for. Bearing in mind that you love your son, you still live under the code of winning and losing matches. I am only interested in three points. So how long do you give him? But I will give you an insight into the way that I think about football. The closest my son will ever come to being dropped is if he ever gets a hat-trick. I certainly wouldn't drop him when he's trying his balls off to get a goal or make one.'

Players also respect Clough because he never gave up on his belief in 'playing football'. Even when his team were in free-fall and headed for relegation, he held onto his beliefs. Stupid stubborn fool. 'Some people think that the way to play football is to kick it up in the clouds and to hope that when it comes down it will land on one of their own players' heads. I think if God had wanted us to play in the clouds he'd have put grass and cows up there.'

But all the goodwill and all the nice words couldn't stop the hands of time. And Clough suddenly found he belonged to a different era. Seeking a midfield playmaker, he tried to sign Gary McAllister. 'I can only assume I upset him when we met because he was wearing cowboy boots and I asked him if he was related to John Wayne.' Actually, the story goes that a fee of £1 million had been agreed, but Clough refused to talk to McAllister's agent. 'I'm talking to you, not your bimbo,' he said after his first question to the player had been answered by the agent. 'The game's changed. We have to deal with these people, but Bill Shankly wouldn't have done.'

Time was up and, with a cruel twist, the Fates told him through his strikers. The 'number 9' apart, there was Lee Glover, Phil Starbuck, Lee Chapman, Nigel Jemson – probably nice boys, but . . . In November 1992, he tried – and failed – to buy a young Nottingham-born striker playing for Bristol City. If he'd have landed Andy Cole . . .

After the golden years of the two European Cups, Forest suffered a fate that, for someone like Clough, was intolerable. They became just another First Division team, another one of the pack chasing Liverpool. To see the truth in this, it's important to recognise (again) their achievement. Put it in contemporary terms. The Forest of the European days was not some Blackburnesque rags-to-riches tale. There was no Jack Walker, no fairy godmother, no millions to invest in an Alan Shearer. Okay, there was a Trevor Francis, but that was it. (Equally, there was no first-round defeat by a team of Swedish part-timers.) And winning the League? Remember, the Liverpool of the late 1970s was a very different kettle of water to the Manchester United of the mid-1990s.

It's difficult to say exactly where it went wrong. That it ultimately comes down to Peter Taylor leaving is obvious – it's that old Morecambe and Wise comparison again – but apart from that? Maybe it went wrong when they bought Trevor Francis for £1 million just before the European Cup final against Malmo. It might seem strange saying that seeing as they won 1–0 courtesy of a Francis goal, but that deal introduced a new element into the proceedings that was to be the ruin of everything – money.

Forest were suddenly in the really big league and the magical sparkle that made Clough and Taylor special didn't seem so necessary any more; who needs magic dust when you've got a million in your chequebook? It's also possible, of course, that they flew too near the sun. Certainly, their judgement in the year after their second European Cup success in Madrid went completely AWOL. In a twelve-month period, they lost Garry Birtles, Ian Bowyer, Martin O'Neill, Larry Lloyd and Trevor Francis. In the next twelve months, Kenny Burns, Frank Gray, John McGovern, Peter Shilton and Gary Mills were sold; John O'Hare and David Needham and Frank Clark retired.

Taylor – the bargain-shopper *extraordinaire* – was as much at fault as Clough. Out went the chequebook and in came Justin Fashanu, Ian

Wallace, Peter Ward, Mark Proctor, Willie Young and three foreign players, Einar Aas, Jurgen Rober and Raimondo Ponte. If you've not heard of these players, there's probably a good reason why. To outsiders, it was funny. Fashanu for a million or something, based on a goal in the opening credits of *Match of the Day*. Wallace for another million, based on absolutely nothing at all. Even Ian's mum would probably have stopped short at £400,000. The youngsters coming through at Forest, people like Steve Wigley and Colin Walsh, must have felt like they'd turned up the day after the party. They never stood a chance.

With Taylor off the boil, Clough was in grief. Left to his own devices, he was the worst shopper in the world. No wonder all you ever saw him in was that manky green sweatshirt. His wardrobe at home was probably full of extortionately expensive purple crimplene suits, fake crocodile-skin shoes and shellsuits. The Ian Wallaces and Justin Fashanus of the sartorial world. As he said, 'I'm a worse judge of centre-forwards than Walter Winterbottom. And he only gave me two caps.'

More likely was the fact that, at heart, Clough and Taylor were a couple of game players, and they'd won the game. What's the point in just doing it again? In all likelihood, they simply got bored. What were they going to win? The World Cup? If you look at the eagerness with which they smashed down their citadel, it seems an obvious answer. Sure, some of the players were getting on, but they weren't shot. Every time – both times – Clough and Taylor scaled the heights, they responded in the same way. At Derby County they walked away unnecessarily. At Forest, they made the team walk away. What they didn't possibly consider was that they were too old to do it again. They'd given their all. The money had been made, the cups won.

'We were able to fulfil our ambitions. My mother was in her sixties before she flew. I sent her off in a helicopter one day to fly to the Channel Islands. When I saw her she said, "Is that flying?" I said it was, and she said to me, "I don't want to travel any other way from now on." That's nice, isn't it?'

Taylor left Clough on 5 May 1982. Officially. The end of the end came much later, just as the beginning of the end had come much earlier. On that day in May, Forest lost at home to Manchester United and Taylor had had enough. It seemed a reasonable decision: he was rich beyond caring and tired of the grief. Retirement seemed a good option but he hadn't counted on what retirement actually meant. An allotment? Bored out of his skull, he turned up six months later . . . as manager of Derby County. Oh dear. Then he did the unforgivable.

It wasn't only that he nicked Clough's one remaining jewel, it was the way that he did it. He did it in a way that reminded Clough of the way it once was. He got his man when the opposition manager – Clough – wasn't looking. Signing John Robertson when Clough was off on a hiking trip wasn't illegal; it was, however, hugely rude and it took the lid off a hundred years' worth of niggles and griefs which had existed between the two men. Like two former lovers arguing about who bought which book, Clough and Taylor bickered – publicly and horribly – about everything, while meaning all the time the same thing: money. 'I pass Peter Taylor on the A52 every day, but if his car broke down I wouldn't pick him up – I'd run him over! In my book, the man's a rattlesnake.' From Taylor's angle, let's not forget ego. As if we could. You say 'Clough' and people's ears prick up; you say 'Taylor' and they start thinking of suit designs.

Reading about Clough is like reading about Bismarck and finding out he had an inspirational right-hand man who inspired his fire. Taylor was more than an adjutant; he was Clough's other half. His yin to Clough's yang. Every time Clough lifted a trophy – and I mean a proper trophy – Taylor was there. And every time Clough screwed up, he was on his lonesome. One without the other was like watching an episode of *The One Ronnie*. And, sadly, the Ronnie you were watching was always Corbett.

Theirs seemed quite a simple operation. Taylor fires up Clough, Clough fires up the players, the players do the business. But if the communication isn't there . . . Clough could go around embracing liberated states like a host at a posh dinner-party. Meanwhile, everyone was starving because no one had thought to get some bread in.

With death comes remorse for, like life itself, you know that when it comes there's no going back. All the would haves, could haves and should haves in the world can't undo what's been done and what's been written. Five more minutes . . . Everyone has experienced the feeling of despair and disbelief that comes on when someone close to them dies. How can it be? How can it be that that person simply ceases to exist? Their face. Their voice. Their smell. How can these things simply cease to be? In his autobiography, Clough did the only thing possible: he dedicated it to Peter Taylor. 'Still miss you badly. You once said, "When you get shot of me there won't be much laughter in your life." You were right.'

It's probably been said that we'll never see his like again; he was a one-off. Well, if that's been said, it's wrong. We've seen his like a hundred times before. Orson Welles made his name by making a film about one of them. Joseph Conrad wrote a book about one. Marlon Brando played one in Coppola's *Apocalypse Now*. The young genius who flows with talent and who makes a fortune on the back of it, who creates an empire of riches and an army of enemies; who, through his success, redefines the medium in which he exists; whose very success forces him into a sort of ivory-tower isolation where he becomes detached from the very things that sparked the genius inside of him. He loses touch with reality and is forced into a corner. The end, when it comes, is as bloody as it is inevitable. Like a beetle tipped over onto its back, he flails against himself to no avail. And as he does so, the termites – his enemies, those he's upset and those consumed with jealousy – quietly assemble and wait to consume his body. All of which takes us back, sadly, to Margaret Thatcher.

Like Thatcher, he was a demagogue who was tolerated until victory turned into defeat. As his team slid down the League and into the jaws of certain relegation, the silhouetted whisperers stood up and the stories spread. He was a lush. He had lost the ability to function properly. He had been found asleep in a ditch near his home. He'd spent his managerial life accepting 'bungs', cash payments for transfer deals. He was, in the end, nothing more than a crook and a drunk.

As ever, the truth matters little. That he drank was no secret. Even I knew that. He'd signed on the dotted line and become an alcoholic in 1962 after that knee injury had forced him to stop playing. He had kept it at bay throughout his working life but, as age crept up, it became harder and harder to resist. So he fell asleep in a ditch? So what? The smart-arses will throw out the old 'those who live by the sword' line, but where lies the greatest indignity: in the great man who declines slowly and publicly, or in the vulture who takes pleasure in seeing it?

As he told Michael Parkinson in a recent interview, 'I was in an environment where people drank. We drank after the match with the opposition. That was social drinking. Then we'd celebrate if we won and drink to drown our sorrows if we lost. That way it becomes a habit. I am not making an excuse, merely stating a simple fact. Also, I was in an occupation where rumours abound. One day I was doing an interview with a journalist and his phone went. After taking the call, he said, "That was my wife. She'd just heard on the news that you are dead."

'Tom Jones once said to me that if he'd knocked off all the birds he was rumoured to have had, he would never have had the time to sing a song. Same with me and drink.' Thing is, Tom's trousers looked better than Clough's face.

*'Asking me what it's like to make money out of transfers is like asking me what it's like to have VD. I don't know. I've never had it.'*

Brian Clough

*'I was told by Mr Venables that Mr Clough likes a "bung". I told him that I thought this was outrageous and that I would not run my company like this. I was told the usual thing was to meet him in a motorway café and he would be handed a bag full of money.'*

Alan Sugar, Spurs chairman, in his court case against Terry Venables

The bungs allegation? When Clough began this managing lark in 1965, football was an infant capitalist, crawling around and making up the rules as it went along. Long gone were the days when Malcolm Allison was down at Clapton dog-track putting some first-names folding on a greyhound owned by the shady brother of a local spiv. By the time Clough and Taylor arrived at Derby and first saw serious wedge, Allison was brewing up a storm at Maine Road and the shady brother was no longer known as 'Dagenham Alf'; he was now known as the manager of the England national team.

The figures mentioned back in the 1960s might not have had as many zeroes as now, but it was money of loose morals. It didn't mind who it was seen with, so long as you promised to show it a good time. If we were honest, we'd admit that it's that sort of money that makes the world go round. But the sooner that the captains of industry (ho hum) who are running football now accept that the rules of today are simply not applicable to yesteryear, the better for all concerned. That's not to condone the taking of bungs, it's just to recognise that it happened. Okay, it was wrong and it mustn't happen again, but let the past lie. And, anyway, how does that phrase go? Let he who is without sin cast the first stone?

There was also a question of Clough selling some 1992 Rumbelows Cup-final tickets to a geezer called John. But why would a man who has made a couple of million out of football want to get involved in selling two thousand tickets through the touts just to end up with a percentage? But then again, why would he sell Darren Wassell to Derby immediately after selling Des Walker to Sampdoria? Why did he sell Teddy Sheringham and buy Robert Rosario? Maybe his judgement had simply gone. The line between super-ego and super-paranoia is sometimes very thin.

Looking at it again, Clough the football entity was more Dorian Gray than Margaret Thatcher. He'd had a charmed existence touched by the angels, achieving success at every turn in the most unlikely places. He didn't give a toss about what people thought because he knew, *he just knew*, that success was there for the taking. But as the trophies accumulated, the picture in the attic turned gradually from the fox-faced sharp young gunslinger of his youth to a puffy, red, bloated, blotchy parody.

When Clough was retired from Forest, he received a silver rose-bowl. 'Very nice,' he said. A silver rose-bowl? Just recap for a minute. He joined Forest in 1975. Two years later they were promoted to Division One. The next season they won the League and the League Cup. They won the League Cup three more times. The European Cup twice. In the eighteen seasons he was there, Forest were out of the top ten only twice. 'Not one of the directors wrote to me. One or two of their wives did, but not the directors themselves. Strange, isn't it?'

Maybe it's strange and maybe it isn't. Gaining respect from his directors was never at the top of his list of priorities. It's doubtful that there were many who'd have adopted him.

'I can't avoid the truth. Can't make it look better than it is. There's only one thing to be said. We're in the shit.' When it came, the end was a sad affair. More in keeping with some Roman tragedy than a dignified exit stage left.

Twenty-four hours before he was sacked – by 'mutual consent' – Clough had been given a vote of confidence by Forest chairman Fred Reacher. It was the final nonsense. I can't imagine anyone needed a vote of confidence less. As Big Jack Charlton said, 'It looks as though he's been hounded out of the game and it's a damn shame. Who's going to replace him? Probably some kind of plastic people.' It's a bit harsh on Clough's successor and disguises the fact that he had to go. Even he now accepts that he should have left after losing the 1991 FA Cup final against Spurs. That would have been fitting. Losing in the competition that was his nemesis. A vote of confidence and a silver rose-bowl? That's sad.

Forest's crime was that they didn't act discreetly. As it says – more or less – in the Bible, 'Do unto others and you'll have them do unto you.' And Forest did unto others as they'd wanted to for quite a long time.

Unlike Thatcher, though, Clough was loved by his people right up to the end. On 1 May 1993, when Forest played their final home game in his charge, 26,000 people – 26,000 fans – turned up to pass on their best wishes.

Clough was . . . it sounds like an epitaph, but it isn't. He's only stopped being a football manager, that's all. He had a great career, a wild, roller-coaster career, and now it's over. That's all. In the thirty years he was in the hot seat, he made three proper mistakes. He shouldn't have left Derby County. He shouldn't have let Peter Taylor go. And he should have quit Forest after that FA Cup final. Really. Taking on Spurs in the FA Cup! That tells you your time has come.

But Brian Clough shouldn't fret. He's got his wealth to protect him and a loving family to nurture him. And it's his family, more than anything, that counts. Working to live is one thing; it's what we must all do. But living to work? That's a Western disease and it's a more pernicious drug than even the demon drink.

In March 1978, in Forest's first momentous season in Division One, Clough nipped off to Spain for a week just as his team were preparing for a FA Cup-tie against Queens Park Rangers. A scouting mission? Some secret preparation? No, a holiday with his family. Asked why, he replied, 'You know what I remember about Bill Nicholson? I remember a story he told me about his daughter's wedding. He looked at her coming down the aisle and thought, "My God, she's grown up and for the last eighteen years I've hardly seen it happen." Well, that's so sad I could have cried. That's not going to happen to me.'

*Chapter 12*

## NOW TAKE MY WIFE . . .

SO NOW THEY'VE RETIRED, AND SPEND THEIR DAYS ON THE CHAT roadshow with Big Mal and The Doc. That they've teamed up is as ironic as it is funny. Like two back-garden-fence neighbours who've spent their lives slagging each other off, they've now joined forces for the common good. They're both knocking on seventy and they're both doing exactly what they want to do. Still.

ALLISON: 'Actually, we had a good lunch today, Tommy and me. We went in at twelve-thirty . . . and came out at quarter to six.'

DOCHERTY: 'That's longer than my last club!'

Boom boom.

The night that I went to see them, the hot topic was Eric Cantona. Asking Big Mal and The Doc what they'd have done, the crowd might as well have asked Margaret Thatcher what she thought about the return of the poorhouse.

DOCHERTY: 'Cantona? He's a great player, make no mistake about that, he's a genius, but you know what they say about genius and insanity. And he's a borderline case, he's got a short fuse. He should have been banned for longer because other players, younger players, will think if he gets away with it . . .'

Pause . . . and . . . then . . . gag.

'The thing that surprised me about Eric Cantona, the thing that surprised me was that a Frenchman was fighting in the first place.'

ALLISON: 'If you don't control your anger, your anger controls you. The biggest mistake that night was that Brian Kidd should have walked him down to the tunnel.'

DOCHERTY: 'The French tunnel.'

ALLISON: 'I'm a great United fan –'

(Someone in the audience shouts something about Cantona being French.)

DOCHERTY: 'He negotiated his contract in English all right, didn't he?'

Huge cheer.

'Cantona's a great player, Ince is a great player . . .' He pauses, looks around and then delivers the line he knows is a south London winner. 'Ince is a yob.'

Hugest cheer.

'Cantona should have had a bigger fine and a suspended sentence. If he'd been sent off again, he should be banned for life. But when you play for a big club, the rules are different. If he'd played for Stockport County, he'd have been banned for life.'

Huger cheer.

'What gets me is that Alex Ferguson says that he's been treated shabbily. He attacks an ITN reporter on holiday and Alex Ferguson says it wasn't his fault. Now what chance do we have when you've got a manager of a top football club condoning what Eric Cantona's done? What example is that to young kids?'

ALLISON: 'Cantona's a joy to watch but he was sent off four times before that and Ferguson didn't fine him once. Maybe if he'd have fined him once or twice or three times he might have thought about it a bit more.'

DOCHERTY: 'If you let these fellows get away with it you're encouraging it. So Manchester United suspend him to the end of the season and fine him £20,000 and then pay him £10,000 a week and send him on holiday to the Caribbean. Very nice thank you. I love all that.'

Earthy common-sense of the sort that people like Norman Tebbit have based a life around. It wasn't like that in my day. When I were a lad . . . A hard day's work for a hard day's pay. You know, all that 'when men were men' stuff.

The rest of it is a series of linked nostalgic one-liners: John Barnes, he's the only man I know to pull a hamstring on *A Question of Sport*; we called Paddy Roche crocus because he only came out once a year; Jim Holton had one of the best right feet in the business. No idea who it belonged to; Jimmy Greaves, he's the fastest man over 5,000 litres . . .

Docherty's banker bet is George Best. You're never alone with a Best gag, and Tom's got more Best gags than Jack Nicklaus had golf clubs.

'We went to dinner last week, but he didn't turn up. He said he was launching a ship in Belfast but it was seven miles out at sea before he'd let go of the bottle.'

'They asked him how many Miss Worlds he'd slept with. He said three. It should have been seven, but he never turned up for the other four.'

'George has started putting Windolene in his whisky. He still gets pissed but at least his eyes are bright and shiny the next morning.'

It's all Christmas-cracker stuff, but it's harmless enough. The rest is self-justification.

BIG MAL: 'If self-preservation is bowing down to people, I'm not interested. Life isn't a rehearsal. If you don't do what you feel at the time, you might not get another chance. All our lives, we've done something we enjoy and we've been paid for it.'

They still are.

*Chapter 13*


# THE ORIGINAL SIN


ON 9 JANUARY 1995, PETER COOK DIED. THE FATHER OF BRITISH
satire, Cook had been a brilliant, innovative comic talent who had revolutionised the concept of comedy, introducing a new, biting political humour,
and laying the path for generations of future comics. Virtually every British
comedian you can think of, from Marty Feldman to John Cleese to Ben
Elton, every satirist from David Frost to Ian Hislop, every comedy show
from *That Was The Week That Was* to *Monty Python*, they all owed a debt to
Peter Cook. Even the so-called 'alternative comedy' boom of the early-
1980s was merely following in Cook's footsteps. He was the seed from
which they all sprouted.

His early career reads like a history of British comedy. When he was
twenty-four, a young pup, Cook set up the ironically named Establishment
Club, an early precursor of the Comedy Store and one of the first clubs
dedicated to making people laugh. Like his cohorts, Dudley Moore,
Jonathan Miller and Alan Bennett, Cook was a Cambridge graduate, but
didn't buy into the British class system which had moulded him. As the
founding father of the magazine *Private Eye*, Cook was one of the first
people to legitimise politicians as a target for comedy. Their hypocrisies and
their mendaciousness helped fuel his humour.

As much as anyone, Cook helped define the Swinging Sixties. Together
with his regular partner Moore, he had success after success: *Beyond the
Fringe*, *Behind the Fridge* and, later, the *Derek and Clive* records. But Cook
never maintained his early pace and, as the 1970s turned into the 1980s,
settled more and more into a life of liquid relaxation. Meanwhile the
infinitely less talented but more disciplined Moore struck gold in
Hollywood as a sex symbol.

And then, suddenly, Cook died. The obituaries were as obituaries are, full
of eulogistic nonsense. You cannot write ill of the dead. You cannot criticise
those who cannot answer back. But Cook's obits – mostly written,
incidentally, by his less-talented contemporaries – were slightly unusual in
that they broke with this rule. Not overtly, you understand, but subtly, more
in inference than actual words. The thing was this: he was supremely talented

and prodigiously gifted. He had been blessed with everything that everyone wants in life. He had had the best start in life that money could buy, wealth and privilege, was fashionably tall and ridiculously good-looking. (Moore, in contrast, the obits pointed out, was short, working class and had a club foot.) And then he fucked up. Worse, he fucked up through choice.

Cook, it was said, had not only climbed to the top of the tree; he had planted an entirely new tree. A forest. But what had he chosen to do? He blew it. While Moore was making *10* and *Arthur*, Bennett was perfecting his professional Northerner bit and writing award-winning plays, and Miller was revolutionising surgery techniques with his right hand and directing radical operas at the ENO with his left, Cook sank into an alcohol-induced slumber and blew it.

Peter Cook committed the greatest sin known to the greed-conscious, aspirational West: he didn't fulfil his potential. And now he was being punished for it.

What none of his admirers-cum-detractors noted was that Cook's genius came from within. His talent was incendiary. He was a burn-out merchant, that's where the fire came from. That Cook's lifestyle was the choice of an intelligent person was not really considered. How could he not have wanted more success? He could have had his own chat show!

That Malcolm Allison isn't a dead, upper middle-class comic is irrelevant. The comparisons are horribly obvious. Maverick genius rebels, history is littered with them. Mould-breaking revolutionaries in their fields, these free spirits are united by one sad – or joyous, depending on your viewpoint – fact: they didn't fulfil their potential. The subtext is obvious. That bastard. If only I'd had that talent . . .

Saying that Malcolm Allison could be doing anything now from coaching Fisher Athletic to managing England is exactly the same as bemoaning the fact that Peter Cook didn't end up with *Cook!*, a thrice-weekly chat show vehicle plugged into the cheap PR circuit. Or maybe a bitch column in the Style section of *The Sunday Times*.

Criticising Allison for his career is a non-starter. In purely footballing terms, he's not been the disaster-zone that history has painted him. As coach with Manchester City, his record was nearly flawless. Four trophies in three years? Bob Paisley would go along with that. And after that, when Joe Mercer left? It's still not so bad. If he hadn't been seduced by Rodney Marsh's tinkerbell charms and tinkered with a winning formula, there's every possibility that another championship trophy would be in the cabinet room at Maine Road. That the Marsh gamble didn't pay off was as much the fault of City's stars as it was of Allison's ridiculously thin boredom threshold.

At Palace he inherited a mess. The team was virtually relegated when he got there. It had the biggest playing staff in the League and those players that were there were – no disrespect – not the full shilling. By the time Allison left, the foundations were in place for the team to be good enough to be dubbed the 'Team of the Eighties'.

Everything else – bar Sporting Lisbon – was a sham. People used him for his publicity value as much as anything. Chairmen like Peter Swales and Ron Bloye knew that hiring Allison meant column inches, attention, bums on seats. Manchester City and Crystal Palace are both 'little' teams forever toiling in the shadow of more illustrious neighbours and their chairmen knew that they needed a gimmick. Why else did Swales replace Allison with John Bond, another sheepskinned rent-a-quote merchant? Swales wanted an Allison, but a controllable one.

So where does that leave the here and now? Allison is, as ever, Allison. Hedonistic, no looking back. 'I really enjoyed managing and I really enjoyed training and I've been very fortunate because I've spent my life doing what I love doing and I've been paid for doing it. I think I'll always love football. I was very fortunate to go into a profession that I love and a job that I love. I spent over fifty years in the game, and it's been a great life.'

Docherty is a little more reflective. 'I think there's room for Malcolm and me and a lot of other managers, John Bond and others, no matter what you might think of them, there's a place for that type of person with a million years of knowledge in the game which is not used. We should be used in a consultancy basis to work with young coaches.

'I just think that people like us, people who are regarded as past their sell-by date – without being disrespectful – that we've still got a tremendous contribution to make to the game, because the one thing young managers lack these days is experience and it's the one thing no one can give you.'

It's a curious thing. In tribal societies – primitive societies – the elders are the wise men and women. They are the ones who are revered as having the knowledge. They've lived life, seen life and know what life is about. Here in the civilised West, we revere youth. We dump the old in special homes, lock them away and wait for them, and their knowledge of life, to die. It's the old story again – in a culture that worships youth, who wants to be reminded of their essential mortality?

And football? Allison: 'It's like a lot of other things. We seem to follow the Americans, you know American football and American basketball. There's lots and lots of drug problems and other problems, you know, and they handle it extremely well. We have a problem because we don't know how to handle it. But Tom and I, we were a bit unlucky. We were born a bit too early for the bungs. Champagne's not cheap and cigars are not cheap and our friends are not cheap . . . it's all very very sad.'

In the roadshow, Big Mal tells this story about when he was a player at West Ham: 'I went to the dogs one night and lost everything. I had 50 bob left in the world. I got the bus home past a row of houses with their lights on and I wished I could lead a normal life like them. The next night I went back and backed seven winners, won £350 and went home in a taxi.'

Some people might say that Allison should have left the story as 'I went to the dogs . . .', but they're probably the ones with the lights on.

# BIBLIOGRAPHY

Malcolm Allison with James Lawton, *Colours of My Life* (Everest Books, 1975)

Peter Ball and Phil Shaw, *Book of Football Quotations* (Stanley Paul, 1993)

Ross Benson with George Best, *The Good, the Bad and the Bubbly* (Pan, 1990)

Brian Clark, *Docherty: Living Legend of Football* (Mandarin, 1991)

Matthew Engel and Ian Morrison, *The Sportspages Almanac*

Tony Francis, *Clough: A Biography* (Stanley Paul, 1987)

Norman Giller, *This Sporting Laugh* (Robson, 1994)

Tom Humphries, *The Legend of Jack Charlton* (Weidenfield & Nicholson, 1994)

Kevin Keegan with Norman Giller, *The Seventies Revisited* (Queen Anne Press, 1994)

John Motson and John Rowlinson, *The European Cup* (Queen Anne Press, 1980)

Patrick Murphy, *His Way: The Brian Clough Story* (Pan, 1993)

Michael Parkinson, *Best: An Intimate Biography* (Arrow, 1975)

Ivan Ponting and Steve Hale, *The Boot-Room: An Anfield Legend* (Bluecoat Press, 1994)

Paul Rowan, *The Team That Jack Built* (Mainstream, 1994)

Gordon Smailes, *Football League Records* (Breedon Books, 1992)

Rob Steen, *The Mavericks* (Mainstream, 1994)

Terry Venables, *The Autobiography* (Michael Joseph, 1994)

*News of the World Football Annual*

*Rothmans Football Yearbook*

Plus various newspapers, videos and magazines – too many to mention.